DAVID DANCED

The Music of the Psalms

By Jace Webster

Copyright © 2013 by Jace Webster

DAVID DANCED
The Music of the Psalms
by Jace Webster

Printed in the United States of America

ISBN 9781628710229

All rights reserved solely by the author. The author guarantees all contents are original and do not infringe upon the legal rights of any other person or work. No part of this book may be reproduced in any form without the permission of the author. The views expressed in this book are not necessarily those of the publisher.

Unless otherwise indicated, Bible quotations are taken from The King James Bible.

www.xulonpress.com

A man who keeps no secrets from God in his heart, and who, in singing his grief, his fears, his hopes and his memories, purifies and purges them all from falsehood. . .

Miguel de Unamuno, 1925

Each man does his utmost in singing what will be a blessing to all. Psalms are sung in the home and rehearsed on the streets. A psalm is learnt without labor and remembered with delight. Psalmody unites those who disagree, makes friends of those at odds, brings together those who are out of charity with one another.

St. Ambrose, 333-397

For My Special Friends
NIKKI and KIMBERLY

INTRODUCTION to the PSALMS

Shouting, fighting, crying, adultery and rejoicing all keep time to the uneven rhythm of life. The Old Testament's Book of Psalms contains every emotion known to man. With music, mystery and mayhem filling chapter after chapter and page after page, this ancient book reads like a novel, leaving one turning pages well into the night. Nothing has ever been written that has such a bold appeal to humanity as the Old Testament Book of Psalms. Neither has any book ever been quoted as often, telling the story of real people, coping with real issues in real time.

David Danced is not meant to be a scholarly text, nor is it full of technical terms, dissecting each word and paragraph. Instead, this is the story of Israel. Openhearted, aching and full of love for God, people, places and emotions leap off the page and into the heart of the reader. Situations from the past find their place in today's world and into the future, expressed by words formed in the crucible of life, tempered with faith and God's revelation. Stirred with emotion, it is easy to identify with the lives and the circumstances of those who wrote these beautiful words. The depth of their love for God and their sheer determination of faith end up being both a rebuke and a healing balm in their lives.

Enter the world of the Israelites, walking with Moses, Solomon, David and most importantly, walking with God.

MAJOR THEMES of the PSALMS

Hold your Bible in your hand and turn to the middle of the book. When opening the Bible, one will find the Book of Psalms right in the middle. This is not only true in the physical sense, but also figuratively, as the Psalms contain truths that are central to Scripture. True, sometimes ungracious, the Psalms are the stories of the human experience. It is the music of Israel, a personal account of learning to *worship* God under the open heavens, in the pit of *despair* or while hiding in a cave. *Anguished* or *exhausted,* there is always a song to express those *painful feelings. Sick, suffering, poor* and *needy,* the *prisoner* and the *exile,* the person in *danger,* or the one in *fear* of *persecution,* will find a symphony in the words of *God's immense mercy* and *forgiveness.* It is a book for the child of God leading into *new experiences* with the Lord.

HISTORY of the PSALMS

The Book of Psalms is not, in its purest sense, a book at all, but rather, a group of songs created over a span of 1,000 years. The oldest known is Psalm 90, written by the hand of Moses, continuing through the period of the Babylonian exile and ending when the Jews returned to Jerusalem to begin the task of rebuilding their homeland in Psalm 126.

The Hebrew word for the book is *Tehillim,* which means "praise". Other psalms in the Hebrew Text are identified by use of the word *tephillot,* meaning prayer. As *The Book of Praise,* it definitely earned its title, as almost every psalm contains some form of praise. Later, that title would change to *The Book of Songs*, finally becoming *The Book of Psalms.*

DATING the PSALMS

The dating of an individual psalm is extremely problematic. Chronology does not exist in the Book of Psalms. On occasion, the situation that prompted the psalm is found in the superscription, thus giving it a pinpoint in history. Usually however, one must examine the literary style, historical language and theological ideas for this information. Even though such gains in knowledge are desirable, if unfound, the book suffers little for their absence. To apply any assumed situation or date and in many cases, the authorship itself, is to do grave injustice to the psalm itself. The focus is to be on the message and its recounting of events.

Manuscripts found in Qumran indicate that the collection as it exists today reached completion before the Maccabean Period in the second century BC. Occasionally called *The Hymn and Prayer Book* of the Second Temple (537 BC-100 BC), it appears applicable to the overall collection as the final editing was done by Ezra after the exile. The Ugarit texts, as well as the Dead Sea Scrolls, show the imagery, style and parallelisms of some of the earlier psalms. Many psalms reflect an ancient Canaanite style and vocabulary. One of the foremost biblical manuscripts, the Codex Alexandrinus, furnishes the designation *Psalter,* based on the Greek word *Psalterion.*

DIVISIONS in the PSALMS

Upon its completion, the Psalter contained 150 Psalms. On this, the Septuagint (Greek translation) and the Hebrew text agree, although they arrive at this number differently.

The Septuagint has an extra psalm at the end. This does not add another psalm to the Psalter however, as the Septuagint also unites Psalms 9 and 10 as a single poem. Also found in both texts is the unification of Psalms 114 and 115, while Psalms 116 and 147 are each divided into two psalms. Psalms number 42 and 43 are treated as two psalms while originally they were one.

Though the Book of Psalms may appear to lack a plan, it is not without a definite order. While it lacks organization in terms of subject matter, its pattern of life provides its form. It appears that a threefold division preceded the final fivefold form. The three books, 1-41, 42-89, 90-150 later comprised five sections. According to the Midrash on the Psalms and

INTRODUCTION to the PSALMS

ancient Jewish commentaries, this fivefold division was done so the Book of Psalms may be made equal to the Five Books of Moses.

The Book of Psalms can be divided into smaller portions in various ways: by author, by date, thematic, style or poetic form. Some are acrostics, starting each verse with a consecutive letter of the Hebrew alphabet. The books can be situational pleadings, victory songs, marching tunes, temple psalms or psalms of distress.

For this reading, the following division type appears most adequate as it expresses the mood of the singer and lends an identity that helps to clarify the purpose of the psalm. The primary types of Psalms identified are: 1) a prayer of an individual; 2) individual praise; 3) prayers of the community; 4) thanks from the community; 5) confessions of faith; 6) hymns which praise God's righteousness; 7) hymns celebrating God's universal reign; 8) songs of Zion; 9) songs concerning the king; 10) traveling songs; 11) liturgical worship and 12) psalms of instruction.

The final form of the Psalter is the result of a process of growth. Long before the book of Psalms reached completion, numerous minor collections were in circulation. Gradually, as people shared and traveled, these small collections joined. Modifications and local nuances changed the psalms through many generations. Moreover, splitting, deleting and changes in the use of psalms have occurred over time. As presented here, the Psalter is to be accepted as complete and inerrant. God would not allow

His word to be presented incorrectly. If the Psalter is acceptable to God, so shall it be acceptable to the world.

AUTHORS of the PSALMS

Some Jews, although probably a small number, believe that all of the psalms were the creation of David, working as a biography of his life. This would cause little detriment to the "letter of the Law" as it takes remarkably little from the spirit and purpose of the book itself. Most biblical scholars accept that there is little reason to question that the Book of Psalms is quite *largely* the work of David, as his name appears in connection with 73 of the Psalms. It has and often still is, referred to as *"The Psalms of David"*.

However, many of the psalms were in existence well before David's time, forming the nucleus of the Jewish worship hymnal. These psalms received enhancement and expansion at the hand of David, as well as at the hands of generation after generation of wandering and worshipping Jews. The collection, in its final form, is believed to have been compiled by the Prophet Ezra.

Read and enjoy these grand expressions of praise. They are one of the many gifts God has given to man. Moses, the Sons of Korah, Asaph and David wrote battle songs, rally songs, songs of confession and melodies of exuberant joy. Sing, praise, march and dance with them, taking each step with the Israelites and their God.

Keep in mind that even though the psalms began over one thousand years ago, there can be seen in them the perfect kingdom, foreshadowed by a limited and imperfect one. Likewise, the righteous man, unlike the perfect One to come, is seen here as no more than a sinner who struggles with faith, trust and temptation.

Many of the psalms appear repetitious and they are just that. Israel and its people often experienced the same situations time after time. This has not changed since the wanderings in the wilderness. Moreover, there has been little change in the way these events were handled. Within almost every psalm the bottom line comes back to faith in God. In that, it can be seen that life then and life now are both repetitive and dependent upon God.

STRUCTURE of the PSALMS

Hebrew poetry lends itself to widespread use. A proverbial saying, a riddle, an orator's appeal and a prayer are all varieties of speech that could slip into the Psalm's rhythm almost effortlessly. The meter is not forced into a prescribed arrangement of strong and weak syllables, but is heard in the sound of three or four stresses in a short sentence or phrase, matched by an answering line of about the same length. The lighter syllables interspersed with the stronger were of no fixed number and the tally of strong beats in a single line could be buried with freedom within a single poem.

Another distinguishing characteristic of Hebrew poetry is the balance of form and sounds, called parallelism. The poet states an idea; then he reinforces that idea by means of repetition, variation, or contrast. Three key types of parallelism exist within the Psalter: 1) synonymous—*repeats* the first line in slightly different words as in Psalm 1:2; 2) antithetic—shows sharp *contrast* with the first line, as seen in Psalm 1:6; and 3) synthetic—the second line completes the first by *supplementing* the original thought, as found in Psalm 7:1.

For every *restriction* put in place by the forms of Hebrew poetry, there are also plenty of *exceptions*. Acrostics occasionally skip a few of the 22 Hebrew letters, while tonal and stylistic changes occur in mid-psalm. In short, there was plenty of room for spontaneity available to the writers. The poetry of the Psalms, with its broad simplicity of rhythm and imagery, survives transplanting into almost any soil. Above all, it has the ability to produce its main text with little loss of either force or beauty.

While the basic style of Hebrew poetry is vastly different from modern poetry, the pattern has a close affinity with the styles of those of the near East. There are numerous similarities in style between the poetry of Israel and that of Egypt and Mesopotamia. The most marked similarities are evident in comparison of the Hebrew songs with the Ugarit's poems. The poetry of Ugarit is primarily the Canaanite-Syrian type as the two cultures were in close contact at one time. The primary similarities are found in metaphors, phrases, rhythms and parallels within the Psalter. Additional similarities include style and phraseology, both religious and theological.

SUPERSCRIPTIONS in the PSALMS

One of the first things noticed about any psalm is the title that bears. Second in importance is the note, or *superscription*, which appears below the title. How to arrive at a proper interpretation of these superscriptions is one of the most vexing problems posed by the Book of Psalms. At times, the authorship of the psalm is in the superscription, such as *"a Psalm of David"* or *"the Sons of Korah"*. The designation of a psalm, a *pilgrimage song,* or *for public worship* may also appear. The superscription may indicate a desired mental or emotional state such as *reflective* or *contemplative.* Still others describe the basic character of the psalm such as a hymn with music—*mizmor*, a simple song—*shir,* or an anthem—*maskil.*

Other superscriptions proceeding psalms refer to the musical instruments used to accompany them. They may also designate which part of the choir is to lead a song, such as soprano, tenor or bass. The meaning of many superscriptions are have become lost or are now unknown, yet when available, the information provides insight into the psalm that would not be otherwise available.

When a historical event is found within a psalm, it should be interpreted in that light. When no historical event appears, there is little hope of restructuring the historical occasion. Assuming the date, situation, writer, or any other part in the psalms will provide more damage than assistance in the understanding of the song.

JESUS in the PSALMS

The Book of Psalms never mentions Jesus, the coming Messiah by name, but His figure appears in a number of psalms as would later become realized. The Psalms form an indispensable background for the ministry of Jesus. Jesus would have learned these psalms as a part of his Jewish devotions. At His baptism, He stated His purpose on earth in words that came from the Psalms. On the cross, the words Jesus spoke in His *dying* moments were words originally voiced in the Book of Psalms. There are about 100 direct references or allusions to the Psalter in the New Testament; many of these refer to the coming Messiah, the Living Jesus and the Eternal Son.

The Psalms speak of Christ, but not as the prophets do. The Book of Psalms is biblical poetry, not to be numbered among the prophetical books. When the Psalter reached its final form, Jesus was easily seen within its pages. The Book of Psalms generally refers to God by use of the word "Lord", while the New Testament "Lord" refers to Jesus. To avoid confusion, God is the name generally used in this text. Moreover, The Psalms also spoke about God and His ways with His people; about God and His ways with the nations; about God and His ways with the righteous and His

INTRODUCTION to the PSALMS

ways with the wicked. What the Psalms said about the Lord's anointed, about His Temple and His holy city, has all been in light of the coming Christ. The psalms reached their fulfillment when Christ came in the flesh and will reach their ultimate conclusion at His second coming.

PSALMS TODAY

Can a Christian read aloud the psalms as his own prayers? The short answer it must surely be no; no more than he should echo the curses of Jeremiah or the protests of Job. A man must speak to God through his own voice and with his own words, not with those of another. Of course, they may be used as a method to find expression of feelings or emotions, prayers for wisdom or methods for praise. He may translate them into affirmations of God's judgment and into denunciations of the spiritually wicked. Throughout the centuries the Psalms have been a source of personal inspiration and spiritual strength. Modified to fit a current situation, the psalms release people from exhaustion and defeat. With emotionally drenched complaints, humble tears, desperate cries and outbursts of pain, the writers of the psalms skillfully expose and express the yearnings of man's deepest thoughts.

In the course of dealing with the adversaries of life, people frequently get frustrated by an inability to find the words to adequately express their emotional pain or mental anguish. When coping with men of flesh and blood who live as enemies of the cross of

Christ or who set themselves up as God's enemies, the instructions of Jesus are to pray, not against them, but for them; to turn them from the power of Satan to God; to repay their evil with goodness and choose none of their ways. Christians must form a relationship with Jesus and the Father; conversation must be individual and not contextual recitation.

By song and spirit, they comfort the lonely, strengthen the weary, bind up the broken hearted and turn the eyes of the downcast upward to their Creator. With hope revived, faith has returned and again life becomes bearable. Today, churches continue to draw from the Book of Psalms. The worship that the Christian church has adopted incorporates not only the lyrics and the instruments of the Psalms, but follows the same pattern of worship. On that note, let all men clap (47:1), lift their hands (141:2), bow (95:6), stand (134:1), shout (47:1) and dance (149:3) in the presence of God.

TODAY, TOMORROW AND FOREVER, THE LORD OUR GOD IS ONE!

THE BOOK of PSALMS

BOOK ONE

PSALMS 1-41
The Genesis Psalms

PSALM 1

¹Blessed [is] the man that walketh not in the counsel of the ungodly, nor standeth in the way of sinners, nor sitteth in the seat of the scornful.
²But his delight [is] in the law of the LORD; and in his law doth he meditate day and night.
³And he shall be like a tree planted by the rivers of water, that bringeth forth his fruit in his season; his leaf also shall not wither; and whatsoever he doeth shall prosper.
⁴The ungodly [are] not so: but [are] like the chaff which the wind driveth away.
⁵Therefore the ungodly shall not stand in the judgment, nor sinners in the congregation of the righteous.
⁶For the Lord knoweth the way of the righteous; but the way of the ungodly shall perish.

PSALM 1
Title: First Psalm of the Righteous
Author: an orphan Psalm, generally attributed to David
Superscription: none
Theme: Wickedness compared to Righteousness

Every line of this psalm, built with the finest hardwood, serves as the "opening door" to the entire Psalter. It stands as a faithful doorkeeper, confronting the obvious and unchangeable truth, shaking out the *chaff* until only the usable grain is left. In parallel construction, the ungodly and sinful stand in comparison to the righteous and godly. God promises to vindicate the righteous and concerns Himself with their ways; the wicked merely drift on to ultimate destruction. Moved and swayed by circumstance, those who desire to work against the will of God have done so of their own choosing. God has offered both positive and negative choices to humanity; right and wrong; blessing and punishment. Each man has the choice to commit himself to what he deems to be of greatest value in his life.

The Psalter and this psalm lead specifically to the beautiful reality in worship—a divine truth that not only informs and gives instruction, but also contains the ultimate judgment that looms beyond it. When taken with the following psalm, there emerge two important concepts: God's Law and His instructions, followed by an awareness of what Yahweh has done for mankind.

Psalm 1 addresses relationships and the company a man keeps. The friends a man chooses serve as a platform from which to seek destiny and success. Godly counsel is a prerequisite to God's prosperity, yet it is wisdom which will bring things to their logical end. God's plan is that the righteous shall prosper. Prosperity is much more than simply financial. It includes prosperity in everything: family, children, marriage, business and ministry. The fulfillment of God's promises cannot come unless a responsible action is first taken by man. No one will righteously prosper until he starts doing what God has required. Many people want the promised results without the responsible commitment. God's answers will not *magically* leap into anyone's schedule. His answers come according to His will and His timing. With intense study and patient pursuit of His promise, God will bring maturity and righteousness to those who seek Him.

PSALM 2

¹Why do the heathen rage, and the people imagine a vain thing?
²The kings of the earth set themselves, and the rulers take counsel together, against the LORD, and against his anointed, [saying],
³Let us break their bands asunder, and cast away their cords from us.
⁴He that sitteth in the heavens shall laugh: the Lord shall have them in derision.

⁵Then shall he speak unto them in his wrath, and vex them in his sore displeasure.
⁶Yet have I set my King upon my holy Hill of Zion.
⁷I will declare the decree: the LORD
hath said unto me, Thou [art] my son;
this day have I begotten thee.
⁸Ask of me, and I shall give [thee] the heathen [for] thine inheritance, and the uttermost parts of the earth, [for] thy possession.
⁹Thou shalt break them with a rod of iron; thou shalt dash them in pieces like a potter's vessel.
¹⁰Be wise now therefore, O ye kings:
be instructed ye judges of the earth.
¹¹Serve the LORD with fear,
and rejoice with trembling.
¹²Kiss the Son, lest he be angry, and ye perish [from] the way, when his wrath is kindled, but a little. Blessed [are] all they that put their trust in him.

PSALM 2
Title: First Messianic Psalm
Author: an orphan Psalm, generally attributed to David
Superscription: none
Theme: The Messiah's Kingdom

This psalm begins with an urgent, yet eternal question. "Why do the heathen rage?" Why do kings and kingdoms imagine that they have the right to force their beliefs and their will on those around them? The evil gather together to plot and scheme against God's chosen ones, offering only chaos and destruction, while persuading others to believe in the "correctness" of their plans. God hears their words and responds quickly with laughter. The wicked shall perish and those who refuse God's wisdom are now in line for the same fate.

The question, although rhetorical, raises some valuable cause for thought. *Why* is everyone angry and what are they angry about? The answer lies in the use of the word "heathen". Those worshipping gods of mud and wood are seeking to push their agenda upon others. The world has invested far too much in this method of business and faith. Though appearing successful at times, the middle and closing of this psalm clearly demonstrate the absurdity of those who would rebel against the Almighty.

God's wrath is a response to the failure of His people to obey His word. God's anger as seen here may sound harsh, but the true comparison is with Christ, whose wrath, like His compassion, is far beyond understanding. His wrath is not only to those fail to obey Him, but have the foolishness to defy Him. It is His hope that discipline may cause the heathen to repent and seek a new way of life. Even so, God's anger is not the same as the anger of a man. Anger is a loss of control. God is never out of control.

On a situational level, this psalm would also fit the coronation of a Davidic king. The kingship of Israel had been prophesied to David and his descendants. This prophecy would see the result of cause and effect as David falls into temptation and falls in line with the unwise kings and experiences the wrath of God. This judgment against David comes as a result of his own choice to sin. David's future lies in the redemption of His people through an exalted royal son. Though unknown to Jews of the time, this highlighted the messianic importance of this psalm. As the second part of the "introduction" to the Book of Psalms, it proclaims the blessedness of all who acknowledge the Lordship of God and take refuge in Him. As quoted in the New Testament, this psalm is applied to Christ as the "great son of David" and God's anointed.

Note: The English word "Messiah" comes from the Hebrew word for "anointed". The anointed one spoken prophetically about here is a King of Israel. Jesus is the true anointed one. Jesus spoke of Himself as the Messiah and it was this declaration that led to His crucifixion. All the nations of the world fall under His rule. The one qualifier is that one must seek for, ask for and accept the Kingship of Jesus. There is an epic responsibility in leading the nations to Christ (2 Corinthians). Christians must unite and utilize the authority, which Jesus, the Messiah of Psalm 2, later conferred upon His church.

PSALM 3

¹A Psalm of David, when he fled from
Absalom his son. LORD, how they are increased that
trouble me! Many [are] they that rise up against me.
²Many [there be] which say of my soul,
[There is] no help for him in God.

³But thou, O LORD, [art] a shield for me;
my glory, and the lifter of mine head.
⁴I cried unto the LORD with my voice,
and he heard me out of his holy hill.
⁵I laid me down and slept; I awaked;
for the LORD sustained me.
⁶I will not be afraid of ten thousands of people, that have set [themselves] against me round about.
⁷Arise, O LORD; save me, O my God: for thou hast smitten all mine enemies [upon] the cheek bone; thou hast broken the teeth of the ungodly.
⁸Salvation [belongeth] unto the LORD:
thy blessing [is] upon thy people.

PSALM 3
Title: First Prayer of Distress
Author: a Psalm of David
Date: When David fled from Absalom
Subscription: *A mizmor* or *song with musical instruments*
Theme: David's Trust in God

This psalm is an excellent example of finding peace in a hopeless situation. The title brings a reminder of the king's personal grief compounded by problems within the kingdom. David faced the rising tide of disloyalty, the rumor that God had withdrawn from him and the precarious state of his kingdom. To be in a shrinking minority is a test of nerve, particularly when the opposition is actively rising and threatening. David exclaims, "how they are increased that trouble me!" Absalom's revolt gave rise to grief and left David surrounded by lies, exasperation and gloom. His greatest need was to have others join in his cause. David looked for those who were in agreement with his ideals, personal strength, support of the kingdom and above all, faithful to the Creator. Sadly, none were to be found.

David's foes are increasing in both number and intensity with each new day. Physically he is in great danger as Saul's armies have been sent to kill him. His spirit struggles under a great weight as he thinks of his beloved son, Absalom—the source of his trouble. He is tired of running, weary of feeling oppressed and exhausted from oncoming taunts every moment of the day and night. His soul lies in pieces around him. However, in the midst of his troubles (3-6), he remembers that God is a shield to defend him. David has confidence in God and gradually that confidence leads him to call God "lifter of my head". Slowly David realizes that it is the Lord, not Absalom, who will determine his future. He sleeps soundly, knowing that God is his helper and protector.

Upon awakening, David realizes that God has sustained him through the night. Fear has subsided and his confidence is increased by this experience. He is now certain that he has nothing to fear from any enemy. His prayer, "arise, O Lord" (7-8), seeks again for God's active power and intervention. As he remembers what God has done for him in the past, He realizes God's faithful care will once again sustain him both day and night.

This is an evening prayer used in a time of chaos. The basic characteristics of this individual lament are waiting for the sequel in Psalm 4, where a sense of relief is finally seen. The eloquent expression of a determined trust in God's protection has made this psalm a favorite throughout the ages—its message of hope is timeless.

PSALM 4

[1] To the chief Musician on Neginoth, A Psalm of David. Hear me when I call, O God of my righteousness: thou hast enlarged me [when I was] in distress; have mercy upon me, and hear my prayer.
[2] O ye sons of men, how long [will you turn] my glory into shame? [How long] will ye love vanity, [and] seek after leasing?
[3] But know, that the LORD hath set apart him that is godly for himself: the LORD will hear when I call unto him.
[4] Stand in awe, and sin not: commune with your own heart upon your bed, and be still.
[5] Offer the sacrifices of righteousness, and put your trust in the LORD.
[6] [There be] many that say, Who will show us [any] good? LORD, lift thou up the light of thy countenance upon us.
[7] Thou hast put gladness in my heart, more than in the time [that] their corn and their wine increased.
[8] I will both lay me down in peace, and sleep: for thou, LORD, only makest me dwell in safety.

PSALM 4
Title: Second Prayer of Distress
Author: a Psalm of David
Subscription: to the chief Musician *on Neginoth or stringed instrument*
Theme: The Safety which is Found in Faith

David's nighttime prayer for deliverance and his hymn of trust in the morning has allowed him to stand boldly while those around him desire his destruction. He is convinced that the Lord alone brings a peaceful mind. God, as the upholder of justice, will honor His covenant to protect the children of Israel. David's authority is questioned as he copes with rumors and false comments made about him. Sadly, some attacks are made by men he once called his friends. Verse 4 yields no response as David appeals to the people's goodwill and common sense. David stands resolute stating that the vindication that matters to him is not in what *they* say, but in what God says.

Seeking rest once again, he retires peacefully on the bosom of God. In the darkness of his soul, he contemplates and prays. David asks for wise counsel regarding those who are slandering his name. God's answer to him in the darkness is that David should *speak to his own conscience* and *sin not.* Regarding his enemies, David is to be silent. As night wears on, David is filled with emotion, slowly separating who he is from what others have said about him. He realizes the truth of his situation: he truly trusted God (5), he was glad in his heart (7) and had complete peace of mind (8). The exhausted David understands that God has proven Himself righteous, capable of deliverance and able to meet his deepest needs.

In contrast to the many that hated and mistrusted him, the King knows (6-8) that God's help will bring gladness beyond imagination. Those surrounding him wish and hope for better times, using their anger to help bring about change. While they wish, David praises God in a classic contrast between inward and outward joy. Outward joy comes through a pleasant set of circumstances. Inward joy and true happiness comes from the gladness of God's presence. Closing on the note of a lullaby: David drifts soundly off to sleep, knowing that the Lord alone is the only source of true peace.

PSALM 5

[1]To the chief Musician upon Neginoth, A Psalm of David. Give ear to my words, O LORD,
consider my meditation.
[2]Hearken unto the voice of my cry, my King, and my God: for unto thee will I pray.
[3]My voice shalt thou hear in the morning, O LORD; in the morning I will direct [my prayer] unto thee, and will look up.
[4]For thou [art] not a God that hath pleasure in wickedness: neither shall evil dwell with thee.
[5]The foolish shall not stand in thy sight:
thou hatest all workers of iniquity.

⁶Thou shalt destroy them that speak leasing: the LORD will abhor the bloody and deceitful man.
⁷But as for, I will come [into] thy house in the multitude of thy mercy: [and] in thy fear will I worship toward thy holy temple.
⁸Lead me, O LORD, in thy righteousness because of mine enemies; make thy way straight before my face.
⁹For [there is] no faithfulness in their mouth; their inward part [is] very wickedness; their throat [is] an open sepulchre; they flatter with their tongue.
¹⁰Destroy thou them, O God; let them fall by their own counsels; cast them out in the multitude of their transgressions; for they have rebelled against thee.
¹¹But let all those that put their trust in thee rejoice: let them ever shout for joy, because thou defendest them: let them also that love thy name be joyful in thee.
¹²For thou, LORD, wilt bless the righteous; with favor wilt thou compass him as [with] a shield.

PSALM 5
Title: First Prayer of Judgment
Author: a Psalm of David
Superscription: to the chief Musician *upon Neginoth or flute*
Theme: A Prayer of Guidance

Once again, the moment David arises, his many treacherous enemies beset him. Everywhere he goes there are men who praise and flatter him in his company, but once out of his sight they are plotting his downfall. David appeals to God, who despises every type of evil (1-5) and who is the defender and the rewarder of good (11-12). This is David's God and he chooses to worship (7) and to serve Him.

This psalm, such as many in the Psalter, addresses the continuing strife between the righteous and the wicked people of the world. There is a calling out to God with the words, "Give ear; consider; harken." Preparation for worship must include a cry to God as the He considers not only words, but also the inner motives of the heart. A twofold contrast in these verses shows the attitude of the righteous toward worship and sin and God's view of worship and sin. God cannot tolerate or travel with evil men and will not allow foolish or arrogant men to stand in His presence. David's prayer is that the wicked will be held accountable, while those who trust in God can share in His unending glory.

Between the lines, David builds a case for consistency and order in daily prayer. The repetition of the phrase "in the morning" equates in this case to an alternate translation meaning *morning by morning*. Also significant is the writer's selection of the Hebrew word *arak,* which means being direct in one's declaration. *Arak* is frequently used in Moses's writings in reference to the priestly duty of putting in order the sacrifices brought to God each day. The usage of the word shows a structured plan similar to one used in battle. These definitions indicate that David's prayers are well thought out and hold purpose and meaning.

Another phrase commonly used by David expresses the depth and spirit of the cry, "my King and my God." As David speaks these words in verse 2, the covenant relationship is expressed. David accepts that he is a man under God's authority, he not one who must struggle for his own ends or by his own means prepare for his future. By God's name and His covenant with His people, their needs are met. David does not fail to acknowledge that if God were bless him according to his own *character* he would be totally undone; thus he lives under God's mercy and worships with trembling.

David launches into prayer against the bloodthirsty and deceitful men spoken of in verse 6 who are now exposed. All the resources of the body are used. Speech-mouth, throat and tongue-are all used to achieve a very specific desire of the heart. Evil will always be vulnerable to the truth, by virtue of its own instability. David cannot forget the danger he is in, but he can (and does) break free from loneliness. He is no longer a solitary man encircled by enemies, but rather he is a man in the company of angels, surrounded by the protection of God.

PSALM 6

¹To the chief Musician on Neginoth upon Sheminith, A Psalm of David. O LORD, rebuke me not in thine anger, neither chasten me in thy hot displeasure.
²Have mercy upon me, O LORD; for I [am] weak: O LORD, heal me; for my bones are vexed.
³My soul is also sore vexed: but thou, O LORD, how long?

⁴Return, O LORD, deliver my soul: oh, save me, for thy mercies' sake.
⁵For in death [there is] no remembrance of thee: in the grave who shall give thee thanks?

⁶I am weary with my groaning; all the night make I my bed to swim; I water my couch with my tears.
⁷My eye is consumed because of grief; it waxeth old because of all mine enemies.
⁸Depart from me, all ye workers of iniquity; for the LORD hath heard the voice of my weeping.
⁹The LORD hath heard my supplication; the Lord will receive my prayer.
¹⁰Let all mine enemies be ashamed and sore vexed: let them return [and] be ashamed suddenly.

PSALM 6
Title: Third Prayer of Distress
Author: a Psalm of David
Superscription: to the chief Musician *on Neginoth or stringed instrument and Sheminith, probably a male choir of tenor or bass singers*
Theme: Prayer of Faith in Distress

This cry from the depths of a broken heart is a prayer for God's mercy and intervention. Tears of pain indicate a time of sickness, bitter grief, fear, humiliation and shame. The grief in this psalm is possibly a result of David's sin with Bathsheba. The psalmist does refer to his enemies, but only briefly, giving rise to the thought that this is not the primary cause of his suffering. He pleads for God's forgiveness as he speaks the words, "rebuke me not, neither chasten me. . . have mercy." Here, he shows an awareness of the disciplinary side of suffering. Sickness is not always a consequence of sin, yet when it is, the pain can be instrumental in bringing the sinner face-to-face with God.

The first half of the psalm shows the writer deeply troubled and alarmed. The second half of the psalm, verses 6 forward, hold no petitions. First, David is weeping before the Lord, crying out, "heal me, deliver my soul, save me." The prayers and tears have not been in vain and later he rejoices in knowing that "the Lord has heard me."

Whatever circumstances are the cause of his grief, this psalm gives words to those who scarcely have the heart to pray. David's depression and exhaustion now overwhelms him and he no longer has the energy to cry out to God. If anything is to save him, it cannot come from his own efforts. All rescues must come from God. As the psalm closes (8-10), he speaks with a confident faith. While he cannot see what lies ahead, he is confident that God has His hand upon him and that the will of God will prevail in his life. This transformation from sadness and sorrow to confidence and victory is a component found in almost every supplicant psalm. The repetition of this pattern is the most telling evidence that God does answer prayer.

Note: The Hebrew word for grave is sheol. *As it is used in verse 5, it refers to the shadowy world of the dead. Though Jews did acknowledge an afterlife, they viewed it as largely negative. Before Christ, death was the end. There would be no more experiences of God's victory, no more praise, just silence. David believes that his ability to praise God is at stake. Only the living can remember God's gracious tenderness and mercy. The Old Testament writers knew that human beings were created for life and they also knew that He alone had power over death. Everyone would die when it was time. For the righteous, death may have been looked upon as a blessing which finally freed them from the wickedness of this world. In this psalm, David pleaded with God to preserve his life, if for no other reason than that he may continue to experience God's presence in his life.*

PSALM 7

¹Shiggaion of David, which he sang unto the LORD, concerning the words of Cush the Benjamite. O LORD my God, in thee do I put my trust: save me from all them that persecute me, and deliver me:
²Lest he tear my soul like a lion, rending [it] in pieces, while [there is] none to deliver.
³LORD my God, if I have done this; if there be iniquity in my hands;
⁴If I have rewarded evil unto him that was at peace with me; (yea, I have delivered him that without cause is mine enemy:)

⁵Let the enemy persecute my soul, and take [it]; yea, let him tread down on my life upon the earth, and lay mine honor in the dust.
⁶Arise, O LORD, in thine anger, lift up thyself because of the rage of mine enemies: and awake for me [to] the judgment [that] thou hast commanded.
⁷Shall the congregation of the people compass thee about: for their sakes therefore return thou on high.
⁸The LORD shall judge the people: judge me, O LORD, according to my righteousness, and according to mine integrity [that is] in me.
⁹Oh let the wickedness of the wicked come to an end; but establish the just: for the righteous God trieth the hearts and reins.
¹⁰My defense [is] of God, which saveth the upright in heart.
¹¹God judgeth the righteous, and God is angry [with the wicked] every day.
¹²If he turn not, he will whet his sword; he hath bent his bow, and made it ready.
¹³He hath also prepared for him the instruments of death; he ordaineth his arrows against the persecutors.
¹⁴Behold, he travaileth with iniquity, and hath conceived mischief, and brought forth falsehood.
¹⁵He made a pit and digged it, and is fallen into the ditch [which] he made.
¹⁶His mischief shall return upon his own head, and his violent dealing shall come down upon his own pate.

¹⁷I will praise the LORD according to his righteousness: and will sing praise to the name of the LORD most high.

PSALM 7
Title: Second Prayer for Judgment
Author: a Meditation of David
Date: Flight from Saul
Superscription: *Shiggaion* or *mournful melody* about the Words of Cush
Theme: Prayer for Deliverance from Enemies

Surrounded and in grave danger, the psalmist writes the first personal lament in the psalter. Through the sadness and suffering, there is heard an element of self-righteousness in the psalmist's words. This gives the idea that religious strife has occasioned this bitter persecution. He believes in his own goodness, continually giving God the option to test and try him. As he protests his own innocence, he asks God to repay his enemies by heaping their own evil deeds upon their heads as just payment. Although personal, there are also corporate aspects, which point to the possibility that several psalms may have been combined to form a single hymn. If the individual speaking is a representative of the nation, the unity of the psalm is preserved.

The psalmist calls for God to *rise up* in verses 6-8. In reality, God never sleeps, but here the call to "rise up" is used in a human sense, virtually in the same way that Jesus used parables. There is a bold picture of the omnipresence of God. He knows that the Lord God has seen the wicked surrounding him, yet feels the need to *remind* God that He needs to judge the evildoers.

There is a combination of personal vindication and the idea of world judgment seen in verses 9-13. While appearing a bit arrogant, David does not mean it to be so. In truth, he is aware of his own limitations and puts his confidence in the Lord. He knows the true nature of God. Boldly he has placed his trust in God, acknowledged his own shortcomings and possibly his guilt, leaving the vengeance to the Lord. With his anger subdued and his trust in God reaffirmed, he knows that God's very nature commands that the upright will be preserved and the wicked will suffer God's wrath.

The focus of the psalm moves to the subject of God's wrath upon the wicked. The need to repent is indicated by the three converging lines of retribution. The first "line" emphasizes the personal aspect of judgment that the sinner must face. In the second picture, the sinner has the same hard logic as Jesus's sayings on the *bad tree or the evil treasure* (Luke 6:43-45). Third, His judgment of that evil makes a man turn away from God. Sin enters a man's life (15) as temptation to act on ungodly thoughts then rises up within the individual, eventually turning into action. Yet for all of the energy expended, wickedness is purely self-defeating.

Praise, like sin, is an act of the will. It is not an exuberance overflowing with words. It is a willing declaration of thanksgiving to God, a willing sacrifice of the heart. Praise comes because God is worthy, not because of any set of circumstances. The doxology ends with an illustration of how faith, when combined with prayer and praise, will produce confidence that all things are to be trusted to God.

PSALM 8

^TTo the chief Musician upon Gittith, A Psalm of
David. O LORD, our Lord, how excellent [is]
thy name in all the earth! who hast set
thy glory above the heavens.
²Out of the mouths of babes and sucklings hast thou
ordained strength because of thine enemies, that
thou mightest still the enemy and the avenger.
³When I consider thy heavens, the work of thy
fingers, the moon and the stars,
which thou hast ordained;
⁴What is man, that thou art mindful of him? and the
son of man, that thou visitest him?
⁵For thou hast made him a little lower than the
angels, and hast crowned him with glory and honor.
⁶Thou madest him to have dominion over
the works of thy hands; thou hast put all
[things] under his feet:
⁷All sheep and oxen, yea, and the beasts of the field;
⁸The fowl of the air, and the fish of the sea, [and
whatsoever] passeth through the paths of the seas.
⁹O LORD, our Lord, how excellent [is]
thy name in all the earth!

PSALM 8
Title: Second Messianic Psalm
Author: a Psalm of David
Superscription: to the chief Musician *upon Gittith an instrument or melody of Gath*
Theme: The Glory of the Lord in Creation

David is overwhelmed as he realizes that the God of the universe cares and concerns Himself with the tiny specks of the earth known as humans. God is infinite and although man is minuscule in relation, God has chosen to make man the pinnacle of His creation and the object of God's watchful care (8:1-9). The question in the psalmist's mind is, "What is man that God should care so much for him?" While sounding almost rhetorical, David's question comes from his heart. In Psalm 144, this mocks the arrogance of the rebel; in Job 7:17 it is a sufferer's plea for respite. There is no note of pessimism here, only astonishment that God is mindful and *does* care for His creations. "God's remembering" always implies His movement *toward* the object of His memory.

Hebrews 2:8 is a reminder that while the world is not yet subjected to man, the Messiah is already crowned with glory and honor. There is the development of thought from the grandeur of God's throne in heaven to the lowest creatures of earth. Man is pictured as being the *centerpiece* for creation. Verses 1 and 2 speak of the glory of God: "How excellent thy name." David sees God in His magnificence at the same time he sees his own smallness. He finds himself surrounded by so much, yet truly, all he has is his knowledge of God's kingship and his ability to praise and glorify his king.

Verses 7 and 8 are illustrations of man's dominion. Not only is man intrinsically distinct from the rest of creation, he has been given authority over all earthly creatures. The ability to exercise authority over the earth is dependent on a willingness to obey the living God, who holds *supreme* authority. Man is glorious, but God alone is *excellent.* God's glory can be seen in the starry heavens and it *is* astonishing that he is mindful of man. God's ways defy prediction. This is clearly seen in the unexpected way that He has given so much power to such weak beings. The psalm ends as it began, with the exclamation of, "how excellent is thy name!"

Note: No scientific discovery by an astronomer or biologist negates the unique significance and value of humans as created beings. Human beings were made a little lower than the angels. There is a distinct separateness of man and animals. Man's authority over the earth makes him accountable for the earth and its inhabitants. This should be the concern of every government and every individual. Mankind must not allow the various forms of life, which the Creator has placed in the hands of man, to pass into oblivion.

PSALM 9

¹To the chief Musician upon Muthlabben, A Psalm of David. I will praise [thee], O LORD, with my whole heart; I will show forth all thy marvelous works.

²I will be glad and rejoice in thee: I will sing praise to
thy name, O thou most High.
³When mine enemies are turned back, they shall fall
and perish at thy presence.
⁴For thou hast maintained my right and my cause;
thou satest in the throne judging right.
⁵Thou hast rebuked the heathen, thou hast
destroyed the wicked, thou hast put out their name
for ever and ever.
⁶O thou enemy, destructions are come to a perpetual end: and thou hast destroyed cities; their
memorial is perished with them.
⁷But the LORD shall endure for ever: he hath prepared his throne for judgment.
⁸And he shall judge the world in righteousness,
he shall minister judgment to
the people in uprightness.
⁹The LORD also will be a refuge for the oppressed,
a refuge in times of trouble.
¹⁰And they that know thy name will put their trust in
thee: for thou, LORD, hast not forsaken
them that seek thee.
¹¹Sing praises to the LORD, which dwelleth in Zion:
declare among the people his doings.
¹²When he maketh inquisition for blood,
he remembereth them: he forgetteth
not the cry of the humble.
¹³Have mercy upon me O LORD; consider my trouble
[which I suffer] of them that hate me, thou that
liftest me up from the gates of death:

¹⁴That I may show forth all thy praise in the gates of the daughter of Zion: I will rejoice in thy salvation.
¹⁵The heathen are sunk down into the pit [that] they made: in the net which they hid is their own foot taken.
¹⁶The LORD is known [by] the judgment [which] he executeth: the wicked is snared in the work of his own hands.
¹⁷The wicked shall be turned into hell, [and] all the nations that forget God.
¹⁸ For the needy shall not always be forgotten: the expectation of the poor shall [not] perish for ever.
¹⁹Arise,O LORD; let not man prevail: but the heathen be judged in thy sight.
²⁰Put them in fear, O LORD: [that] the nations may know themselves [to be, but] men.

PSALM 9
Title: First Praise/Prayer Psalm
Author: a Psalm of David
Superscription: to the chief Musician *upon Muthlabben a tune described in the Septuagint meaning, "the secrets of the son"*
Theme: Giving Thanks for the Lord's Righteous Judgments

This psalm, along with Psalm 10, forms an acrostic. Acrostic psalms are those in which the initial letters of successive verses follow the order of the 22-letter Hebrew alphabet. This device was often used to assist the memory. Only the first eleven letters are used here, but the acrostic continues (although somewhat imperfectly) in Psalm 10. According to the Roman church, the Septuagint and the Vulgate, Psalms 9 and 10 are a single hymn. Protestant and Hebrew writings contend that the division is appropriate, as Psalm 9 is purely national, while Psalm 10 is strongly personal. Regardless of divisions, these psalms complement one another in topic and focus.

David gives wholehearted thanks to God because his enemies have been condemned. In knowing God's ways, he has no doubt as to the outcome. In verses 4-8, the writer is grateful that He shall judge the world in righteousness. This is a picture of the final judgment, visualized as a present judgment. God will bless those who trust Him (9-12) and the psalmist seeks those who will join him in praise. David begins by making a declaration of God's loving care, both past and present. Ancient and Near Eastern writings agree that thanksgiving for deliverance is an integral part of worship. In many cultures, it is believed that fervent prayer and thanksgiving will *motivate* the Lord to act on behalf of His people.

True to this concept, verses 13 and 14 are an appeal for God's favor. Such a lament is unusual within an expression of thanksgiving, but it may be natural for one which expresses such sincere gratitude. The great redemptive miracles are remembered, but also the less obvious counterparts that focus around daily experiences. Where lesser men boast of success and talk of their own capabilities, David sees God as his rescuer in verse 3 and sings of His justice in verse 4.

In verse 13, the psalm moves towards a quieter climax, progressing from personal praise into a bold appeal for action. David has firmly fixed his mind on God, remembering the glories of the past, the beauty of the present and hope for the future. Faith and trust in God are more than mere antidotes to his own suffering, but more importantly, they address man's fallen moral state. The psalm closes (19-20) with the recognition that man, on his own, is as dust (Genesis 3:19) and nothing more than a mere breath (Psalm 39:11; 144:12). David admonishes all people to continually praise God and give Him thanks for all victories. Men are as the steam off a hot cup of soup, starting as a feverous heat, cooling quickly then disappearing, while God continues to sit as King forever.

PSALM 10

¹Why stand is thou afar off, O LORD? [Why] hidest thou [thyself] in times of trouble?
²The wicked in [his] pride doth persecute the poor: let them be taken in the devices
that they have imagined.
³For the wicked boasteth of his heart's desire, and blesseth the covetous, [whom] the Lord, abhorreth.
⁴The wicked, through the pride of his countenance, will not seek [after God]: God [is]
not in all of his thoughts.
⁵His ways are always grievous; by judgments [are] far above out of his sight: [as for] all his enemies,
he puffeth at them.

⁶He hath said in his heart, I shall not be moved: for [I shall] never [be] in adversity.
⁷His mouth is full of cursing, deceit, and fraud: under his tongue [is] mischief and vanity.
⁸He setteth in the lurking places of the villages: in the secret places, doth he murder the innocent: his eyes are privily set against the poor.
⁹He lieth in wait secretly as a lion in his den: he lieth in wait to catch the poor: he doth catch the poor, when he draweth him into his net.
¹⁰ He croucheth, [and] humbleth himself, that the poor may fall by his strong ones.
¹¹ He hath said in his heart, God hath forgotten: he hideth his face; he will never see [it].
¹² Arise, O LORD; O God, lift up thine hand: forget not the humble.
¹³Wherefore doth the wicked condemn God? he hath said in his heart, Thou wilt not require [it].
¹⁴Thou hast seen [it]: for thou beholdest mischief and spite, to requite [it] with thy hand: the poor, committeth himself unto thee; thou art the helper of the fatherless.
¹⁵Break thou the arm of the wicked and the evil [man]: seek out his wickedness [till] thou find none.
¹⁶The LORD [is] King for ever and ever: the heathen are perished out of his land.
¹⁷LORD, thou hast heard the desire of the humble: thou wilt prepare their heart,
thou wilt cause thine ear to hear:
¹⁸To judge the fatherless and the oppressed, that the man of the earth may no more oppress.

PSALM 10
Title: The First Appeal to Jehovah to Punish the Wicked
Author: a Psalm of David
Superscription: none
Theme: Confidence in God's Ability to Overcome Evil

This psalm has both a literary and a textual affinity with the preceding psalm, although the mood is entirely different. The enemy is no longer the wicked of other nations, but is now seen in a heartless and morally bankrupt society. Almost prophetically, he mentions that the secularization of any nation—with its removal of any mention of God in schools, businesses, or politics—is taking a giant step towards its ultimate downfall.

David is grieved that the passion towards God is nealy absent. The faithful are the target of intimidation and put to death for expressing a belief in God. Injustice seems rampant. The arrogance of man (1-11) dominates the lives of so many individuals. Such people are betrayed by their own choice. As long as they prosper in this self-righteous life, they defy God, especially with their words. Greedily they serve unrestrained appetites, victimizing others and take no account of God or His laws. Perhaps their blasphemy (3) and repeated assurances of impunity (4, 6, 11, and 13) betray a basic disquiet. They utter the bold words, "There is no God" (4). This is the language of the prideful. He worships only himself and his desires, treating the defenseless as his natural prey.

The wicked ones cannot be restrained in society. The psalmist speaks of his own pain and the pain he feels for his nation. He feels as if his God is a great distance away, standing far off while the tyrant prospers. It is the function of this psalm to touch the nerve of this problem and to keep it alive against the comfort of familiarity or complicity with the corrupt world. Verses 12 through 18 have the psalmist crying, "Arise, O Lord, lift thy hand." This intense appeal cries for direct action by God. Although the attitude of prayer keeps breaking through, verse 13 (which is an echo of verse 1) leaves the question unanswered.

At psalm's end, the writer resolves to face his troubles, confident that he does not face them alone. His fear and anger have turned into an affirmation (16-18). Verse 16 looks abroad to the nations (similar to Psalm 9) and the psalm closes with the reminder that no man who is of the earth can do anything in his own strength. David knows that eventually justice will come. God will strengthen their hearts (17) until the time of judgment. God will do as He has promised. Regardless of what David can see, he still believes in God's righteousness. The Apostle Paul would later be in this same position in 2 Corinthians 12:8-10.

PSALM 11

¹To the chief Musician, [A Psalm] of David. In the LORD put I my I trust: how say ye to my soul, Flee [as] a bird to your mountain?
²For, lo, the wicked bend [their] bow, they make ready their arrow upon the string, that they may privily shoot at the upright in heart.
³If the foundations be destroyed, what can the righteous do?
⁴ The LORD [is] in his holy temple, the LORD'S throne [is] in heaven: his eyes behold, his eyelids try, the children of men.
⁵The LORD trieth the righteous: but the wicked and him that loveth violence his soul hateth.
⁶Upon the wicked, he shall reign snares, fire and brimstone, and an horrible tempest: [this shall be] the portion of their cup.
⁷For the righteous LORD loveth righteousness; his countenance doth behold the upright.

PSALM 11
Title: First Psalm of Trust
Author: a Psalm of David
Date: While David was Hiding from Saul
Superscription: to the chief Musician
Theme: Faith in the Lord's Goodness

Grave peril confronts the psalmist; enemy armies encircle him with the sole purpose of taking his life. While hiding in a mountain cave, David meditates upon how the crisis might be resolved. His reflection gives rise to deep thought and noble expression of his confidence in the Lord. His words of assurance flow into a psalm of truly uncommon eloquence.

His current circumstances are strikingly similar to those that occur in several episodes of David's life. In this instance, as much as David would like to get away from all of this and flee to the mountains, it is impossible because he is surrounded, both literally and figuratively by his circumstances. This is a test (4-5) of a righteous person's patience and faith when he sees wicked men committing injustice. The Lord waits briefly to see who will remain loyal to His ways. He will act, but His action is not always immediate.

Scheming plans give way to the underhanded power of his enemies, causing the men with David to fear that their very foundations are crumbling and that running and hiding is the only recourse available. The advice of David's peers seems well meant, much as Peter advised the Lord to stay out of Jerusalem. Yet, running and hiding are not the answer. David realizes that he is the mainstay of his people and he must save his life and secure their future at all costs. In focusing on the days ahead, David can clearly see the overpowering realities that face him. He is distressed, but not defeated.

Running from his enemies would only serve to undermine David's faith. He remains confident that God's throne is established in the holy temple and that God is not blind to what goes on in the world. If God sees, then just punishment shall come upon the wicked, even as it did upon Sodom. Such a confession of confident trust in the Lord's righteousness comes at a time when wicked adversaries seem to have the upper hand. Yet David testifies of his unshakable trust in the Lord, who is the only true refuge. The righteous Lord will save His people, giving them a place in His presence. His judgment, however, will rain down upon wicked.

The psalm echoes its beginning with God-His character is holy, righteous and just. God's nature is permanent and unchangeable. He loves those who imitate His characteristics. The first line of the psalm shows where the believer's safety lies in the worldly sense, while the last line shows where his safety lies in the spiritual sense—with God.

PSALM 12

¹To the chief Musician upon Sheminith, A Psalm of David. Help, LORD; for the godly man ceaseth; for the faithful fail from among the children of men.
²They speak vanity everyone with his neighbor:
[with] flattering lips [and]
with a double heart do they speak.
³The LORD shall cut off all flattering lips, [and] the tongue that speaketh proud things:
⁴Who have said, With our tongue, we will prevail; our lips [are] our own: who [is] Lord over us?
⁵For the oppression of the poor, for the sighing of the needy, now I will arise, saith the LORD; I will set [him] in safety [from him that] puffeth at him.

⁶The words of the LORD [are] pure words: [as] silver tried in a furnace of earth, purified seven times.
⁷Thou shalt keep them, O LORD, thou shalt preserve them from this generation for ever.
⁸The wicked walk on every side, when the vilest men are exalted.

PSALM 12
Title: Fourth Prayer of Distress
Author: a Psalm of David
Superscription: to the chief Musician *upon Sheminith, a male choir; or eight stringed instrument*
Theme: Man's Infidelity and God's Continuing Grace

Evil men and their actions are the focus of Psalm 12. The author clearly states that he is sick and tired of hearing lies, gossip, frivolous chatter and useless flattery. He wishes that all of them would have their lips cut off. Rumors and falsehoods are not only scandalous; they are contrary to the word of God. Although a man has control over his tongue, it is evident to David that most have been remiss in using this ability. Unfortunately, continued focus on self-will and disregard of the needs to others will only lead to oppression and ultimately the loss of the desire for God and His righteousness. Surrounded by men whose word cannot be trusted (1-4) the psalmist puts his faith in the very dependable wisdom of God, who is still worshiped by a faithful minority.

The writer is speaking on behalf of faithful, godly men—those who have been used and vilified by the ones who speak idle vows and promises, then indulge in hateful and malicious behaviors. The empty talk, smooth talk and doubletalk by the evil men are designed to manipulate the hearer rather than to communicate with him. The power of propaganda is seen as the psalm opens. It is as though the man of God has looked up to find himself surrounded by wickedness, with God as his only ally. Another man standing in this position as a minority of one might have responded differently, but David, who is not retreating, signals God for help.

The Bible does not underestimate the power of big talk (3-4); but instead makes it clear that the Lord despises it. Both the Old and New Testaments illustrate the potency of a weapon such as speech. Beginning with the serpent in Eden, to the predicted persecutor found in Revelation 20, the need to monitor the tongue is recognized repeatedly. There is plenty of reason to see why the biggest supporter of the apocalyptic beast is the false prophet.

The final verse returns to the main theme—emphasizing the value and power of words. When the lifestyle and possessions of unrighteous and evil persons are idolized, the arrogant and the prideful will seize every opportunity to flaunt them. Where the wicked prowl, pride will increase. In cities where immorality is *attractive* and *glamorized* by civic leaders, elected officials, media personalities and other public personalities, it can be overwhelming.

Believers, however, can see such people for who they truly are and in doing so, make a conscious choice to reject their ways and follow God.

David stands determined in his faith. He sees what is in the world, yet he knows that God is there and what He has promised, He will perform. The words of the Lord are pure words, they are as silver that has been purified in the furnace not just once, but seven times—far above the .9999 fine that the human world considers *perfect*. In heated situations, the only way to come through is with a love that is pure, like the word of God. As the song ends, the problem remains unresolved, but David has found a definite assurance and relief in trusting the word of God.

PSALM 13

¹To the chief Musician, A Psalm of David. How long wilt thou forget me, O LORD? for ever? how long wilt thou hide thy face from me?
²How long shall I take counsel in my soul, [having] sorrow in my heart daily? how long shall mine enemy be exalted over me?
³Consider [and] hear me, O LORD my God: lighten mine eyes, lest I sleep the [sleep of] death;
⁴Lest mine enemy say, I have prevailed against him; [and] those that trouble me rejoice when I am moved.
⁵But I have trusted in thy mercy; my heart shall rejoice in thy salvation.
⁶I will sing unto the LORD, because he hath dealt bountifully with me.

PSALM 13
Title: Fifth Prayer of Distress
Author: a Psalm of David
Date: Time of Absalom's Revolt
Superscription: to the chief Musician
Theme: The Salvation of the Lord

This psalm is an excellent example of an individual lament. David is having a faith struggle. He asks of God, "How long?" The fourfold repetition of this phrase clearly shows the writer's intense agony and the depth of his anguish. The cry is poignant in itself, but the lines which follow analyze his torment in terms of his relation to God, to himself and to his enemy. It is logical that the "divine forgetting" and "hiding" are a reference to the idea that God was withholding any form of practical assistance or relief. This psalm, eloquent and painful, is at its heart deeply personal.

David's behavior at Absalom's revolt carries a note of instruction. Though admittedly less than perfect, David has done his best to remain righteous, generous, responsible and submissive to God. Now he is trapped between doubting his faith and feeling that God is not going to act on his behalf. Feeling abandoned, he goes before God and asks, "How long?" He is completely distressed over God's apparent disinterest in him and despite his earnest prayers (3-4), no help appears to be forthcoming. In the depth of pain, he asks if he must bear this agony forever and if only death will end his suffering.

This psalm slowly transitions from doubt to trust. In these few stanzas are seen the deepest longings of a troubled soul. Although a personal enemy is behind the scenes, his troubles encompass much more than that. He struggles as he realizes how much his enemies will rejoice to see him forgotten and ignored by the God of Israel. There is no sign of physical sickness, although the problem may very well have caused him to be in a state of severe mental stress. In the midst of doubt and dejection, he prays for God to understand his problem and to bring the brightness back into his life. He much prefers the glory of God to the "valley of the shadow of death".

In verses 5 and 6 David has not heard from God, yet a sense of relief comes upon him as he clings to his faith. The pressure of life remains, but his future is no longer in the hands of his enemies, but in God's alone. David places his faith in God's bountiful love. It is with a full heart that David pledges his love and turns his attention away from the temporary failure of his faith. God has not responded as he would like, but he trusts in God's timing, love and promise of a joyous outcome. It is in this moment that he has found his true peace.

PSALM 14

[1]To the chief Musician, [A Psalm] of David. The fool hath said in his heart, [There is] no God. They are corrupt, they have done abominable works, [there is] none that doeth good.

²The LORD looked down from heaven upon the children of men, to see if there were any that did understand, [and] seek God.
³They are all gone aside, they are [all] together become filthy: [there is]
none that doeth good, no, not one.
⁴Have all the workers of iniquity no knowledge? who eat up my people [as] they eat bread, and call not upon the LORD.
⁵There were they in great fear: for God [is] in the generation of the righteous.
⁶Ye have shamed the counsel of the poor, because the LORD [is] his refuge.
⁷Oh that the salvation of Israel [were come] out of Zion! when the LORD bringeth back the captivity of his people, Jacob shall rejoice,
[and] Israel shall be glad.

PSALM 14
Title: First Psalm of Instruction
Author: a Psalm of David
Superscription: to the chief Musician
Theme: Foolishness of the Unrighteous;
Judgment of God

This psalm is a remarkable example of how the Psalter developed. With the exception of minor textual variations, especially in verse 6, Psalm 14 is almost identical to Psalm 53. Since the latter is from a later collection, it substitutes *Elohim* for *Yahweh*. Both of these psalms show the disgusting and depraved condition of man when laid side by side with the glorious and majestic spirit of God. In showing the corrupt state of humankind, the Apostle Paul (Romans 3:10) refers to this psalm when he states "there are none that are good-no not one."

David refers to the man who is "the *fool*". The *fool* indicates not only an atheist, but also one who is foolish in what he thinks and how he acts. The fool rarely, if ever, thinks of God and lives as if His existence were fantasy. The words "corrupt", "abominable" and "filthy" all point to the depravity of such an individual, pictured here as being typical in Israel. They are thought to be wise and relatively intelligent men, yet make a mindful decision to choose moral perversion as a lifestyle. Those who are godless feel at liberty to take advantage of others who are at their mercy, either financially or socially. This psalm's focus on the lifestyle of the arrogant and infamous has links to both Psalms 10 and 12 of the Psalter.

Delving still further into the folly of the godless, it is obvious (4-6) that corruption has not circumvented those in the temple priesthood simply because of their position. The very ones who should serve the people by calling upon God on their behalf are instead at the front of the pack, leading the charge to devour the righteous.

The prayer in verse 7 may have been added strictly for liturgical purposes, or it may just be a small glimmer of hope experienced by the psalmist; a hope that men would possess the knowledge that there was One greater Who governs the universe. This is quite a perfect closure for the collection of prayers that began with Psalm Three.

PSALM 15

¹A Psalm of David. LORD, who shall abide in thy tabernacle? who shall dwell in thy holy hill?
²He that walketh uprightly, and worketh righteousness, and speaketh the truth in his heart.
³[He that] backbiteth not with his tongue, nor doeth evil to his neighbor, nor taketh up a reproach against his neighbor.
⁴In whose eyes a vile person is contemned; but he honoureth them that fear the LORD. [He that] sweareth to [his own] hurt, and changeth not.
⁵[He that] putteth not out his money to usury, nor taketh reward against the innocent. He that doeth these [things] shall never be moved.

PSALM 15
Title: Second Psalm of the Righteous
Author: a Psalm of David
Superscription: none
Theme: Who may Approach the Lord

Psalm 15 is a wisdom psalm: a commentary on man's duty to God and his fellow man as set forth in Deuteronomy 6:5 and Leviticus 19:18. This psalm literally spells out the ethical and moral characteristics which would entitle (or at least allow) a man to be admitted to the place of worship. The godly man must be righteous, honest, trustworthy and always seeking justice. More importantly, the man who desires to be in the presence of God must be able to put such moral and ethical principles into daily practice.

The pattern of question and answer here may be a model used in certain sanctuaries in the ancient world. The worshiper would ask the conditions of admittance into the synagogue and the priest would reply. While the expected answer might have been a list of ritual requirements (as seen in Exodus 19:10-15), here it appears to be more than that. Focus is on the pertinent question, "Lord, who may abide in thy tabernacle?" A man must possess integrity, be true to God's character and prove himself able to restrain his words. His allegiance to God is beyond question. The brief comment on usury refers to charging *excessive* interest on money which is loaned to others.

If an acceptable answer is given, the worshiper has testified that he is worthy to worship in the Holy Temple. He declares himself to be one who not only fulfills his duties to God, but also possesses the remaining virtues as they refer to man's duty toward his fellow man. With these attributes, the personal and moral wisdom of the worshiper will be seen in daily life. God's standards must be met if man is to be a guest in God's house. While it is unknown if any were denied entry to the Temple, it also remains unclear just how many were able to answer sufficiently and truthfully.

PSALM 16

¹Michtam of David. Preserve me,
O God: for in thee do I put my trust.
²[O my soul], thou hast said unto the LORD, Thou [art] my Lord: my goodness [extendeth] not to thee;
³[But] to the saints that [are] in the earth, and [to] the excellent, in whom [is] all my delight.
⁴Their sorrows shall be multiplied [that] hasten [after] another [god]: their drink offerings of blood will I not offer, nor take up their names into my lips.
⁵The LORD [is] the portion of mine inheritance and of my cup: thou maintainest my lot.
⁶The lines are fallen unto me in pleasant [places]; yea, I have a goodly heritage.
⁷I will bless the LORD, who hath given me counsel: my reins also instruct me in the night seasons.
⁸I have set the LORD always before me: because [he is] at my right hand, I shall not be moved.
⁹Therefore my heart is glad, and my glory rejoiceth: my flesh also shall rest in hope.
¹⁰For thou wilt not leave my soul in hell; neither wilt thou suffer thine Holy One to see corruption.
¹¹Thou wilt show me the path of life: in thy presence [is] fullness of joy; at thy right hand [there are] pleasures for evermore.

PSALM 16
Title: Third Messianic Psalm
Author: a Psalm of David
Superscription: to the chief Musician *on Michtam*
Theme: The Messiah's Victory

This is a messianic psalm, which also contains a prayer of self-keeping. In accordance with the dominant ideas, it could also be called a psalm of trust. In this regard, it has a thematic link with Psalm 23. Together, these two psalms show that faith, trust and obedience are the essential characteristics which must be possessed by those who bring their prayers to God. This prayer is not for deliverance from an enemy, but for continued happiness. David takes great delight in the saints who have placed their trust in God. Contrasted with this is the state of multiplied sorrows, which is the sad lot of those who have gone after other gods.

Apostasy and idolatry were widespread at this time in history and considered as "right" behavior in many cultures. Against this background of paganism, David compares the happiness of faith in God with the plight of those who have slipped into idolatry. His great hope amplifies his present and unchanging trust in God. To express his joy, the psalmist uses phrase after phrase to show his jubilance. He shares his awareness that to have communion with God is not only to enjoy guidance (7) and stability (8), but the hope of resurrection and endless bliss (11).

David speaks of the life he enjoys by the gracious provision of God. These words of assurance sum up his faith: with the Lord as a resting place, even the grave cannot rob him of his life. David is overcome with emotion as he thinks of being face-to-face with God. His exuberance grows into the certainty of his being able to enjoy this intimacy forever. This psalm is unsurpassed for the beauty and the prospects it opens up. By following God, the path of life (and its circumstances) are placed in God's hands, not only after the grave, but with joy and beauty in this life. This allows the believer to enter God's presence today and to stay with Him forever.

Note: David prophetically declares that the Holy One, Jesus the Christ, would be resurrected from the dead, bodily and without corruption. This was the exuberant announcement of Peter on the day of Pentecost found in the Book of Acts 2:27. At Antioch (Acts 13:35) Paul shares the sufficiency of the atoning blood which was shed on the cross. Jesus has completed the work He came to do and has broken the power of death. He has introduced a promise of eternal life to all who will receive Him as Messiah.

PSALM 17

¹A prayer of David. Hear the right, O LORD, attend unto my cry, give ear unto my prayer, [that goeth] not out of feigned lips.
²Let my sentence come forth from thy presence; let thine eyes behold the things that are equal.

³Thou hast proved mine heart; thou hast visited [me] in the night; thou hast tried me, [and] shalt find nothing; I am purposed [that] my mouth shall not transgress.
⁴Concerning the works of men, by the word of thy lips I have kept [me from] the paths of the destroyer.
⁵Hold up my goings in thy paths, [that] my footsteps slip not.
⁶I have called upon thee, for thou wilt hear me, O God: incline thine ear unto me, [and hear] my speech.
⁷Show thy marvelous lovingkindness, O thou that savest by thy right hand them which put their trust [in thee] from those that rise up [against them].
⁸Keep me as the apple of the eye, hide me under the shadow of thy wings.
⁹From the wicked that oppress me, [from] my deadly enemies, [who] compass me about.
¹⁰They are enclosed in their own fat: with their mouth they speak proudly.
¹¹They have now compassed us in our steps; they have set their eyes bowing down to the earth;
¹²Like as a lion [that] is greedy of his prey, and as it were a young lion working in secret places.
¹³Arise, O LORD, disappoint him, cast him down: deliver my soul from the wicked, [which is] thy sword:
¹⁴From men [which are] thy hand, O LORD, from men of the world, [which have] their portion in [this] life, and whose belly thou fillest with thy hid

[treasure]: they are full of children, and leave the rest of their [substance] to their babes.
¹⁵As for me, I will behold thy face in righteousness: I shall be satisfied, when I awake, with thy likeness.

PSALM 17
Title: Sixth Prayer of Distress
Author: a Prayer of David
Superscription: none
Theme: Prayer and Confidence in Salvation

Verses 1 through 5 are an appeal for justice. The psalmist prays that God will hear his prayer, which he presents with lips that are *free of deceit*. He begs for a just examination of the evidence from the One who knows his innocence. "Deliver my soul" is an appeal for the mercy of God. David repeats his cry, this time with direct reference to his enemies. He requests that God demonstrate His loving kindness by keeping him safe and hiding him from those who mean him harm. This is a prelude to a call for protection, which dominates the second half of this psalm.

The first mention of David's dangerous situation is in verse 7, which leads into a vivid account of the enemies surrounding him and a strong plea for their overthrow. David laments his unjust treatment and remains adamant that he is innocent of the charges brought against him. God is clearly his last Court of Appeal and his only hope. His absolute confidence in God is seen throughout, especially in the final verse.

David is not complacent, but is deeply concerned for his integrity and the truth of God. He searches his heart and decides that his piety is not pretense (1 John 3:18-21). He appeals to God to adjudicate his case. As an innocent man, David calls for the total destruction of those who stand against him. His prayer is seemingly answered as there are insights into what has been stored up for the wicked.

The encounter with God (13) is a familiar pattern of judgment, followed by an interesting methodology (14) of how to handle one's enemies. Simply, allow *God* to *disappoint* them in all their endeavors. The men who resist David are those who are *fat* in their pride and will reap only the rewards that the earthly life can provide. David is seeing beyond the earth's rewards and longs for the day when he will see God and become a man in God's own likeness. Once again, the short-term gain of worldly men is put to shame when compared with the eternal gifts of God.

Note: When this psalm was written, the Jews had no concept of the resurrection of Jesus-only that He would care for them forever. The significance of righteousness for seeing God face-to-face is not purely judicial. Only like can communicate with like (Titus 1:15; Matthew 5:8). The promise of seeing Him as He is gives the assurance that, barring refusal, man may become like Him (1 John 3:2). David is the apple of God's eye in verse 8. The word "apple" used in this way refers to the pupil-the part of the eye which one instinctively protects. Thus, God protects David instinctively.

PSALM 18

¹To the chief Musician, [A Psalm] of David, the servant of the LORD, who spake unto the LORD the words of this song in the day [that] the LORD delivered him from the hand of all his enemies, and from the hand of Saul: And he said, I will love thee, O LORD, my strength.
²The LORD [is] my rock, and my fortress, and my deliverer; my God, my strength, in whom I will trust; my buckler, and the horn of my salvation, [and] my high tower.
³I will call upon the LORD, [who is worthy] to be praised: so shall I be saved from mine enemies.
⁴The sorrows of death compassed me, and the floods of ungodly men made me afraid.
⁵The sorrows of hell compassed me about: the snares of death prevented me.
⁶In my distress I called upon the LORD, and cried unto my God: he heard my voice out of his temple, and my cry came before him, [even] into his ears.
⁷Then the earth shook and trembled; the foundations also of the hills moved and were shaken, because he was wroth.
⁸There went up a smoke out of his nostrils, and fire out of his mouth devoured: coals were kindled by it.
⁹He bowed the heavens also, and came down: and darkness [was] under his feet.
¹⁰And he rode upon a cherub and did fly: yea, he did fly upon the wings of the wind.

¹¹He made darkness his secret place; his pavilion round about him [were] dark waters [and] thick clouds of the skies.
¹²At the brightness [that was] before him his thick clouds passed, hail [stones] and coals of fire.
¹³The LORD also thundered in the heavens, and the Highest gave his voice; hailed [stones] and coals of fire.
¹⁴Yea, he sent out his arrows, and scattered them; and he shot out lightings, and discomfited them.
¹⁵Then the channels of waters were seen, and the foundations of the world were discovered at thy rebuke, O LORD, at the blast of the breath of thy nostrils.
¹⁶He sent from above, he took me, he drew me out of many waters.
¹⁷He delivered me from my strong enemy, and from them which hated me: for they were too strong for me.
¹⁸They prevented me in the day of my calamity: but the LORD was my stay.
¹⁹He brought me forth also into a large place; he delivered me, because he delighted in me.
²⁰The LORD rewarded me according to my righteousness; according to the cleanness of my hands hath he recompensed me.
²¹For I have kept the ways of the LORD, and have not wickedly departed from my God.
²²For all his judgments [were] before me, and I did not put away his statutes from me.

²³I was also upright before him, and I kept myself from mine iniquity.
²⁴Therefore hath the LORD recompensed me according to my righteousness, according to the cleanness of my hands in his eyesight.
²⁵With the merciful thou wilt show thyself merciful; with an upright man thou wilt show thyself upright;
²⁶With the pure thou wilt show thyself pure; and with the froward thou wilt show thyself froword.
²⁷For thou wilt save the afflicted people; but wilt bring down high looks.
²⁸For thou wilt light my candle: the LORD my God will enlighten my darkness.
²⁹For by thee I have run through a troop; and by my God I have leaped over a wall.
³⁰[As for] God, his way, [is] perfect: the word of the LORD is tried: he [is] a buckler
to all those that trust in him.
³¹For who [is] God save the LORD? or who [is] a rock save our God?
³²[It is] God that girdeth me with strength, and maketh my way perfect.
³³He maketh my feet like hinds' [feet], and setteth me upon my high places.
³⁴He teacheth my hands to war, so that a bow of steel is broken by mine arms.
³⁵Thou hast also given me the shield of thy salvation: and thy right hand hath holden me up, and thy gentleness hath made me great.
³⁶Thou hast enlarged my steps under me, that my feet did not slip.

³⁷I have pursued mine enemies, and overtaken them: neither did I turn again until tell they were consumed.
³⁸I have wounded them that they were not able to rise: they are fallen under my feet.
³⁹For thou hast girded me with strength unto the battle: thou hast subdued under me those that rose up against me.
⁴⁰Thou hast also given me the necks of mine enemies; that I might destroy them that hate me.
⁴¹They cried, but [there was] none to save [them: even] unto the LORD, but he answered them not.
⁴²Then, did I beat them small as dust before the wind: I did cast them out as the dirt in the streets.
⁴³Thou hast delivered me from the strivings of the people; [and] thou hast made me the head of the heathen: a people [whom] I have not known, shall serve me.
⁴⁴As soon as they hear of me, they shall obey me: the strangers shall submit themselves unto me.
⁴⁵The strangers shall fade away, and be afraid out of their close places.
⁴⁶The LORD liveth; and blessed [be] my rock; and let the God of my salvation be exalted.
⁴⁷[It is] God that avengeth me, and subdueth the people under me.
⁴⁸He delivereth me from mine enemies: yea, thou liftest me up above those that rise up against me: thou hast delivered me from the violent man.
⁴⁹Therefore will I give thanks unto thee, O LORD, among the heathen, and sing praises unto thy name.

⁵⁰Great deliverance giveth he to his king; and showeth mercy to his anointed, to David, and to his seed for evermore.

PSALM 18
Title: First Psalm of Deliverance
Author: a Psalm of David
Date: David Delivered from Saul
Superscription: to the chief musician:
spoken by David
Theme: The Sovereignty of God

This psalm is the *longest* psalm in *Book One* of the Psalter. The structure is composed of three major divisions: 1) the Lord's deliverance of David from his mortal enemies, 2) the moral grounds upon which the Lord saved David and 3) David's thanks for the help of the Lord. This psalm is remarkably similar to Psalm 14 and bears comparison to 2 Samuel 22.

The outburst of love and praise in verses 1 through 3 and the cataclysmic terms in which he describes God's rescue (7-19) give some idea of his peril and desperation. The center of the psalm shows God in the midst of David's battle, leading him through danger, death and perdition. David becomes fully aware that he owes his life, his triumphs, his throne and *everything else* he possesses to God (28-50). God has blessed David personally, but in doing so, God has also blessed all of Israel. They are blessed for His name's sake—just as the church is blessed by Christ, not due to man's righteousness, but for His.

David's praise rests firmly on what God means to him. He shows God as a helper, bringing an end to, rather than stirring up, oppression. He recalls when he called upon God in his distress and fear. In response to his call to God, the earth shook, the Lord thundered and deliverance came. This is similar to the power of God encircling the former slaves as Moses was given the Ten Commandments at Mt. Sinai (Exodus 19:16-18; 20:18, 21; 24:16-18).

Smoke, as in Isaiah 6, is deemed as God's reaction to unacceptable behaviors. The *nostrils* as used here have a Hebrew origin used to describe anger. Deuteronomy 4:24 equates a raging fire with divine jealousy and intolerance. In Ezekiel 10:2 hailstones and coals are rained down from God's throne on a doomed city. While seeming prideful and arrogant, David declares that each of his deliverances was *according to my righteousness, my faithfulness and my uprightness.* God trained him and prepared the way for his success. He asks rhetorically, "Who is a rock, except our God?"

Although every Davidic King might make this psalm his own, it belonged especially to David. This testimony was, and is, a testimony to Christ. David was the chosen offspring of Abraham and the head of the nations (43-45), but only in a partial sense. This psalm looks far beyond the time of David to the throne of God's greater son, Jesus.

The Lord lives! Blessed be my rock!

PSALM 19

¹To the chief Musician, A Psalm of David. The heavens declare the glory of God; and the firmament showeth his handiwork.
²Day unto day uttereth speech, and unto night showeth knowledge.
³[There is] no speech nor language, [where] their voice is not heard.
⁴Their line is gone out through all the earth, and their words to the end of the world. In them has he set a tabernacle for the sun,
⁵Which [is] as a bridegroom coming out of his chamber, [and] rejoiceth as a strong man to run a race.
⁶His going forth [is] from the end of the heaven, and his circuit unto the ends of it: and there is nothing hid from the heat thereof.
⁷The law of the LORD [is] perfect, converting the soul: the testimony of the LORD [is] sure, making wise the simple.
⁸The statutes of the LORD [are] right, rejoicing the heart: the commandment of the LORD [is] pure, enlightening the eyes.
⁹The fear of the LORD [is] clean, enduring for ever: the judgments of the LORD [are] true [and] righteous altogether.
¹⁰More to be desired. [are they] than gold, yea, than much fine gold: sweeter also than honey and the honeycomb.

¹¹Moreover by them is thy servant warned: [and] in keeping of them [there is] great reward.
¹²Who can understand [his] errors? cleanse thou me from secret [faults].
¹³Keep back thy servant also from presumptuous [sins]; let them not have dominion over me: then shall I be upright, and I shall be innocent from the great transgression.
¹⁴Let the words of my mouth, and the meditation of my heart, be acceptable in thy sight, O LORD, my strength, and my redeemer.

PSALM 19
Title: Second Praise/Prayer Psalm
Author: a Psalm of David
Superscription: to the chief Musician
Theme: A Supreme Revelation of God

God's personality and nature is made known to man through His written word. God's word is perfect, sure, true, gives joy and is sweeter than honey. In two movements, this exquisitely written psalm tells the true relationship of God to the world He has created. First is the realization that God is as revealed in His creation of the universe. The second focus is the absolute clarity of the word of God. This theology is as powerful as its poetry. Often quoted in Romans 10:18 and restated in Romans 15:21, this psalm states that God's eternal power is perceived in the things that He has made. As His "life" is in all creation, there is no place He cannot be, no voice He cannot hear and no person He cannot reach.

The second truth is that the Law was given as a comprehensive method of revealing God's desire for humanity. God has attested to the truth of the scriptures (John 5:39), which stand as a declaration of His promises. The absolute trustworthiness of the Bible (7) is clearly stated. The word of God is described as being perfect, accurate and dependable. The written word of God is *inerrant,* meaning that the scriptures are 100% perfect. In spite of the personal character of the original writers of the scriptures, the Author is God; there are no mistakes and no changes are needed. The watchful eye of the Holy Spirit has ensured that through endless translations and a multitude of generations, the Bible is spiritually and fundamentally the same as it has always been. Even literary critics with no faith in the Bible's truth or value attest to its being the most completely reliable book from antiquity.

In verse 13, David mentions *presumptuous sins.* The word "presumptuous" means *disrespectful, brazen* and *impudent.* These types of sins are relatively easy to recognize, but the balance of the definition may lead to a more vague type of sin. These sins are brought about by feeling too familiar, comfortable or overconfident in the knowledge of God. As David meditates on God's teaching, he sees how a person's words are a reflection of the inner man, serving as both a warning and a guide. His greatest desire is to follow and please God and to show this in his daily life.

The personal plea of "Cleanse Thou me" shows that David knows he is in continual need of God's guidance. The psalm closes with David requesting the strength to overcome all types of sin and to be found acceptable by God. To be *acceptable in thy sight* literally means *may my actions bring delight to you*. Praise and thanksgiving bring joy to the Lord, but daily strength and obedience truly delight Him.

PSALM 20

¹To the chief Musician, A Psalm of David. The LORD,
hear thee in the day of trouble;
the name of the God of Jacob defend thee;
²Send thee help from the sanctuary,
and strengthen thee out of Zion;
³Remember all thy offerings,
and accept thy burnt sacrifice;
⁴Grant thee according to thine own heart,
and fulfill all thy counsel.
⁵We will rejoice in thy salvation, and in the name of
our God, we will set up [our] banners:
the LORD fulfill all thy petitions.
⁶Now know I that the Lord saveth his anointed; he
will hear him from his holy heaven with the saving
strength of his right hand.
⁷Some [trust] in chariots, and some in horses: but
we will remember the name of the LORD our God.
⁸They are brought down and fallen:
but we are risen and stand upright.
⁹Save, LORD: let the king, hear us when we call.

PSALM 20
Title: Second Psalm of Trust
Author: a Psalm of David
Superscription: to the chief Musician
Theme: The Promise of God's Assistance

The sounds of war fill the air! The soldiers of David prepare to march against their enemies, yet they take no steps until they have honored God. In the beginning, the congregation approaches God (1-5) and offers a corporate invocation of blessing. In reply, a single voice, perhaps that of the King himself, tells of the certainty of God's answers.

David describes how God will protect them through the power of His name. He is the one true sanctuary to Israel. God has bestowed upon Israel His gift of salvation, His saving strength and His great power. The banners of each tribe are set as standards by which to proclaim their upcoming victory. Faith and trust in God are not regarded in Israel as something magic that would make their armies invincible, but the use of His name invited Him to be involved in the Israelite's battle.

In the original Hebrew, *"grant thee according to thine own heart"* differs only slightly from its use in Psalm 41 where it signifies God's answer to petitions put before Him. However, the use of the phrase in both psalms wonderfully links them together as both prayer and thanksgiving on either side of a crisis. The phrase, *"let the king hear us when we call"* reflects directly back to the opening of the psalm. The time of trouble frustration, anger, depression, etc., has been made into a time of prayer and a reaffirmation of trust.

PSALM 21

¹To the chief Musician, A Psalm of David. The king shall joy in thy strength, O LORD; and in thy salvation, how greatly shall he rejoice!
²Thou hast given him his heart's desire, and hast not withholden the request of his lips.
³For thou preventest him with the blessings of goodness: thou settest a crown of pure gold on his head.
⁴He asked life of thee [and] thou gavest [it] him, [even] length of days for ever and ever.
⁵His glory [is] great in thy salvation: honor and majesty hast thou laid upon him.
⁶For thou hast made him most blessed for ever: thou hast made him exceedingly glad with thy countenance.
⁷For the king trusteth in the Lord, and through the mercy of the most High he shall not be moved.
⁸Thine hand shall find out all thine enemies: thy right hand shall find out those that hate thee.
⁹Thou shalt make them as a fiery oven in the time of thine anger: the LORD shall swallow them up in his wrath, and the fire shall devour them.
¹⁰Their fruit shalt thou destroy from the earth, and their seed from among the children of men.
¹¹For they intended evil against thee: they imagined a mischievous device, [which] they are not able [to perform].

¹²Therefore shalt thou make them turn their back, [when] thou shalt make ready [thine arrows] upon thy strings against the face of them.
¹³Be thou exalted, LORD, in thine own strength: [so] we will sing and praise thy power.

PSALM 21
Title: Fourth Messianic Psalm
Author: a Psalm of David
Superscription: to the chief Musician
Theme: Rejoice in the Salvation of the Lord

Sing praise to Almighty God for victory! In this psalm, supplication gives way to celebration and thanksgiving due to a recent victory. Although not quite as obvious in the original Hebrew, the English translation indicates that Psalms 20 and 21 are paired as petition and answer. The similarities include the use of two main blocks of material. Here the people sing praises of the King, while in Psalm 20 the people's prayer was added to the prayers of the King. The words *"in thy strength"* are found in both psalms, thus proclaiming the King's trust in the Lord and the security afforded to him by God's unfailing love. Each verse contributes to the list of things God has done for and through the King.

Verses 1-7 recount the relationship of God to King David. The word *"he"* in these verses refers to David. The King speaks (4) of the glorious gift of his present life and to the future that he believes God has in store for him. (At this time, the Hebrews had little conception of an afterlife.) To an Old Testament reader it may have appeared as a reference to the future family line of the dynasty, which was promised to David in 2 Samuel 7:16. The New Testament, however, fills every aspect of this picture in the coming of *the Most Excellent King*—the Messiah for whom the entire verse is true beyond any type of exaggeration.

The word *"fire"* refers to the final judgment as in Malachi 4:1. In 2 Peter 3:7 of the New Testament, the words *"a fiery oven"* are used as they are here. There is a decisive spirit willing to seek out the enemy, aggressively finding and utterly destroying *everyone* who attacks God's kingdom. Worldly ruination of all evil far outruns the power of any earthly King, thus the allusion to the coming Messiah. The Book of 2 Thessalonians (1:7-9) may have *borrowed* from this passage as it borrows the theme of Christ appearing with fire and judgment.

A change of mood comes at the end of the verse where all other words fade into complete praise. David knows that the day will come when the entire world will be subject to the rule and command of the Father. The close of Psalm 21 resembles the ending of Psalm 20; there is no place that is beyond the reach of God.

PSALM 22

[1]To the chief Musician upon Aijeleth Shahar, A Psalm of David. My God, my God, why hast thou forsaken me? [why art thou so] far from helping me, [and from] the words of my roaring?

²O my God, I cry in the daytime, but thou hearest not; and in the night season, and am not silent.
³But thou [art] holy, [O thou]
that inhabitest the praises of Israel.
⁴Our fathers trusted in thee: they trusted,
and thou didst deliver them.
⁵They cried unto thee, and were delivered:
they trusted in thee, and were not confounded.
⁶But I [am] a worm, and no man; a reproach of men,
and despised of the people.
⁷All they that see me laugh me to scorn: they shoot out the lip, they shake the head, [saying],
⁸He trusted on the LORD [that] he would deliver him: let him deliver him, seeing he delighted in him.
⁹But thou [art] he that took me out of the womb:
thou didst make me hope [when I was]
upon my mother's breasts.
¹⁰I was cast upon thee from the womb; thou [art]
my God from my mother's belly.
¹¹Be not far from me; for trouble [is] near;
for [there is] none to help.
¹²Many bulls have compassed me: strong [bulls]
of Bashan have beset me round.
¹³They gaped upon me. [With] their mouths,
[as] a ravening and roaring lion.
¹⁴I am poured out like water, and all my bones are out of joint: my heart is like wax; it is melted
in the midst of my bowels.
¹⁵My strength is dried up like a potsherd; and my tongue cleaveth to my jaws; and thou hast brought me into the dust of death.

¹⁶For dogs have compassed me: the assembly of the wicked have enclosed me: they pierced
my hands and my feet.
¹⁷I may tell all my bones: they look
[and] stare upon me.
¹⁸They part my garments among them,
and cast lots upon my vesture.
¹⁹But be not thou far from me, O LORD: O my strength, haste thee to help me.
²⁰Deliver my soul from the sword; my darling from the power of the dog.
²¹Save me from the lion's mouth: for thou hast heard me from the horns of the unicorns.
²²I will declare thy name unto my brethren: in the midst of the congregation I will praise thee.
²³Ye that fear of the LORD, praise him; all ye the seed of Jacob, glorify him; and fear him,
all ye the seed of Israel.
²⁴For he hath not despised nor abhorred the affliction of the afflicted; neither has he hid his face from him; but when he cried unto him, he heard.
²⁵My praise [shall be] of thee in the great congregation: I will pay my vows before
them that fear him.
²⁶The meek shall eat and be satisfied: they shall praise the LORD that seek him:
your heart shall live forever.
²⁷All the ends of the world shall remember and turn unto the LORD: and all the kindreds of the nations shall worship before thee.
²⁸For the kingdom [is] the LORD'S: and he [is] the

governor among the nations.
²⁹All [they that be] fat upon the earth shall eat and worship: all they that go down to the dust shall bow before him: and none can keep alive his own soul.
³⁰A seed shall serve him; it shall be accounted to the Lord for regeneration.
³¹They shall come, and shall declare his righteousness unto a people that shall be born, that he hath done [this].

PSALM 22
Title: Fifth Messianic Psalm
Author: a Psalm of David
Superscription: to the chief Musician *upon Aijeleth Shara*
Theme: The Suffering and Praise of the Messiah (occasionally referred to as the Passion Psalm)

Although not a recognized continuation, Psalm 22 bears much of the same symbolism and wording of the previous psalm. It is a peculiar mixture of praise and complaint. Sin is not referenced; there is no claim to self-righteousness and there is no request for personal vengeance. In all of these areas, the psalmist is silent. David is feeling intense oppression from those around him and begins to feel that God has forgotten about him. Even in this, however, there is a quiet confidence that no matter how he *feels*, the *knowledge* that God is near sustains him.

Verses 6-18 describe in colorful similes the pain and distress David feels, although again, no specific reason is given. David is encountering the strong enslaving the weak, the many imposing their ideals on the few and those of little or no wealth being ensnared by the rich. The context suggests the motives that encourage men to these behaviors include the pressure of a crowd mentality (12), greed (18) and perverted desires. These verses indicate that although the immediate focus of the trouble is King David, the entirety of humanity seems to be severely separated from the God who brought them from Egypt.

With the words *"I will declare your name to the brethren,"* the psalmist turns from complaints of suffering to the expression of the praise which is in his heart. Praise provides a powerful place where God can delight in His people. David's desire is to proclaim loud and long his personal dependence upon the Lord. He can envision the circle of joy expanded to include all of humankind (27-31) and every generation. At the deepest level, this psalm speaks of the Messiah, who will later become the response to David's prayer. In time, all of the world in every generation will bend their knees to the coming Christ.

Note: This psalm is great for personal and group worship. Unquestionably, some of the most remarkable and exciting things about honest and sincere praise is taught here. Here is the remedy for times of loneliness, abandonment or depression. The answer is to praise! Prayers, simple and honest, are the testimony to a living God Who abides with His children. This fact can create faith and trust and lead to deliverance from Satanic harassments, torments or bondage. The psalm, written for the early church is fully applicable to the New Testament life. Finally, the vision extends to unborn generations (30), in terms which anticipate the preaching of Jesus; God's righteousness revealed in the flesh.

PSALM 23

¹A Psalm of David. The LORD [is] my shepherd;
I shall not want.
²He maketh me to lie down in green pastures:
he leadeth me beside the still waters.
³He restoreth my soul: he leadeth me in the paths of
righteousness for his name's sake.
⁴Yea, though I walk through the valley of the shadow
of death, I will fear no evil: for thou [art] with me;
thy rod and thy staff they comfort me.
⁵Thou preparest a table before me in the presence
of mine enemies: thou anointest my head with oil;
my cup runneth over.
⁶Surely goodness and mercy shall follow me all the
days of my life: and I will dwell in the house
of the LORD for ever.

PSALM 23
Title: Sixth Messianic Psalm
Author: a Psalm of David
Superscription: none
Theme: The Lord Cares for His People

Often known as the "Psalm of the Divine Shepherd", this is perhaps the best-loved chapter in the Book of Psalms. As a view of trust, this psalm has no peer and it is impossible to estimate its effect upon man through the centuries. Its beauty and its message are beyond exhaustion. God is the *Great Shepherd* (John 10) who provides and meets the needs of all. By following Him, there is security from harm and the special gifts that God bestows upon His own.

The Lord is my Shepherd is engraved on headstones across the country. It is also engraved on the hearts of His people by virtue of His tender care and continuing watchfulness. The most impressive feature of this metaphor lies in the Shepherd Himself. He leads into rest and reviving, into the struggles of life and through the dangerous places. The Shepherd provides for the needs of the sheep and keeps them from harm. David speaks throughout the psalm, freely declaring that God is his Shepherd. The most personal line, *I shall not want,* is extremely far reaching. In this single sentence contains the reality that the believer will not have a lack of anything. No lack of joy, happiness, sustenance, or anything else that makes life both possible and pleasant. He leads toward still, calm waters where the weary may rest. God would not be a good shepherd if in fact He had not intended that He and the flock should be bound up with each other.

"He restoreth my soul" (3) is an expression open to more than one interpretation. It may picture the straying sheep brought back as in Isaiah 49:5, which is often translated as *"repent"* or *"be convicted"*. On the other hand, *"my soul"* usually means "my life" and *"restore"* often has a physical or psychological sense, as in Isaiah 58:12. The *dark valley* is not necessarily one God has chosen, but one that He has allowed. Knowing that He is also in the dark valley, never leaving the faithful to fend for themselves is a fact that takes much of the sting out of any ordeal. *Green pastures* bring comfort, which brings the compassion that enables man to sigh with one who is grieving. In this sense comfort is more than a *polite* sympathy, but a deep, emotional empathy. It is shedding tears with those who cry and coming alongside those who walk in fear.

Every detail, from the well-set table (5-6) to the overflowing cup, is an assurance of peace. Goodness and mercy are the center of God's heart and they will be with man throughout every day of life. The final word, *forever* anticipates the New Testament where death will be defeated and eternity will be spent in everlasting joy in the presence of God and His Son.

PSALM 24

¹A Psalm of David. The earth [is] the LORD'S, and the fullness thereof; the world, and they that dwell therein.
²For he hath founded it upon the seas, and established it upon the floods.
³Who shall ascend into the hill of the LORD? Or who shall stand in his holy place?
⁴He that hath clean hands, and a pure heart; who hath not lifted up his soul unto vanity nor sworn deceitfully.
⁵He shall receive the blessing from the LORD, and righteousness from the God of his salvation.
⁶This [is] the generation of them that seek him, that seek thy face, O Jacob.
⁷Lift up your heads, O ye gates; even lift [them] up, ye everlasting doors; and the King of glory shall come in.
⁸Who [is] this King of glory? The LORD strong and mighty, the LORD mighty in battle.
⁹Lift up your heads, O ye gates; even left [them] up, ye everlasting doors; and the King of glory shall come in.
¹⁰Who is this King of glory? The LORD of hosts, he [is] the King of glory.

PSALM 24
Title: First Psalm of God
Author: a Psalm of David
Date: When the Ark of the Covenant was Brought to Jerusalem
Superscription: none
Theme: The King of Glory and His Kingdom

This is a processional song written for that miraculous day in the life of David—the day when the Ark of the Covenant was first brought into Jerusalem. Further telling of this occasion is in 2 Samuel 6:12-15. David sang, danced and shouted praises as the Ark was brought to its permanent home. The question and answers of this song were probably chanted by Levites. In verses 7 through 10, we can see the divine entrance as it is occurring. *"Lift up your heads"* refers to the top of the lentils or tops of the portals through which one enters.

The emphasis of this psalm is a delineation of who may approach the house of God and enter to pray. Who is worthy to stand in God's presence (1-3)? Were it not for the fact that God was the God of Abraham, Isaac and Jacob there would be no hope, for until the crucifixion of Jesus, none could be counted as worthy. It is only because of Abraham's covenant with God that man may come into His holy presence. God must not be approached lightly. The same standards of ethical conduct are demanded today, with special emphasis placed on the character of worship. A warning reminds the faithful of the sovereignty of God over the earth and all creatures.

It cautions against limiting God. He is the creator and sustainer of the earth. He can do all things.

To *ascend* and *stand* presents a beautiful vision of worship. What a joy to be silent and simply bask in God's holy presence. Ascending the holy hill (3) is a parallel to trust; leaving the present position and moving forward toward God. *Righteousness* from God encompasses both prosperity and justification. The man who has all of his affairs under God's rule has God's blessing. The summons *"to the gate"* indicates the way to forgiveness.

This stirring challenge and response cannot help but bring forth introspection on the part of the worshiper. Is he indeed one who is worthy? Has he invited God to search him, has he been approved by God as one who is righteous? This psalm, quoted in 1 Chronicles 16, looks as far back as Abraham and as far forward as the reign of the Messiah. If in truth God is holy, the challenge that is heard at the ancient doors in not merely a quibble question, but is a point of meditation for all who would call Him Lord.

PSALM 25

¹[A Psalm] of David unto thee, O LORD,
do I lift up my soul.
²O my God, I trust in thee: let me not be ashamed,
let not mine enemies triumph over me.
³Yea, let none that wait on thee be ashamed: let
them be ashamed, which transgress without cause.
⁴Show me thy ways, O LORD; teach me thy paths.

⁵Lead me in thy truth, and teach me: for thou [art]
the God of my salvation;
on thee do I wait all the day.
⁶Remember, O LORD, thy tender mercies and thy
loving kindnesses; for they [have been] ever of old.
⁷ Remember not the sins of my youth, nor my transgressions: according to thy mercy remember thou
me for thy goodness' sake, O LORD.
⁸Good and upright [is] the LORD: therefore will
he teach sinners in the way.
⁹The meek, he will guide in judgment:
and the meek will he teach his way.
¹⁰All the paths of the LORD [are] mercy and truth
unto such as keep his covenant and his testimonies.
¹¹For thy name's sake, O LORD,
pardon mine iniquity; for it [is] great.
¹²What man [is] he that feareth the LORD? him shall
he teach in the way [that] he shall choose.
¹³His soul shall dwell at ease; and his
seed shall inherit the earth.
¹⁴The secret of the LORD [is] with them that fear
him; and he will show them his covenant.
¹⁵Mine eyes [are] ever toward the LORD; for he shall
pluck my feet out of the net.
¹⁶Turn thee unto me, and have mercy upon me; for I
[am] desolate and afflicted.
¹⁷The troubles of my heart are enlarged: [O] bring
thou me out of my distresses.
¹⁸Look upon mine affliction and my pain;
and forgive all my sins.

¹⁹Consider mine enemies; for they are many; and they hate me with cruel hatred.
²⁰O keep my soul, and deliver me: let me not be ashamed; for I put my trust in thee.
²¹Let integrity and uprightness preserve me; for I wait on thee.
²²Redeem Israel, O God, out of all his troubles.

PSALM 25
Title: Seventh Prayer of Distress
Author: a Psalm of David
Superscription: none
Theme: Prayer for Deliverance and Forgiveness

There are two dominant themes within this psalm: guilt and a need for guidance. The tone is subdued as the psalmist expresses his need for God's forgiveness. Enemies, seldom absent from David's life, oppose the way he runs the kingdom and the way he lives his personal life. The psalmist is endlessly harassed by the attack of his enemies and disquieted in his own conscience. Deeply aware of his need, he returns to God, asking for His help.

Instruction in the will of God is the first plea of this psalm. He desires to know the foundations of right decisions—a foundation which will train him to distinguish good from evil (Hebrews 5:4). Keenly aware of his sin, the psalmist begins to feel the effects of guilt. Eventually he reaches the point of obedience and humility, knowing that he is a sinner who requires God's teaching. God instructs sinners, not because of their goodness, but because He is good and upright (8), thus He has obligated Himself to reproduce these qualities in others.

God, however, does not work on man's time schedule and calls upon the psalmist to wait in hope. To wait is to accept that things happen in God's timing and by respecting this, one is waiting in anticipation rather than in resignation. It may be in one of these *waiting* times when David, in verses 8-14, meditates upon the combination of emotional, intellectual and moral attributes of God. Many of His characteristics are derived from His responses to His people in the past. He is just; He is righteous, loving and true to His word. David then reflects upon a man's trusting and reverential heart, which is the proper response to the love of God.

The passages of this psalm are intricately woven. David prays when his enemies try to betray him with falsehoods and lies. Prayer brings God's mercy, love, faithfulness and goodness. God brings relief and deliverance. If David must wait, as he does so, he focuses on the ability of God to deliver him from the trials of his life. His profession of faith and trust lead him to celebrate the love of Yahweh. Many petitions here are everlasting and timeless. This psalm should be read and read often.

PSALM 26

¹[A Psalm] of David. Judge me, O LORD; for I have walked in mine integrity: I have trusted also in the LORD; [therefore] I shall not slide.
²Examine me, O LORD, and prove me;
try my reins and my heart.

³For thy lovingkindness [is] before mine eyes:
and I have walked in thy truth.
⁴I have not sat with vain persons,
neither will I go in with disassemblers.
⁵I have hated the congregation of evildoers;
and will not sit with the wicked.
⁶I will wash mine hands in innocency:
so I will compass thine altar, O LORD:
⁷That I may publish with the voice of Thanksgiving,
and tell of all thy wondrous works.
⁸LORD, I have loved the habitation of thy house,
and the place where thine honor dwelleth.
⁹Gather not my soul with sinners,
nor my life with bloody men:
¹⁰In whose hands [is] mischief,
and their right hand is full of bribes.
¹¹But as for me, I will walk in mine integrity: redeem me, and be merciful unto me.
¹²My foot standeth in an even place: in the congregations I will bless the LORD.

PSALM 26
Title: First Testimony/Prayer Psalm
Author: a Psalm of David
Superscription: none
Theme: A Prayer for Redemption

David has lived a consistent life of trust and obedience to God. He is not claiming perfection or being self-righteous, only stating the facts as he views them. Though unclear, this prayer hints that threats are being made by the liars and violent men of the city. *"Examine me and prove me"* verifies David's commitment to Yahweh and displays the genuineness of his heart. David claims to have walked in the truth, avoided any contact with renegades and to have followed the Law of Moses. In contrast to the behavior of his enemies, he believes that he is "quite an example" to others.

If these verses sound overtly arrogant, then David's meaning is obscured. Hating evil company is not simply a matter of social preference, but of spiritual choice and activity. David's character and kingdom were both at stake and his circle of associates would tip the scales. His heart is with God, but the heart may be misled when it comes to the selection of one's friends and allies.

This is the secret of true independence, as Paul was to find out in the cross current of criticism and intrigue, (reference 1 Corinthians 4:3-5). When David thought of his ways in detail, not merely of his *overall* loyalty, his plea to be *searched* and *known* became no longer a demand, as in verse 2, but a surrender. This is also seen in Psalm 139:23.

At psalm's close, there is a well-rounded view of a godly person's ability to love God without entering into fear. David shows that his will is to persist in his walk with God. He is certain that in the end he will be vindicated. He now focuses on the future, saying, "*I* will *walk in integrity."* Again, this is not self-righteousness but a promise, since the second element is humility along with a heartfelt confession of his own.

So the song which began defensively ends with praise and joy, adding one's voice to those of the multitudes of fellow believers.

Note: The word "habitation" as it is used here refers to the place where God dwells. In the wilderness, God's glory had dwelt visibly in the tabernacle. In Judaism, the word for dwelling is shekinah *and this word became a standard term when describing the glory of God. In a Messianic foreshadowing of Christ, John 1:14 Jesus announces His existence in the cloud and the fire: the word became flesh and dwelt among us; we have beheld His glory, glory as of the only Son from the Father.*

PSALM 27

¹[a Psalm] of David. The LORD [is] my light and my salvation; whom shall I fear? the LORD [is] the strength of my life; of whom shall I be afraid?
²When the wicked, [even] mine enemies and my foes, came upon me to eat up my flesh,
they stumbled and fell.
³Though an host should encamp against me, my heart shall not fear: though war should rise against me, in this [will] I [be] confident.
⁴One [thing] have I desired of the LORD, that I will seek after; that I may dwell in the house of the LORD all the days of my life, to behold the beauty of the LORD, and to inquire in his temple.

⁵For in the time of trouble he shall hide me in his pavilion: in the secret of his tabernacle shall he hide me; he shall set me up upon a rock.
⁶And now shall mine head be lifted up above mine enemies round about me: therefore will I offer in his tabernacle sacrifices of joy; I will sing, yea,
I will sing praises unto the LORD.
⁷Hear, O LORD, [when] I cry with my voice: have mercy also upon me, and answer me.
⁸[When thou saidst], Seek ye my face; my heart said unto thee, Thy face, LORD, will I seek.
⁹Hide not thy face [far] from me; put not thy servant away in anger: thou hast been my help; leave me not, neither forsake me, O God of my salvation.
¹⁰When my father and my mother forsake me, then the Lord will take me up.
¹¹Teach me thy way, O LORD, and lead me in a plain path, because of mine enemies.
¹²Deliver me not over unto the will of mine enemies: for false witnesses are risen up against me, and such as breathe out cruelty.
¹³[I had fainted], unless I had believed to see the goodness of the LORD in the land of the living.
¹⁴Wait on the LORD: be of good courage, and he shall strengthen thine heart: wait,
I say, on the LORD.

PSALM 27
Title: Eighth Psalm of Distress
Author: a Psalm of David
Superscription: none
Theme: A Joyous Declaration of Faith

This vibrant and picturesque psalm expands on the themes which surround it. Psalms 26 and 28 focus upon the protection of the Lord, the awe of being in His house and the joy of worship. If a man has his priorities in the correct order, (4, 8) he has nothing to fear from the Lord, (1-3, 5-6). He is keenly aware of whom to turn to in times of trouble (7-12) and his hope is well-founded (13-14). The vivid contrast (1-6 and 7-14) has brought many commentators to determine that this psalm is a composite of earlier psalms. Composite or single, the energy and spirit of this song is apparent.

The beginning of the psalm asks, "Whom shall I fear?" This states that he is not underrating the power of those who fight against him. The need of a stronghold or refuge is a reminder that even life may be lost at the hands of their enemies. In verses 7-14 there is an anxious cry of fear, "Hear, O Lord". These words shift the mood entirely from triumph to a deep distress when David is facing an utter lack of hope as in 1 Samuel 23:26. The best methods of avoiding fear of enemies, of habits, or temptations lies in being absorbed by God's purpose and His will. This is the essence of worship as well as the foundation of discipleship.

Even though the psalmist is mired in depression, feeling forsaken and rejected, his trust in God will not fail. From the brink of distress, he returns his thoughts to God. Once again, he settles in with patience, waiting for God to work out His will in this situation. David is a worshiper seeking God's face. He is committed to walk the path God has given him, despite the fact that every step he takes seems to cause problems. He is bound up with God, yet, although it is distasteful, he knows that he is also bound up in the world. He has learned that the best method of avoiding fear of enemies, of habits, or temptations lies in being absorbed by God's purpose and His will. This is the essence of worship as well as the foundation of discipleship.

PSALM 28

¹[a Psalm] of David. Unto thee will I cry, O LORD, my rock; be not silent to me: lest, [if] thou be silent to me, I become like them that go down into the pit.
²Hear the voice of my supplications, when I cry unto thee, when I lift up my hands toward thy holy oracle.
³Draw me not away with the wicked, and with the workers of iniquity, which speak peace to their neighbors, but mischief [is] in their hearts.
⁴Give them according to their deeds, and according to the wickedness of their endeavors: give them after the work of their hands;
render to them their desert.

⁵Because they regard not the works of the LORD, nor the operation of his hands, he shall destroy them, and not build them up.
⁶Blessed [be] the LORD, because he hath heard the voice of my supplications.
⁷The LORD [is] my strength and my shield; my heart trusted in him, and I am helped: therefore my heart greatly rejoiceth; and with my song I will praise him.
⁸The LORD [is] their strength, and he [is] the saving strength of his anointed.
⁹Save thy people, and bless thine inheritance: feed them also, and lift them up forever.

PSALM 28
Title: Third Prayer for Judgment
Author: a Psalm of David
Superscription: none
Theme: Rejoicing in Answered Prayer

This psalm is the story of prayer and its answer. Danger leads to a cry for help and a plea for the punishment of evil men. The psalmist is in deep despair. He is not afraid of death, but of an unmerited disgrace brought about by those who hate and despise him. This psalm, like many other laments, exposes the continual strife between those of David's faith and those who are strangers or pagans. He prays for deliverance from the constant peril which he faces at the hands of his heathen enemies. While lingering upon the fate which will eventually overcome the wicked, at the same time he fears that he will suffer the same consequences.

In verses 1 and 2 the psalmist pleads with God to *"be not silent."* He desperately asks for God to hear the sound of his cry and to answer him. To a Hebrew, the lack of an answer indicated that God *has not* or *will not* hear a man's petition. The urgent nature is emphasized by the fear that unless he hears from God, he will die. David prays for protection, but his emphasis quickly changes to a request for reprisal and retaliation upon his enemies. Nothing burns so deeply as injustice and nothing should. The verses are not vindictive, but express the feelings of any wholesome or reverent conscience. David is reaching with trust as a child strains to the arms of a parent. At the same time, he is asking God to intercede for him (Exodus 17:9) by calling down God's wrath upon the heads of his enemies.

The psalm transitions from prayer to an attitude of gratitude in verses 6 and 7. This outburst of excitement and praise is interpreted as confirmation that the prayer has been answered. It is possible that this joyous thanksgiving may have been added later, but may be simply the inner confidence that God has heard and is no longer silent. David gives thanks for the protection of his kingdom. He is more than just a private citizen and as the Lord's *anointed* (a term which grew into the word Messiah), he represented the kingdom as well. God's grace toward him and toward the people was bound together. A final prayer makes brings the realization that nothing is as precious as knowing that God considers Israel and its people as His most valuable possession.

PSALM 29

¹A Psalm of David. Give unto the LORD, O ye mighty, give unto the LORD glory and strength.
²Give unto the LORD the glory due unto his name; worship the LORD in the beauty of holiness.
³The voice of the LORD [is] upon the waters: the God of glory thundereth: the LORD [is] upon many waters.
⁴The voice of the LORD [is] powerful; the voice of the LORD [is] full of majesty.
⁵The voice of the LORD breaketh the cedars; yea, the LORD breaketh the cedars of Lebanon.
⁶He maketh them also to skip like a calf; Lebanon and Sirion like a young unicorn.
⁷The voice of the LORD divideth the flames of fire.
⁸The voice of the LORD shaketh the wilderness; the LORD shaketh the wilderness of Kadesh.
⁹The voice of the LORD maketh the hinds to calve, and discovereth the forests: and in his temple doth everyone speak of [his] glory.
¹⁰The LORD sitteth upon the flood; yea, the LORD sitteth King forever.
¹¹The LORD will give strength unto his people; the LORD will bless his people with peace.

PSALM 29
Title: First Psalm of Praise
Author: a Psalm of David
Subscription: none
Theme: Praise for the Holiness and Majesty of God

The voice of God, in its awe-inspiring majesty, rings clearly through this psalm. It is easy to picture the violent thunderstorm as it comes in from the sea, down the length of Canaan and away into the desert. As the thunder quietly dies, the Lord sits in judgment over His world. In all of the metaphors of nature, God is clearly seen: the thunder, the rain, the lightening and the wind that sets the forests in motion. Everyone is encouraged to give the Lord endless glory! Among the scriptures, this stands as a beautiful picture of the beauty and power of God. (There are however, parallels in terminology with Canaanite Psalms from 1400-1300 BC discovered in Syria.)

God is above and over nature, commanding it with His words in the same manner as He created the earth and all that is upon it. This psalm is often recited on the day of Pentecost as it refers to the "flames of fire" in Acts 2:2-5. In praise to the King of creation, the psalm speaks of the winter storms of the Mediterranean going from west to east across the Lebanon range and merging with the winds of Northern Kadesh.

As seen here, the most powerful experiences to the Hebrews were earthquakes and raging seas. The actions of nature continually reminded them of His power and glory and caused them to meditate on the strength of the Lord. All creation urges the singing of praise. The psalm closes with the promise that the God who rides the floods will give strength to His people and will bless them forever.

PSALM 30

^{1}A Psalm [and] Song [at] the dedication of the house of David. I will extol thee, O LORD; for thou hast lifted me up, and hast not made
my foes to rejoice over me.
^{2}O LORD my God, I cried unto thee,
and thou hast healed me.
^{3}O LORD, thou hast brought up my soul from the grave: thou hast kept me alive, that I should
not go down to the pit.
^{4}Sing unto the LORD, O ye saints of his, and give thanks at the remembrance of his holiness.
^{5}For his anger [endureth but] a moment;
in his favor [is] life: weeping may endure for a night, but joy [cometh] in the morning.
^{6}And in my prosperity I said, I shall never be moved.
^{7}LORD, by thy favor, thou hast made my mountain to stand strong: thou didst hide thy face, [and] I
was troubled.
^{8}I cried unto thee, O LORD;
and unto the LORD I made supplication.
^{9}What profit [is there] in my blood, when I go down to the pit? shall the dust praise thee?
Shall it declare thy truth?

> ¹⁰Hear, O LORD, and have mercy upon me:
> LORD, be thou my helper.
> ¹¹Thou hast turned for me my mourning into
> dancing; thou hast put off my sackcloth,
> and girded me with gladness;
> ¹² To the end that [my] glory may sing praise to thee,
> and not be silent. O LORD my God,
> I will give thanks unto thee for ever.

PSALM 30
Title: Third Praise/Prayer Psalm
Author: a Psalm of David
Date: (Probably) the Dedication of the House of David
Superscription: a Song of Dedication
Theme: The Blessing of Answered Prayer

This psalm gives the definition of joy: loud singing, rejoicing in triumph, cheering and praising God in loud voices and with thanksgiving. As seen in Proverbs 11, this joyous outburst describes the inward feelings experienced by the righteous. When God eliminates the wicked of the world, Zephaniah 3:17 literally says that God will dance over His chosen people with singing.

Several occasions may have initiated this psalm: 1) the dedication of David's personal palace after he had conquered Jerusalem, (2 Samuel 5:11, 7:2), 2) the dedication of God's house in verses 1-12, 3) a deliverance from an enemy as in 1 Chronicles 21, or a celebration of good health from a debilitating illness, possibly one which was life threatening.

Not knowing the origin of the psalm makes it much less restrictive. It also came to be applied to the exile which had been experienced by Israel, celebrating their return to Zion. In Jewish liturgical practice (from Talmudic times), it is chanted at Hanukkah. Hanukkah is the feast celebrating the rededication of the Temple by Judas Maccabee after its desecration by Antioch Epiphanies. As a part of the celebration, appropriate speeches and songs (Deuteronomy 20:5; Ezra 6:16) were also commonplace.

The psalmist says of God in verses 1-3, "I will extol thee, O Lord." The vivid cry of "thou hast brought up my soul" would be applicable in any situation where God had intervened on behalf of His people. The term *"strong mountain"* (7) is more accurately expressed as *"my mountain stands strong"*. This is the metaphor for both David's kingdom and for his personal life. It is clear that the frailty of the king makes him of little or no use to the people unless he is linked to the Creator. The words of verse 10 are eternal, showing simply that David is a man in need of God's grace.

The closing verses look back at the first five verses which, enhanced by the remembrances of God's glory and goodness of verses 6-10, end the psalm. There is a reflection back to the spirit of David, who danced before the Lord with all his might. This praise, which has the effervescence of dancing, also has silence and persistence; more persistence than David himself could imagine when he included the word *"forever"*. Knowing how to praise the Lord, in joy or in silence, will always give the spirit the power to say, *"I shall never be moved!"*

PSALM 31

¹To the chief Musician, a Psalm of David. In thee, O LORD, do I put my trust; let me never be ashamed: deliver me in thy righteousness.
²Bow down thine ear to me; deliver me speedily: be thou my strong rock,
for an house of defense to save me.
³For thou [art] my rock and my fortress; therefore for thy name's sake lead me, and guide me.
⁴Pull me out of the net that they have laid privily for me: for thou [art] my strength.
⁵Into thine hand I commit my spirit: thou hast redeemed me, O LORD God of truth.
⁶I have hated them that regard lying vanities: but I trust in the Lord.
⁷I will be glad and rejoice in thy mercy: for thou hast considered my trouble;
thou hast known my soul in adversities;
⁸And hast not shut me up into the hand of the enemy: thou hast set my feet in a large room.
⁹Have mercy upon me, O LORD, for I am in trouble: mine eye is consumed with grief,
[yea], my soul and my belly.
¹⁰For my life is spent with grief, and my years with sighing: my strength faileth because of mine iniquity, and my bones are consumed.

¹¹I was a reproach among mine enemies, but especially among my neighbors,
and a fear to mine acquaintance:
they that did see me without fled from me.
¹²I am forgotten as a dead man out of mind:
I am like a broken vessel.
¹³For I have heard the slander of many: fear [was] on every side: while they took counsel together against me, they devised to take away my life.
¹⁴But I trusted in thee, O LORD: I said,
Thou [art] my God.
¹⁵My times [are] in thy hand:
deliver me from the hand of mine enemies,
and from them that persecute me.
¹⁶Make thy face to shine upon thy servant:
save me, for thy mercies' sake.
¹⁷Let me not be ashamed, O LORD; for I have called upon thee: let the wicked be ashamed,
[and] let them be silent in the grave.
¹⁸Let the lying lips be put to silence;
which speak grievous things proudly and
contemptuously against the righteous.
¹⁹[Oh] how great [is] thy goodness, which thou hast laid up for them that fear thee: [which] thou hast wrought for them that trust in
thee before the sons of men!
²⁰Thou shalt hide them in the secret of thy presence from the pride of man: thou shalt keep them secretly in a pavilion from the strife of tongues.
²¹Blessed [be] the LORD: for he hath showed me his marvelous kindness in a strong city.

²²For I said in my haste, I am cut off from before thine eyes: nevertheless thou heardest the voice of my supplications when I cried unto thee.
²³O love the LORD, all ye saints: [for] the LORD preserveth the faithful, and plentifully rewardeth the proud doer.
²⁴Be of good courage, and he shall strengthen your heart, all ye that hope in the LORD.

PSALM 31
Title: Ninth Prayer of Distress
Author: a Psalm of David
Superscription: to the chief Musician
Theme: The Lord is a Fortress in Times of Trouble

The first eight verses have made this psalm the voice of many worshipers throughout Jewish and Christian history. The change in verse 9 puts a different tone into the psalm, highlighting that this psalm was composed by a variety of authors. The latter section is more indicative of a single writer. The psalm, however, makes no dependence upon the writers, but is instead a description of the soul of man. It speaks of man's interests, tears, turmoil and at last, his triumph.

This expressive psalm has been the testimonial of many notable characters in both the Old and New Testament. In a moment of deep crisis (6), Jonas draws upon it. Like the prophet Jeremiah the psalmist feels *tossed out* and of no value to God—a clear description of his own plight. There is no other psalm which tells of greater "steadiness" or "sturdiness" of the Lord. Jesus applied Psalm 31:15 to his own circumstances; in Luke 23:46 He echoed the words of verse 5: "Into your hands I commit my spirit." Christians who may be suffering at the hands of non-believers are invited to share in these words and turn sorrow into a new and joy-filled life.

As David remembers his earlier days, he also remembers that beneath those frightening times was the reality of his refuge in God. Trust for God deepens (1-5) with David's recollection (6-8) of how God had continually given him courage and strength. What started as a psalm of surrender now strays to the strong enmity of a faithful individual against the multitudes. This peace is short-lived, however, as again in verses 9-13 he is quickly dragged back to the present dilemma. Coming away from his confident feelings, the topic shifts back to pleas of deliverance from his cruel enemies. He starts with the words, "Have mercy on me." The continual abhorrent behavior of his enemies carries him as a river from hopelessness (12) to terror (13) to the murderous acts and thoughts which are "fathered" by hatred.

David places his life back into the secure hands of God, finding that his heart is settled as he accepts God's sovereignty. It is with a renewed confidence that he is able (23-24) to give help and encouragement to others. He now shares in the Covenant benefits that God has offered to those who are faithful. Thus, with the Lord's approval he is once again able to stand against his enemies with no regard for the accusations of others.

David calls the saints to walk in integrity and uprightness, trusting in the Lord. Those who refuse to have humble reliance on the Lord must arrogantly scheme to make their own way. They have become a law unto themselves, as in Deuteronomy 8:16-19. Reliance on the ability of self is just another form of pagan worship and those who are proud are the same as those who are wicked. Even in his current situation, the psalmist knows that if he depends on God, the wicked will be defeated.

Note: The title Rabbi is the derivation of the word rab. *In general, Rabbi has been meant as "my teacher". A more exact explanation shows that it means "my great one" (full of knowledge, master, great instructor). Thus, the Lord did not allow His followers to call Him by this lofty title. He stressed that there is but one Rabbi and that is God.*

PSALM 32

¹[A Psalm] of David, Maschil. Blessed [is he whose] transgression [is] forgiven, [whose] sin [is] covered.
²Blessed [is] the man,
unto whom the LORD imputeth not iniquity,
and in whose spirit [there is] no guile.
³When I kept my silence, my bones waxed old
through my roaring all the day long.

⁴For day and night thy hand was heavy upon me: my
moisture is turned into the draught of summer.
⁵I acknowledged my sin unto thee, and mine iniquity
have I not hid. I said, I will confess
my transgressions unto the LORD;
and thou forgavest the iniquity of my sin.
⁶For this shall everyone that is godly pray unto thee
in a time when thou mayest be found:
surely in the floods of great waters
they shall not come nigh unto him.
⁷Thou [art] my hiding place; thou shalt preserve me
from trouble; thou shalt compass me about
with songs of deliverance.
⁸I will instruct thee and teach thee in the way which
thou shalt go: I will guide thee with mine eye.
⁹Be not as the horse, [or] as the mule, [which] have
no understanding: whose mouth must be held in
with bit and bridle, lest they come near unto thee.
¹⁰Many sorrows [shall be] to the wicked:
but he that trusteth in the LORD,
mercy shall compass him about.
¹¹Be glad in the LORD, and rejoice, ye righteous: and
shout for joy, all [ye that are] upright in heart.

PSALM 32
Title: Second Psalm of Instruction
Author: a Psalm of David
Superscription: *Maschil an instructing or musing*
Theme: Forgiveness

This psalm is the second of the seven *Instructional Psalms*. There is only a vague overtone in which it may be suggested that this psalm was used by a group. It appears to be a dialog between God and David. Jews, Christians and others who read this word are allowed to become privy to this conversation. This psalm comes with the admonishment to *speak to the Lord* while He may be found (Isaiah 55:6) and not to provoke Him, even in the face of punishment. In this way, joy can come to the sinful one because of his complete pardon from God. A God who forgives is a God who can be thoroughly trusted. In Canaanite mythology, the sea and death were the two great enemies of Baal; the imagery which comes from scripture and mythology are often placed side by side to depict threats and distress.

Without mythology, one can easily see the value of being righteous and the importance of practicing this truth. Romans 4:6-8 shows that the word *"imputes"* (or reckons) implies that God's treatment of man as righteous is His gift, having nothing to do with what a man's actions deserve. The word *reckoned* is the same word in Genesis 15:6 and is used to teach that the gift of God is received by faith alone. Any idea, however, that we are free *to continue in sin that grace may abound* is firmly excluded by the emphasis and focus on sincerity at the close of this verse.

The psalm ends on a note of gladness with a reminder for Israel to become a teachable people. Forgiveness from God is good; fellowship with God is better and when one has experienced the heavy hand of discipline in life, how much more can one appreciate the gentle touch of God.

*Note: Four words are used for sin: **"transgression"**, which means a **willful disobedience**; "sin" refers to **missing the mark**; "iniquity" implies some form of **perversity**; "guile" suggests **self-deception**. Each of these is a moral offense, but is still covered by God's mercy and forgiveness.*

PSALM 33

¹Rejoice in the LORD, O ye righteous:
[for] praise is comely for the upright.
²Praise the LORD with harp: sing unto him with the
psaltery [and] an instrument of ten strings.
³Sing unto him a new song; play skillfully
with a loud noise.
⁴For the word of the LORD [is] right;
and all his works [are done] in truth.
⁵He loveth righteousness and judgment: the earth is
full of the goodness of the LORD.
⁶By the word of the LORD were the heavens made;
and all the host of them by the breath of his mouth.

⁷He gathereth the waters of the sea together as an heap: he layeth up the depth in storehouses.
⁸Let all the earth fear the LORD: let all the inhabitants of the world stand in awe of him.
⁹For he spake, and it was [done];
he commanded, and it stood fast.
¹⁰The LORD bringeth the counsel of the heathen to naught: he maketh the devices of
the people of none effect.
¹¹The counsel of the LORD standeth for ever,
the thoughts of his heart to all generations.
¹²Blessed [is] the nation whose God [is] the LORD;
[and] the people [whom] he hath
chosen for his own inheritance.
¹³The LORD looketh from heaven;
he beholdeth all the sons of men.
¹⁴From the place of his habitation he
looketh upon all the inhabitants of the earth.
¹⁵He fashioneth their hearts alike;
he considereth all their works.
¹⁶There is no king saved by the multitude of an host:
a mighty man is not delivered by much strength.
¹⁷An horse [is] a vain thing for safety: neither shall
he deliver [any] by his great strength.
¹⁸Behold, the eye of the LORD [is] upon them that
fear him, upon them that hope in his mercy;
¹⁹To deliver their soul from death,
and to keep them alive in famine.
²⁰Our soul waiteth for the LORD:
he [is] our help and our shield.

²¹For our heart shall rejoice in him,
because we have trusted in his holy name.
²²Let thy mercy, O LORD, be upon us,
according as we hope in thee.

PSALM 33
Title: Fourth Praise/Prayer Psalm
Author: anonymous
Date: (Possibly) the Deliverance of Judah
Superscription: none
Theme: The Lord in Creation

This psalm is a perfect example of what it is to praise God for *what* He does and more importantly, for *who* He is. The entire psalm is filled with descriptions of the Lord as creator, sovereign, judge and savior to the world. The voices of the Levitical choir are heard in this song, perhaps with the leader speaking verses 1-3, followed by the choir (4-19) and a response from the people in verses 20-22. This psalm seems somewhat misplaced in Book One, but it stands here as the answer to verse 11 of the preceding psalm. This answer converts a personal experience into a corporate hymn of thanksgiving. The fact that there are 22 verses may refer to the Hebrew alphabet, but there is no acrostic arrangement.

The initial circumstance is unknown, but reference to a *new song* suggests a nationwide deliverance, such as Judah experienced in a time of Jehoshaphat or Hezekiah. The phrase *"new song"* is seen six times in the psalms and has many parallels to Paul's visions. Every new experience of God brings with it a new vision. The apostle John, in his vision, heard a *new song* in heaven (Revelation 5:9-10; 14:3). The *new song* is a wonderful and spontaneous outburst of praise and joy.

As described in the psalm, the reason for the outburst of praise (4-9) is a result of the awesome work which God has done. God cannot be separated from either His works or His word. To know that nothing ever existed except by God's command (6, 9) is to be faced with the grandeur of creation. We were not made for self-glory or as a necessity of God, but as a work of His choice. There are no scientific facts which conclusively support the evolutionary model of humanity. The word of God is faithful, upright, loving and full of justice; these are the evolutions of God.

Many thoughts and feelings are expressed here in their purest form: patience (20); confidence (20); buoyant (1) and well formed (21). The name of God as used here was revealed in Exodus 34:5 and serves to focus worship on the giver rather than on the gift. All hope and praise is to be given to God for such a hope will never give itself to disappointment (Romans 5:5). Stand firm, even as the world stands firm because it is ordered to do so by the word of God. The word by which God governs all things is not chaotic, devious or erratic. Under His rule, order and goodness are present in all creation.

The Lord sees what all men think and he understands the thoughts of evil or deceitful men. He recognizes tyranny just as He recognizes the needs of His own people. God's rule is based on His perfect knowledge, (13-15), His perfect control of all things

(16) and above all, His perfect love (18). Even now, facing life in a corrupt and warring world, force is not the answer. *Moreover*, in the unusual circumstance where evil and wicked do succeed, the Old Testament assures us that it does not do so by its own ability, but only because God has allowed it to be so.

PSALM 34

¹[A Psalm] of David, when he changed his behavior before Abimelech; who drove him away, and he departed. I will bless the LORD at all times: his praise [shall] continually [be] in my mouth.
²My soul shall make her boast in the LORD: the humble shall hear [there of], and be glad.
³O magnify the LORD with me,
and let us exalt his name together.
⁴I sought the LORD, and he heard me, and delivered me from all my fears.
⁵They looked unto him, and were lightened: and their faces were not ashamed.
⁶This poor man cried, and the LORD heard [him], and saved him out of all of his troubles.
⁷The angel of the LORD encampeth round about them that fear him, and delivereth them.
⁸O taste and see that the LORD [is] good: blessed [is] the man [that] trusteth in him.
⁹O fear the LORD, ye his saints: for [there is] no want to them that fear him.

¹⁰The young lions do lack, and suffer hunger:
but they that seek the LORD
shall not want any good [thing].
¹¹Come, ye children, hearken unto me: I will teach
you the fear of the LORD.
¹²What man [is he that] desireth life,
[and] loveth [many] days, that he may see good?
¹³Keep thy tongue from evil,
and thy lips from speaking guile.
¹⁴Depart from evil, and do good;
seek peace and pursue it.
¹⁵The eyes of the LORD [are] upon the righteous,
and his ears [are open] unto their cry.
¹⁶The face of the LORD [is] against them that do evil,
to cut off the remembrance of them from the earth.
¹⁷[The righteous] cry, and the Lord heareth, and
delivereth them out of all their troubles.
¹⁸The LORD [is] nigh unto them that are of a broken
heart; and saveth such as be of a contrite spirit.
¹⁹Many [are] the afflictions of the righteous: but the
LORD delivereth him out of them all.
²⁰He keepeth all his bones:
not one of them is broken.
²¹Evil shall slay the wicked: and they that hate the
righteous shall be desolate.
²²The LORD redeemeth the soul of his servants: and
none of them that trust in him shall be desolate.

PSALM 34
Title: Second Psalm of Deliverance
Author: a Psalm of David
Date: When Abimelech Drove David Away
Superscription: David's Behavior toward Abimelech
Theme: Happiness for Those Who Trust in God

This psalm glows with relief and gratitude for David's miraculous escape from his son Abimelech. David had successfully executed his plan for escape by acting as if he were mad. Although Abimelech wanted him dead, he would not have his father's blood on his hands. This psalm is an acrostic, similar in structure to Psalm 25 and both contain similar thoughts of thanksgiving as those expressed in the Book of Proverbs.

The summons to praise rings out in the first three verses. David has determined that he will praise God continually. The invitation is extended to those who exhibit humility and are willing to accept a commitment to praise the Lord. David owes his life to God. Trials and adversity are ever constant in his life, yet he is always aware that God has been beside him and carried him through. He states confidently that what the Lord (Yahweh) has done for him, He will also do for all men who both fear and praise His holy name.

The word *"taste"* as used in verse 8 is the same as the metaphor used in 1 Peter 2:3 when Peter calls men to examine and perceive the wonders of the Lord. In verse 5, the word *"radiant"* is likened to Isaiah 60:5 where it speaks of a mother's face at the sight of a long lost child. Verse 14 again refers to the troubles speech can cause when it is misused. James 1:26 further expounds upon this important point. Other phrases in verses 12-16 will later be quoted by Peter in his letters to the churches.

The lesson here answers questions regarding the enjoyment of life. The good things of life which are joyful (12) are inextricably linked with the good that is done (14). The actual apex of the psalm comes in verse 15 where God's face is turns toward man-His eyes see even those things which have been so carefully hidden. His ears are always open and although He is ever aware of man's failings, He takes prayer to be serious and legitimate. The final verses again emphasize the chasm between the lovers of God and those who have rejected Him.

Note: There is a distinct Messianic foreshadowing in verses 17-22. Jesus, like His Father before Him (as they cannot be separated), delivered the people, drew near to the brokenhearted, healed the righteous and as He was crucified, not one of His bones was broken.

PSALM 35

¹[A Psalm] of David. Plead [my cause], O LORD,
with them that strive with me:
fight against them that fight against me.
²Take hold of shield and buckler,
and stand up for mine help.

³Draw out also the spear, and stop [the way] against them that persecute me: say unto my soul,
I [am] thy salvation.
⁴Let them be confounded and put to shame that seek after my soul: let them be turned back and brought into confusion that devise my hurt.
⁵Let them be as chaff before the wind: and let the angel of the LORD chase [them].
⁶Let their way be dark and slippery: and let the angel of the LORD persecute them.
⁷For without cause they have hid for me their net [in] a pit [which] without cause
they have digged for my soul.
⁸Let destruction come upon him at unawares; and let his net that he hath hid catch himself: into that very destruction let him fall.
⁹And my soul shall be joyful in the LORD:
it shall rejoice in his salvation.
¹⁰All my bones shall say, LORD, who [is] like unto thee, which deliverest the poor from him that is too strong for him, yea, the poor and the needy
from him that spoileth him?
¹¹False witnesses did rise up; they laid to my charge [things] that I knew not.
¹²They rewarded me evil for good [to]
the spoiling of my soul.
¹³But as for me, when they were sick, my clothing [was] sackcloth: I humbled my soul with fasting; and my prayer returned into mine own bosom.

¹⁴I behaved myself as though [he had been] my friend [or] brother: I bowed down heavily, as one that mourneth [for his] mother.
¹⁵But in mine adversity they rejoiced, and gathered themselves together: [yea], the abjects gathered themselves together against me, and I knew [it] not; they did tear [me], and ceased not:
¹⁶With hypocritical mockers in feasts, they gnashed upon me with their teeth.
¹⁷Lord, how long wilt thou look on? rescue my soul from their destructions, my darling from the lions.
¹⁸I will give thee thanks in the great congregation: I will praise thee among much people.
¹⁹Let not them that are mine enemies wrongfully rejoice over me: [neither] let them wink with the eye that hate me without a cause.
²⁰For they speak not peace: but they devise deceitful matters against [them that are] quiet in the land.
²¹Yea, they opened their mouth wide against me, [and] said, Aha, aha, our eye hath seen [it].
²²[This] thou hast seen, O LORD: keep not silence: O LORD, be not far from me.
²³Stir up thyself, and awake to my judgment, [even] unto my cause, my God and my Lord.
²⁴Judge me, O LORD my God, according to thy righteousness; and let them not rejoice over me.
²⁵Let them not say in their hearts, Ah, so would we have it: let them not say, We have swallowed him up.
²⁶Let them be ashamed and brought to confusion together that rejoice at mine hurt: let them be

clothed with shame and dishonor that magnify [themselves] against me.

²⁷Let them shout for joy, and be glad, that favor my righteous cause: yea, let them say continually, Let the LORD be magnified, which hath pleasure in the prosperity of his servant.

²⁸And my tongue shall speak of thy righteousness [and] of thy praise all the day long.

PSALM 35
Title: Fourth Prayer for Judgment
Author: a Psalm of David
Superscription: none
Theme: The Lord is the Avenger of His people

This psalm of judgment put forth by David contains 18 requests for God's judgment on the wicked and evil people of the world. David openly displays the misery and frustration of those who must continually suffer injustice. He watches the wrongdoers prosper in every aspect of life, while also seeing the anguish of the righteous. As a faithful man, David refuses to become isolated, angry or bitter, stating that in every circumstance there is joy in the Lord.

This song bears an echo of the Song of Moses (Exodus 15:11) and of Paul who, in his recollection of the resurrection (2 Corinthians 1-8), discovered that he could find peace in the darkest of places. Many other verses in the New Testament show this psalm to be a witness of an unspoken prophecy of things to come. It has often been said that the New Testament is the Old Testament fulfilled. These verses definitely lay the groundwork for things to come.

Each of the imprecatory Psalms-15, 58, 59, 69, 109 and 137-wish anguish upon their enemies. The fact that these are not God's pronouncements, but rather the prayers for God to destroy his enemies, puts this psalm on a collision course with the teachings of Jesus. Jesus spoke of *loving* those who do evil. Can both of these ideas be correct? The short answer is *yes*. In the Old Testament God's goal was to build a *nation* that would later receive the coming Christ. Unfortunately, His imperfect humans did not always cooperate and anger and wrath fell upon them in discipline. God's focus, through Jesus, is the *transformation* of individuals rather than teaching basic lessons.

The psalmist vigorously prays for God to uphold him, being confident that the course of his life truly is a transformation to righteousness. He calls on God to punish his enemies (1-6, 17, 26) and to clear his good name. He makes his case before God in verses 7, 11-16, 17 and 25. He begs of God to *"plead my cause"*, but he wants justice on his own terms. He totally resents everything about his enemies and wants God to totally obliterate them, but to make sure that they suffer along the way. Once this is done, the psalmist promises to praise God (10, 18, 28) and tell of His righteous actions. Verses 11-18 are a continuation of his appeal to God and his desire for the destruction of his enemies. While this may refer to a second incident, the hopes of the psalmist are the same.

The psalm ends on a happy note. Happy, holy and at peace are those who seek the Lord. God is pleased to see His servants prosper! The Hebrew word translated here as *"prosperity"* has several meanings, such as safety, wellness, happiness and peace. When prosperity comes to His children, purchased by the blood of Jesus, one can only imagine His joy.

PSALM 36

¹To the chief Musician, [A Psalm] of David, the servant of the LORD. The transgression of the wicked saith within my heart, [that there is] no fear of God before his eyes.
²For he flattereth himself in his own eyes, and until his iniquity be found to be hateful.
³The words of his mouth [are] iniquity and deceit: he hath left off to be wise, [and] to do good.
⁴He deviseth mischief upon his bed; he setteth himself in a way [that is] not good; he abhorreth not evil.
⁵Thy mercy, O LORD, [is] in the heavens; [and] thy faithfulness [reacheth] unto the clouds.
⁶Thy righteousness [is] like the great mountains; thy judgments [are] a great deep: O LORD, thou preservest man and beast.
⁷How excellent [is] thy lovingkindness, O God! therefore, the children of men put their trust under the shadow of thy wings.

⁸They shall be abundantly satisfied with the fatness
of thy house; and thou shalt make them drink
of the rivers of thy pleasure.
⁹For with thee [is] the fountain of life:
and in thy light shall we see light.
¹⁰O continue thy lovingkindness unto them
that know thee; and thy righteousness
to the upright in heart.
¹¹Let not the foot of pride come against me, and let
not the hand of the wicked remove me.
¹²There are the workers of iniquity fallen: they are
cast down, and shall not be able to rise.

PSALM 36
Title: Second Psalm of the Wicked
Author a Psalm of David
Superscription: to the chief Musician
Theme: God's Perfection/Man's Wickedness

Beyond any in the Psalter, this is a genuine picture of human wickedness with all its depravity when it is compared to the righteous behavior of the true servants of the Most High. This psalm takes place at a time when the singer is being menaced and harassed and yet places all his faith is God, living with the assurance of victory. There are two well-defined pictures: one of *godliness* and one of *godlessness*. The writer uses a somewhat harsh poetic language as he describes the wicked among men. The characteristics of the righteous are shown in a gentler tone, in line with the gentleness of the Lord. Some suggest that this is the result of two poems being conjoined; that thought is neither clear nor necessary as the language and thought of the conclusion in verses 10-12 revert to the style and tone of the beginning.

The opening words mean literally "an Oracle of Transgression". This hints that the author is taking great efforts to expose the sinner, along with his evil misdeeds. The portrait is of one who is completely dedicated to a sinful life. A believer sets his pathway toward God; the sinner scoffs even at the terror of the Lord. A blatant dismissal of God is truly the culmination of wickedness. The wicked man has become too arrogant to detect his faults or to detest himself. His feeling of well-being makes him reckless, exposing and further motivating his craving for sinful thoughts and actions.

Like Scottish plaid, these light and dark colors weave a pattern in the text. Those who struggle and scheme to accumulate the goods of this world may be successful for a short time. Yet the brighter light, the light of God, will come upon His children and they will see the true light of life. That greater light is Jesus as is seen in John 8:12. The last verse claims the victory; it speaks as if the future was the present and the results were already visible. This is the same faith that is declared in Hebrews 11:1 as putting our confidence in the things we hope for; being certain of things we cannot see. His prayer and praise signified that he was ready to invoke the name of God and, having invoked the name of the Holy One, he is ready to accept the future; in his mind the matter is settled.

PSALM 37

¹[A Psalm] of David.
Fret not thyself because of evildoers, neither be thou envious against the workers of iniquity.
²For they shall soon be cut down like the grass, and wither as the green herb.
³Trust in the LORD, and do good; [so] shalt thou dwell in the land, and verily thou shalt be fed.
⁴Delight thyself also in the LORD; and he shall give thee the desires of thine heart.
⁵Commit thy ways unto the LORD; trust also in him; and he shall bring [it] to pass.
⁶And he shall bring forth thy righteousness as the light, and thy judgment as the noonday.
⁷Rest in the LORD, and wait patiently for him: fret not thyself because of him who prospereth in his way, because of the man who bringeth wicked devices to pass.
⁸Cease from anger, and forsake wrath: fret not thyself in any wise to do evil.
⁹For evildoers shall be cut off: but those that wait upon the LORD, they shall inherit the earth.
¹⁰For yet a little while, and the wicked [shall] not [be]: yea, thou shalt diligently consider his place, and it [shall] not [be].
¹¹But the meek shall inherit the earth; and shall delight themselves in the abundance of peace.
¹²The wicked plotteth against the just, and gnasheth upon him with his teeth.

¹³The Lord shall laugh at him:
for he seeth that his day is coming.
¹⁴The wicked have drawn out the sword, and have bent their bow, to cast down the poor and needy, [and] to slay such as be of upright conversation.
¹⁵Their sword shall enter into their own heart, and their bows shall be broken.
¹⁶A little that the righteous man hath [is] better than the riches of many wicked.
¹⁷For the arms of the wicked shall be broken: but the LORD upholdeth the righteous.
¹⁸The LORD knowest the days of the upright: and their inheritance shall be for ever.
¹⁹They shall not be ashamed in the evil time: and in the days of famine they shall be satisfied.
²⁰But the wicked shall perish, and the enemies of the LORD [shall be] as the fat of lambs: they shall consume; into smoke shall they consume away.
²¹The wicked borroweth, and payeth not again: but the righteous showeth mercy, and giveth.
²²For [such as be] blessed of him shall inherit the earth; and [they that be] cursed of him shall be cut off.
²³The steps of the [good] man are ordered by the LORD: and he delighteth in his way.
²⁴Though he fail, he shall not be utterly cast down: for the LORD upholdeth [him with] his hand.
²⁵I have been young, and [now] am old; yet have I not seen the righteous forsaken, nor his seed begging bread.

²⁶[He is] ever merciful, and lendeth;
and his seed [is] blessed.
²⁷Depart from evil, and do good;
and dwell for evermore.
²⁸For the LORD loveth judgment, and forsaketh not his saints; they are preserved for ever: but the seed of the wicked shall be cut off.
²⁹The righteous shall inherit the land,
and dwell therein for ever.
³⁰The mouth of the righteous speaketh wisdom,
and his tongue talketh of judgment.
³¹The law of his God [is] in his heart;
none of his steps shall slide.
³²The wicked watcheth the righteous,
and seeketh to slay him.
³³The LORD will not leave him in his hand, nor condemn him when he is judged.
³⁴Wait on the LORD, and keep his way, and he shall exalt thee to inherit the land: when the wicked are cut off, thou shalt see [it].
³⁵I have seen the wicked in great power, and spreading himself like a green bay tree.
³⁶Yet he passed away, and, lo, he [was] not: yea, I sought him, but he could not be found.
³⁷Mark the perfect [man], and behold the upright: for the end of [that] man [is] peace.
³⁸But the transgressors shall be destroyed together: the end of the wicked shall be cut off.
³⁹But the salvation of the righteous [is] of the LORD: [he is] their strength in the time of trouble.

⁴⁰And the LORD shall help them, and deliver them, he shall deliver them from the wicked, and save them, because they trust in him.

PSALM 37
Title: Third Psalm of Instruction
Author: a Psalm of David
Superscription: none
Theme: The Heritage of the Righteous

Psalm 37 is an acrostic poem which is full of the proverbial sayings of the wisdom writers. Described here are people flagrantly disobeying God's law, enjoying their wealth and seemingly suffering no rebuke from God. The psalmist adamantly warns the people *not* to envy them. The wicked are in a far from enviable position and their time will soon be up. For those true to God, however, blessings and security await. This message is found again in the proverbial sayings of 10-40, which paint the contrast between the wicked and the righteous. In spite of his own warnings to others, David struggles with the *unfairness* connected with the prosperity of the wicked. Although tempted to doubt God's goodness, he quiets his own mind by appealing to patience and trust. The words *"don't fret"* are used here as a reminder that fretting only causes worry and worry causes doubt.

Verses 1-11 focus on the *mind* of the believer. Moving into the *physical* world, David makes a contrast between the two lifestyles and their future. Nearly every verse, to the end of the psalm, names the *wicked* or the *righteous*: their attributes or their future. Meaningless possessions, arrogance and self-righteousness lead to self-annihilation. David goes on to catalog the destiny of the wicked. The fate of evil doers is to be *cut down*, to *wither,* to be *cut off*, have their *arms broken* and eventually, *neither he nor his seed will be found* upon the earth—the same earth which will be inherited by the righteous.

Verses 21-31 show the rewards that God promises to the righteous. They shall *dwell in the land* and *be fed* (3), have *the desires of their heart* (4), *inherit the earth* (9), *have an abundance of peace* (11) and *be upheld by the Lord*. In addition, according to the psalmist, even in his old age he has never seen the righteous forsaken and his children have never had to beg. God is their sufficiency. While the wicked watch for an opportunity to trap others, the righteous wait to watch their defeat. Be patient, for the fate of both the godly and the ungodly of this world have already been determined by a just God.

The call to do good (27) is not as flighty as it may seem. When a man faces struggle, he is tempted to fight with his own strength and rely upon his own intellect. This is wasted energy. In every conflict, the Lord is on the side of justice (28) and there is nothing capricious about His support. Men live in a very unstable world. This instability can cause even the righteous man to give in to his selfish desires and become ungodly, joining the men whose portion is of the world. There will be difficulties, but God's hand is a stable place in which to take refuge. From Him (39) and in Him (40) there is safety and shelter.

PSALM 38

¹A Psalm of David, to bring to remembrance. O
LORD, rebuke me not in thy wrath:
neither chasten me in thy hot displeasure.
²For thine arrows stick fast in me,
and thy hand preset me sore.
³[There is] no soundness in my flesh because of
thine anger; neither [is there any]
rest in my bones because of my sin.
⁴For mine iniquities are gone over mine head:
as an heavy burden they are too heavy for me.
⁵My wounds stink [and] are corrupt
because of my foolishness.
⁶I am troubled; I am bowed down greatly;
I go mourning, all the day long.
⁷For my loins are filled with a loathsome [disease]:
and [there is] no soundness in my flesh.
⁸I am feeble and sore broken: I have roared by
reason of the disquietness of my heart.
⁹Lord, all my desire [is] before thee;
and my groaning is not hid from thee.
¹⁰My heart panteth, my strength faileth me: as for
the light of mine eyes, it is also gone from me.
¹¹My lovers and my friends stand aloof from my
sore; and my kinsman stand afar off.

¹²They also that seek after my life lay snares [for me]: and they that seek my hurt speak mischievous things, and imagine deceits all the day long.
¹³But I, as a deaf [man], heard not; and [I was] as a dumb man [that] openeth not his mouth.
¹⁴Thus I was as a man that heareth not, and in whose mouth [are] no reproofs.
¹⁵For in thee, O LORD, do I hope:
thou wilt hear, O LORD, my God.
¹⁶For I said, [Hear me], lest [otherwise] they should rejoice over me: when my foot slippeth,
they magnify [themselves] against me.
¹⁷For I [am] ready to halt, and my sorrow [is] continually before me.
¹⁸For I will declare mine iniquity;
I will be sorry for my sin.
¹⁹But mine enemies [are] lively, [and] they are strong: and they that hate me
wrongfully are multiplied.
²⁰They also that render evil for good are mine adversaries; because I follow [the thing that] good [is].
²¹Forsake me not, O LORD: O my God,
be not far from me.
²²Make haste to help me, O Lord my salvation.

PSALM 38
Title: Tenth Prayer of Distress/Third Penitential Psalm
Author: a Psalm of David
Superscription: to the chief Musician, Jeduthun
Theme: Remembrance of God's Goodness

Similar in content to Psalm 32, this psalm is both a confession of sin and a prayer for God's help. While the time and situation of this psalm are unknown, David is clearly and admittedly aware that his own sinful actions are the reason for this agony. Sin has resulted in physical sickness (3, 5, 7) as well as his mental suffering (2, 4, 6).

David's burden is both inward and outward, a torment of mind and body. The description of a serious skin disease makes this comparable to the suffering of Job. As he struggles through these trials, his friends desert him, admonish him and refuse his company. They have no sympathy for him, nor do they desire to assist in the restoration of the penitent sinner. As in Galatians 6:1, his friends and enemies turn against him and he becomes a cause of laughter. Those around him seem to have forgotten that they are not immune to sin and its consequences.

Forsaken, abandoned and filled with deep regret, he cries out to God for help (21-22). Before God, he stands, figuratively naked, not hiding his sin or his shame or trying to minimize any of his actions. He makes no claim of his innocence as he cries out from the depths of his soul. Pleading for mercy, he knows that in God alone is there hope. This psalm shows that even *the man after God's own heart* could be caught up and sin and wind up in despair. He is humbled by his sin, as in Isaiah 1:6, but is overwhelmed to discover how simply he became a victim of sin. This sin, which started out as a mere trickle of thought, is now revealed to him (4) as a wild and raging sea.

Seeing his sin clearly exposed, he determines to renew his faith and follow God once again. Following the Law of God is generally an unpopular choice, (John 15:18) as the believer's faith is elusive to the unbeliever. Even while facing God's discipline, David stands firmly. His words confess a sinner's *weakness and instability*, the only constant behaviors of humankind. His final plea poetically shows David's ability to wait on God. The theme of waiting is seen in both the beginning and the ending of this psalm, thus reinforcing its value. The psalm ends with no physical resolution, but David's calmness does not depend on situation, but on faith alone.

PSALM 39

¹To the chief Musician, [even] to Jeduthun, A Psalm of David. I said, I will take heed to my ways, that I sin not with my tongue: I will keep my mouth with a bridle, while the wicked is before me.
²I was dumb with silence, I held my peace, [even] from good; and my sorrow was stirred.
³My heart was hot within me, while I was musing the fire burned: [then] spake I with my tongue,

⁴LORD, make me to know mine end, and the measure of my days, what it [is; that]
I may know how frail I [am].
⁵Behold, thou hast made my days [as] an handbreadth; and my age [is] as nothing before thee: verily every man at his best state
[is] altogether vanity.
⁶Surely every man walketh in a vain show: surely, they are disquieted in vain: he heapeth up [riches], and knoweth not who shall gather them.
⁷And now, Lord, what wait I for?
my hope [is] in thee.
⁸Deliver me from all transgressions: make me not the reproach of the foolish.
⁹I was dumb, I opened not my mouth;
because thou didst [it].
¹⁰Remove thy stroke away from me: I am consumed by the blow of thine hand.
¹¹When thou with rebukes dost correct man for iniquity, thou makest his beauty to consume away like a moth: surely every man [is] vanity.
¹² Hear my prayer, O LORD, and give ear unto my cry; hold not thy peace at my tears:
for I [am] a stranger with thee, [and] a sojourner, as all my fathers [were].
¹³O spare me, that I may recover strength, before I go hence, and be no more.

PSALM 39
Title: Second Testimony/Prayer Psalm
Author a Psalm of David
Superscription: to the chief Musician, *Jeduthun and Ethan-Choir Leaders*
Theme: Wisdom and Forgiveness

Jeduthun, whose name appears in several psalm subtitles, was one of David's three prominent choir leaders, as seen in 1 Chronicles 16:41. These choir leaders were called upon to direct the corporate worship. This psalm appears to be a sequel to Psalm 38, but it may be an entirely different situation. It may only be its placement here that indicates continuity. Pondering the pain and injustices of life (1-6) brings up a feeling of anger and indignation. The world is so incredibly unfair! These feelings, however, seem to look different in the twilight of life as one can see death's door in the future. In old age, there comes the realization that life is little more than a flash in time and he is little more than a sojourner on the earth. The psalmist, as a traveler is completely reliant on the hospitality of God. He is greatly tempted to complain against God (10), but, like Job, he must avoid the trap of temptation which will cause him to accuse God of foolish behavior among His people.

The writer, for all of his resolution to keep silent, lets his thoughts burst out in verses 1-3. He does not *want* to dishonor God, but he feels death at his door, his life no more than a puff of wind (5-6). He *needs* to say *something*. He cries out to God for reassurance (4), forgiveness (8) and removal of the troubles that plague him (10-13). The prayer asks for help to understand the vanity and frailty of life. He begs God to lead him back to quiet confidence and to be rid of these awful thoughts. Slowly, he begins to reformulate the problem from the perspective of a learner (4) and a man of prayer (7).

What is man (Job 7:17) that the Great Almighty would care for him? The words here are spoken with touching loyalty (1) and in submission (7). Such songs in the night begging for answer and clarity reveal something of the bewilderment of man. Once again, the psalm has no resolution. The truth was only made clear when the word became flesh.

PSALM 40

¹To the chief Musician, A Psalm of David.
I waited patiently for the LORD;
and he inclined unto me, and heard my cry.
²He brought me up also out of an horrible pit, out of
the miry clay, and set my feet upon a rock,
[and] established my goings.
³And he hath put a new song in my mouth, [even]
praise unto our God: many shall see [it], and fear,
and shall trust in the LORD.
⁴Blessed [is] that man that maketh the LORD his
trust, and respecteth not the proud,
nor such as turn aside to lies.

⁵Many, O LORD my God, [are] thy wonderful works [which] thou hast done, and thy thoughts [which are] to us-ward: they cannot be reckoned up in order unto thee: [if] I would declare and speak [of them], they are more than can be numbered.
⁶Sacrifice and offering thou didst not desire; mine ears hast thou opened: burnt offering and sin offering hast thou not required.
⁷Then said I, Lo, I come: in the volume of the book [it is] written of me,
⁸I delight to do thy will, O my God: yea, thy law [is] with in my heart.
⁹I have preached righteousness in the great congregation: lo, I have not refrained my lips, O LORD, thou knowest.
¹⁰I have not hid thy righteousness within my heart; I have declared thy faithfulness and thy salvation: I have not concealed thy lovingkindness and thy truth from the great congregation.
¹¹Withhold not thou thy tender mercies from me, O LORD: let thy lovingkindness and thy truth continually preserve me.
¹²For innumerable evils have compassed me about: mine iniquities have taken hold upon me, so that I am not able to look up; they are more than the hairs of mine head: therefore my heart faileth me.
¹³Be pleased, O LORD, to deliver me: O LORD, make haste to help me.
¹⁴Let them be ashamed and confounded together that seek after my soul to destroy it; let them be

driven backward and put to shame
that wish me evil.
¹⁵Let them be desolate for a reward of
their shame that say unto me, Aha, aha.
¹⁶Let all those that seek thee rejoice and be glad in
thee: let such as love thy salvation say continually,
The LORD be magnified.
¹⁷But I [am] poor and needy; [yet] the Lord thinketh
upon me: thou [art] my help and my deliverer;
make no tarrying, O my God.

PSALM 40
Title: Seventh Messianic Psalm
Author: a Psalm of David
Superscription: to the chief Musician
Theme: Persevering in Trial

The theme of waiting, which began in Psalm 37 with its anguish and frustration having carried through Psalms 38 and 39, now reaches an exciting climax. The psalm begins much like Psalm 1, centering around God's magnificent works. Verses 4 and 5 focus on the goodness of God. David knows that God's thoughts and actions are impossible to fathom and too numerous to be counted (6). The only offering that one could bring was the offering of self-giving and self-sacrifice.

Verse 11 verifies that David's troubles are not over. He remembers that on his own, he is truly inadequate. As a powerful king he states, *"I am poor."* This type of humility is required when entering into the presence of God. With the Law of God in his heart

(8), he is utterly crushed by sorrow and iniquity (12), but still understands that God maintains the cause of the afflicted. To be lowly in status, to be poor, weak or ailing is not an indication of a lack of faith any more than wealth indicates goodness. The Old and New Testaments agree that what matters in a man's life are right actions, which come from right motives.

David's words, *"Lo, I come"* are found in the highest point of the psalm. Waiting is again David's lot and the psalm ends with a prayer of distress oddly tinged with confidence. There is a note of urgency, yet one of underlying joy, as David remembers a wider circle and a cause much bigger than his own pressing needs. These words indicate a shadowing of the coming of the Christ and can be compared with the tentative *"Here I am"* spoken by Moses in Isaiah 6:8. Both statements show that the duty of the believer is to trust in God for the outcome of any situation.

Note: The ending of the psalm is quite similar to Psalm 70 and carries a Messianic reference (see verses 7 and 8; Hebrews 10:17). David's declaration is one which none but the Messiah could fulfill. The Book of Hebrews applies these verses to Jesus offering Himself on the cross as the ultimate and final sacrifice.

PSALM 41

¹To the chief Musician, a Psalm of David. Blessed [is]
he that considereth the poor: the LORD
will deliver him in time of trouble.

²The LORD will preserve him, and keep him alive; [and] he shall be blessed upon the earth: and thou wilt not deliver him unto the will of his enemies.
³The LORD will strengthen him upon the bed of languishing: thou wilt make all his bed in his sickness.
⁴I said, LORD, be merciful unto me: heal my soul; for I have sinned against thee.
⁵Mine enemies speak evil of me, When shall he die, and his name perish?
⁶And if he comes to see [me], he speaketh vanity: his heart gathereth iniquity to itself; [when] he goeth abroad, he telleth [it].
⁷All that hate me whisper together against me: against me do they devise my hurt.
⁸An evil disease, [say they], cleaveth fast unto him: and [now] that he lieth he shall rise up no more.
⁹Yea, mine own familiar friend, in whom I trusted, which did eat of my bread, hath lifted up [his] heel against me.
¹⁰But thou, O LORD, be merciful unto me, and raise me up, that I may requite them.
¹¹By this I know that thou favorest me, because mine enemy doth not triumph over me.
¹²And as for me, thou upholdest me in mine integrity, and settest me before thy face for ever.
¹³Blessed [be] the LORD God of Israel from everlasting, and to everlasting. Amen, and Amen.

PSALM 41
Title: Eighth Messianic Psalm
Author: a Psalm of David
Date: The Time of Absalom's Usurpation in 2 Samuel 15
Superscription: to the chief Musician
Theme: The Blessings and Sufferings of the Righteous

Psalm 41 is a meditation upon and a prayer for God's blessings. Its messages correspond closely with the *Beatitudes* found in the New Testament. *"Blessed is he that considereth the poor"* is line one of this psalm and corresponds to *"blessed are the merciful" found* in Jesus's Sermon on the Mount. Happy is the man who lends assistance to those in need and when troubled, he will place his reliance upon God. Such a man will be delivered from his struggles, prospered in his dealings and blessed in his ways. David uses his own life as an illustration of God's goodness. Unknown to David, he is not only telling his own story, he is also telling the story of the coming Christ.

David's appeal is a plea for mercy and for physical healing. As his kingdom is in complete chaos, he sees that his enemies have taken pleasure in watching his failures. Even his closest friends have turned on him, much as Judas Iscariot later betrayed his master and friend (John 13:18 and Acts 1:16). David knew that he was not always in the right, but facing those who stood against him only made him weaker in his own conscience. He is forced to turn to the only place where he can find rest: to God and His unrelenting goodness. In the Lord's hands he knows he will be given more *mercy* (4, 10) and *care* than he would have received from a friend. God, whom he has wronged, is David's help and comfort; those whom David has treated kindly now turn their backs to him. He painfully learns that those he has called *"friend"* will not stand with him when he needs them.

In a crisis, David does not pray that God will destroy his enemies, but for the strength and courage to stand up to them himself. It is only through such strength that he can be certain that God's favor is with him. This is somewhat unusual in the Psalms as it is more common that God is asked to punish a man's enemies. David, however, as king, has authority to act judicially, even though he used that power with great restraint. Beyond David's own circumstances, the comparison to his reactions and Jesus's betrayal can be readily seen. The contrast here is between *judicial justice* and *atoning grace*.

Note: This psalm, as we have seen, is a reference to Jesus in almost every way. It is interesting to note that the coming of Christ was prophesied in this psalm, written approximately 500 years before the Book of Zechariah, which was written about 500 years before the coming of Jesus. The words of these writers form a single prophecy which was to be lived out by Jesus. Both David and Zechariah spoke of the betrayal by a friend. Zechariah goes so far as to indicate what Judas would receive in payment (Matthew 26:15) and how the money would be used to buy the Potter's Field as seen in Matthew 27:6-10. Obviously, prophecy is true, regardless of the length of time between prophecy and manifestation. This prophecy leaves little doubt that God was, is and will be forever intertwined with the lives of His people.

NOTES ON BOOK ONE
Themes from Psalms 1 through 41 include:

- Knowing God and believing He is everywhere and in everything
- There is no hiding from God
- It is difficult to follow His direction; it offends the nature of the flesh
- Putting ultimate value on material items is the beginning of sin
- Meditation and sincere prayer change lives
- The word of God is complete and infallible
- Every situation offers a choice of where faith is placed
- It is crucial to admit and repent of sin
- Accept God's forgiveness with humility

BOOK TWO

PSALMS 42-72
Referred to as the Exodus Book

PREFACE TO BOOK II

The second book in the five-part Book of Psalms is only a section of a much larger collection. Several collections of psalms are represented here, while many have been lost to time. This reasoning comes from the fact that *Elohim* (referring to God) is used over 164 times in verses 42-83, while the word *Yahweh* appears only 30 times in Book Two. Book Two introduces the *Sons of Korah* and *Asaph*—David's choirmasters. This book includes four anonymous psalms and one which is ascribed to Solomon. The only Psalm of David (51) refers to his indiscretions with Bathsheba. Of special importance to believers is the reminder that a sin against another is a sin against God.

PSALM 42

¹To the chief Musician, Maschil, for the sons of Korah. As the hart panteth after the water brooks, so panteth my soul after thee, O God.
²My soul thirsteth for God, for the living God: when shall I come, and appear before God?
³My tears have been my meat day and night, while they continually say unto me, Where [is] thy God?
⁴When I remember these [things], I pour out my soul in me: for I had gone with the multitude, I went with them to the house of God, with the voice of joy and praise, with a multitude that kept holy day.
⁵Why art thou cast down, O my soul? and [why] art thou disquieted in me? hope thou in God: for I shall yet praise him [for] the help of his countenance.
⁶O my God, my soul is cast down within me: therefore I will remember thee from the land of Jordan, and of the Hermonites, from the hill Mizar.
⁷Deep calleth unto deep at the noise of thy waterspouts: all thy waves and thy billows are gone over me.
⁸[Yet] the LORD will command his loving kindness in the daytime, and in the night his song [shall be] with me, [and] my prayer unto the God of my life.
⁹I will say unto God, my rock, Why hast thou forgotten me? why go I mourning because of the oppression of the enemy?
¹⁰[As] with a sword in my bones, mine enemies reproach me; while they say daily unto me, Where [is] thy God?

> [11] Why art thou cast down, O my soul? and why art thou disquieted within me? hope thou in God: for I shall yet praise him, [who is] the health of my countenance, and my God.

PSALM 42
Title: Fourth Psalm of Instruction
Author: for the Sons of Korah
Superscription: to the chief Musician *Maschil-a reflective tune*
Theme: Seeking God in Times of Distress

The nature of Psalm 42 is a deep, strong, powerful longing for God. One can hear David's painful yearning as he describes his thirst for God. Exiled in the North (42:6), his anguish is multiplied as he is encircled by wicked men who mock the psalmist and God. In verses 1-3 he cries out to God for help in easing his sorrow. He believes that God has forgotten him, or worse that God has taken His hand away and rejected him altogether.

He begins to contrast his past happiness with his current disastrous situation. The imagery continues as he describes the feeling of great waves and breakers overcoming him. Even as the deer cannot disguise her thirst, neither can the psalmist hide his passion for God and his desire to be with Him. He wonders about his future, yet somehow, he holds on to hope. The psalmist remembers the days when he led crowds of people on pilgrimages or when he stood among his brethren at a great festival. The memories are both pleasant and sorrowful.

The refrain in verse 5, "Why art thou cast down, O my soul?" hints that he will later discover the answer to his anguish. He knows God's hand is involved in his suffering, at least to the extent that he has allowed it. The psalm takes the writer back and forth between question and answer, finally ending in faith. He has answered his own question. Disquieted though he may be, the best thing that he can do is to praise God. He is deeply aware that he cannot *see* or even *feel* God around him, yet he knows that He surrounds him in his turmoil. This is the magnificent *formula of faith* which he uses as he faces humiliation.

PSALM 43

¹Judge me, O God, and plead my cause against and ungodly nation: O deliver me from
the deceitful and unjust man.
²For thou [art] the God of my strength:
why dost thou cast me off? why go I mourning
because of the oppression of the enemy?
³O send out thy light and thy truth: let them lead
me; let them bring me unto thy holy hill,
and to thy tabernacles.
⁴Then will I go unto the altar of God,
unto God my exceeding joy: yea, upon the harp I will
praise thee, O God, my God.
⁵Why art thou cast down, O my soul? and why art
thou disquieted within me? hope in God:

for I shall yet praise him, [who is] the health of
my countenance, and my God.

PSALM 43
Title: Eleventh Prayer of Distress
Author: for the Sons of Korah
Superscription: none
Theme: Prayer to God when in Trouble

This is a prayer for restoration. The psalmist places his case in God's hands when he says to God, "Judge me, O God, and plead my cause." There are two main ideas that alternate within this psalm. Miserable as he is, the first desire is for freedom from persecution. Secondly, but just as imperative is his longing for God's temple in Jerusalem. The verses, repeated from the previous psalm, echo the confident hope that God will answer his prayer.

Psalm 43 holds a growing reliance on things that cannot be seen. Has God actually forgotten him? Although the storm of suffering shows no sign of abating and the psalmist is ever plunged into darkness, he remembers the promises of God. He pleads with God to deliver him from this hopeless situation and return him to the city of the Temple.

Even though he is far away from home, he knows he can still receive the blessings of God just as if he were standing upon His holy hill. His discouragement slowly turns a corner and he becomes truly confident of God's love and guidance. Therefore it is, homeward bound or not, the psalmist can praise God for

His glory and ever-present help. Outwardly, nothing has changed. He is still an exile and still far away from home, but inwardly he has won the battle.

Note: In some churches, 43:1 is sung on Passion Sunday, recalling the last trip Jesus took to Jerusalem.

PSALM 44

¹To the chief Musician for the sons of Korah, Maschil. We have heard with our ears, O God, our fathers have told us, [what] work thou didst in their days, in the times of old.
²[How] thou didst drive out the heathen with thy hand, and plantedst them; [how] thou didst afflict the people, and cast them out.
³For they got not the land in possession by their own sword, neither did their own arm save them: but thy right hand, and thine arm, and the light of thy countenance, because thou hadst a favor unto them.
⁴Thou art my King, O God: command deliverances for Jacob.
⁵Through thee will we push down our enemies: through thy name we will tread them under that rise up against us.
⁶For I will not trust in my bow, neither shall my sword save me.
⁷But thou hast saved us from our enemies, and hast put them to shame that hated us.
⁸In God we boast all the day long, and praise thy name for ever.

⁹But thou hast cast off, and put us to shame;
and goest not forth with our armies.
¹⁰Thou makest us to turn back from the enemy: and
they which hate us spoil for themselves.
¹¹Thou hast given us like sheep [appointed] for meat;
and hast scattered us among the heathen.
¹²Thou sellest thy people, for nought, and dost not
increase [thy wealth] by their price.
¹³Thou makest us a reproach to our neighbors,
a scorn and a derision to them
that are round about us.
¹⁴Thou makest us a byword among the heathen, a
shaking of the head among the people.
¹⁵My confusion [is] continually before me, and the
shame of my face hath covered me,
¹⁶For the voice of him that reproacheth and blasphemeth; by reason of the enemy and avenger.
¹⁷All this is come upon us; yet, have we not forgotten
thee, neither have we dealt falsely in thy covenant.
¹⁸Our heart is not turned back, neither have our
steps declined from thy way;
¹⁹Though thou hast sore broken us in the place of
dragons, and covered us with the shadow of death.
²⁰If we have forgotten the name of our God, or
stretched out our hands to a strange god;
²¹Shall not God search this out? for he knoweth
the secrets of the heart.
²²Yea, for thy sake are we killed all the day long; we
are counted as sheep for the slaughter.
²³Awake, why sleepest thou, O Lord? arise,
cast [us] not off for ever.

²⁴Wherefore hidest thou thy face, [and] forgetteth
our affliction and our oppression?
²⁵For our soul is bowed down to the dust:.
Wherefore our belly cleaveth unto the earth.
²⁶Arise for our help, and redeem us for
thy mercies' sake.

PSALM 44
Title: Fifth Psalm of Instruction
Author: for the Sons of Korah
Superscription: to the chief Musician
Theme: Redemption Remembered

While national in scope, this psalm is permeated with a deep sense of self-justification. The humiliation and disgrace they suffer at the hands of enemies is taken as *just cause* for the people of God to rebuke His decisions. They are disgraced (13-16) at the hands of others and cannot seem to understand why (17-22). In oral tradition and in the Scriptures the stories of God, His rescues and His power in days past, are known to all in the congregation. No victory, it is said, has occurred without the presence of God (1-3). Now faced with this overwhelming defeat, the people contend that God has deserted them. However, despite urgent prayers, no assistance from God seems to be forthcoming.

The psalmist employs a cutting sarcasm here, saying that what God has done is nothing short of handing his people over to the enemy. He has forgotten Israel and He has forgotten His covenant with them. The word *"forget"* in Hebrew indicates being inactive, just as to *remember* is to acknowledge and act accordingly (Ecclesiastes 12:1).

Their claim is repeated stating that the nation of Israel has never failed to recognize God and have at all times remained faithful to Him. This remains questionable, yet filled with self-righteousness (23), the psalmist cries, "Cast us not off for forever, awake!" They are not implying that God has actually gone to sleep, but rather that He pays no attention to them. More painful than defeat in battle is the inner defeat (15) and a complete loss of confidence in themselves and in God.

What appears to be God's withdrawal is simply God's refusal to be controlled by man's expectations. The crux of the psalm is in verse 22 with the phrase, "for thy sake". This thought is not developed here, but it implies the thought that suffering may be a way of developing character rather than a punishment. If this is the goal of the psalm, a reversal as well as a victory may be a sign of fellowship with Him, not alienation or abandonment. The psalm ends not with the despair of the defeated, but with the conviction that regardless of the outcome, they are more than conquerors (Romans 8:36).

PSALM 45

¹To the chief Musician upon Shoshannim, for the sons of Korah, Maschil, A Song of loves. My heart is indicting a good matter: I speak of the things which I have made touching the King: my tongue [is] the pen of a ready writer.

²Thou art fairer than the children of men: grace is poured into thy lips: therefore,
God hath blessed thee forever.
³Gird thy sword upon [thy] thigh, O [most] mighty,
with thy glory and thy majesty.
⁴And in thy majesty ride prosperously because of truth and meekness [and] righteousness; and thy right hand shall teach thee terrible things.
⁵Thine arrows [are] sharp in the heart of the king's enemies; [whereby] the people fall under thee.
⁶Thy throne, O God, [is] for ever and ever: the scepter of thy kingdom [is] a right scepter.
⁷Thou lovest righteousness, and hatest wickedness: therefore God, thy God, hath anointed thee with the oil of gladness above thy fellows.
⁸All thy garments [smell] of myrrh, and aloes, [and] cassia, out of the ivory palaces,
whereby they have made thee glad.
⁹Kings daughters [were] among thy honorable women: upon thy right hand did stand
the queen in gold of Ophir.
¹⁰Hearken, O daughter, and consider, and incline thine ear; forget also thine own people,
and thy father's house;
¹¹So shall the king greatly desire thy beauty: for he [is] thy Lord; and worship thou him.
¹²And the daughter of Tyre [shall be there] with a gift; [even] the rich among the people
shall entreat thy favor.
¹³The king's daughter [is] all glorious within: her clothing [is] of wrought gold.

¹⁴She shall be brought unto the king in raiment of needlework: the virgins her companions that follow her shall be brought unto thee.
¹⁵With gladness and rejoicing shall they be brought: they shall enter into the king's palace.
¹⁶Instead of thy fathers shall be thy children, whom thou mayest make princes in all the earth.
¹⁷I will make thy name to be remembered in all generations: therefore shall the people praise thee for ever and ever.

PSALM 45
Title: Ninth Messianic Psalm
Author: for the Sons of Korah
Superscription: to the chief Musician sung *to "the lilies" a song of love*
Theme: The Glories of the Messiah's Bride

Psalm 45 is a beautiful nuptial song. It may have some reference to the marriages of either David or Solomon. Some believe the occasion to be the wedding of King Ahab of Israel to Jezebel, Princess of Tyre (1-2). There is no possible way to identify the King or the period in history, but later Jewish interpreters proclaimed this psalm to be Messianic, as did the early Christians (Hebrews 1:8, 9). These verses are but a foretaste of God's bringing His people to glory, to reign on earth (Revelation 6:10) with their master, the King, whose praise and adoration will be endless.

The eulogy of the groom (2:9) portrays his character, attributes and kindness. The description shows that he has power in both spiritual and military matters. However, compliments and praises to the Royal King suddenly give way to divine honors (6), which will be seen in their full value at the coming of the Messiah. This event prophetically anticipates the relationship of Christ and His bride, as in Ephesians 5:32 and Revelation 19:7. The glory of the event shines through and beneath the surface, the event that *will* come is being vaguely witnessed by the Israelites.

Advice is given to the bride (10-15) as she is brought into the view of the King. The bride, her attendants, their grace and the beauty of their clothing are fitting for this occasion. The words *"to forget"* mean more than just leaving her parents as it did in Genesis 2:24. Here, the King was often from another nation or culture, so she had to be willing to break with her own past to marry—just as Christians now must give up their identification with the world in order to be the bride of Christ.

In the description of the royal wedding, old things are giving way to a new beginning, which is fundamental to all marriages. As a counterpart to Genesis 2:24, the husband has, as his duty, the requirement to break with his former home and give all to his wife. The bride for her part is to submit herself to her King (husband). The bride-to-be is escorted to her King in her radiance and purity—the equivalent of the apostle Paul's prayer for Christians to present themselves as a pure bride to her one true husband, Jesus, as seen in 2 Corinthians 11:2.

PSALM 46

¹To the chief Musician for the sons of Korah, A Song upon Alamoth. God [is] our refuge and strength, a very present help in trouble.
²Therefore we will not fear, though the earth be removed, and though the mountains be carried into the midst of the sea;
³[Though] the waters, thereof roar [and] be troubled, [though] the mountains shake with the swelling thereof.
⁴[There is] a river, the streams whereof shall make glad the city of God, the holy [place] of the tabernacles of the most high.
⁵God [is] in the midst of her; she shall not be moved: God shall help her, [and that] right early.
⁶The heathen raged, the kingdoms were moved: he uttered his voice, the earth melted.
⁷The LORD of hosts [is] with us; the God of Jacob [is] our refuge.
⁸Behold the works of the LORD, what desolations he hath made in the earth.
⁹He maketh wars to cease unto the end of the earth; he breaketh the bow, and cutteth the spear in sunder; he burneth the chariot in the fire.
¹⁰Be still, and know that I [am] God: I will be exalted among the heathen, I will be exalted in the earth.
¹¹The LORD of hosts [is] with us; the God of Jacob [is] our refuge.

PSALM 46
Title: Tenth Messianic Psalm
Author: for the Sons of Korah
Superscription: *a Song-Alamoth (a chorus of young women)*
Theme: God: Refuge of His People; Destroyer of Nations

The psalm claims the superiority of God: His power over nature (1-3); His power over the attackers of the city; (4-7; 8) His power over the entire world (8-11). It energetically anticipates both the beginning and the end to wars which are waged against the people of God. This psalm was composed in a time of crisis, giving it a unique strength among the psalms. As frequently occurs, the exact occasion for the writing of this psalm cannot be determined. With the crisis unidentified, speculation is of little value. It may have been written following Sennacherib's attack on Jerusalem (2 Chronicles 32), in the face of an overwhelming natural disaster, or possibly in an anticipation of the coming Messiah.

Verses 4 and 5 have a parallel in Revelation 22:1-5 where the perfect city of God is realized. The psalmist rejoices in knowing that God resides with His people (1, 4-5, 7, 11) and protects them from their enemies. The sequence of the psalm shows that tranquility and peace are on the far side of judgment. This agrees with Old Testament prophecy and apocalypse (as found in Isaiah 6:10-13; 9:5; Daniel 12:1-2) and also the New Testament (as found in 2 Peter 3:12).

The admonition which closes the psalm, *"to be still"*, is not necessarily a comfort for the harassed, but rather a rebuke to the anxious people of the world to be silent. People are to refrain from useless striving and lack of confidence. These words resemble the command which was spoken at another turbulent time as Jesus spoke to the raging sea, saying, *"Peace, be still!"* God desires peace for His people. The psalm, with its historical facts unknown, echoes the refrain of the people that peace will come with confidence in God.

Note: The words, "God is our refuge and strength" is a primary theme of this Psalm. This line later inspired Luther to write the words, "A Mighty Fortress is Our God", a leading song used during the Christian Reformation.

PSALM 47

¹To the chief Musician, A Psalm for the sons of Korah. O clap your hands, all ye people; shout unto God, with the voice of triumph.
²For the LORD most high [is] terrible;
[he is] a great King over all the earth.
³He shall subdue the peoples under us, and the nations under our feet.
⁴He shall choose our inheritance for us,
the excellency of Jacob, whom he loved.
⁵God is gone up with a shout, the LORD with the sound of a trumpet.

⁶Sing praises to God, sing praises:
sing praises unto our King, sing praises.
⁷For God [is] the King of all the earth:
sing ye the praises with understanding.
⁸God reigneth over the heathen: God sitteth upon
the throne of his holiness.
⁹The princes of the people are gathered together,
[even] the people of the God of Abraham: for the
shields of the earth [belong] unto God:
he is greatly exalted.

PSALM 47
Title: Eleventh Messianic Psalm
Author: for the Sons of Korah
Superscription: to the chief Musician
Theme: Praise Him who Rules the Earth

This psalm belongs to a group of psalms, the balance of which are found clustered in Psalms 92-100. It rejoices that the king who reigns in Canaan is the same king who reigns over all the earth. Coming from the time of a monarchy, this song was used for corporate worship in the temple. Its usage is for either the Feast of Tabernacles or the dedication of the first temple in Jerusalem. Later this song was sung during the Festival of the New Year.

The mention of Jacob, whom he loves, begs the question if the object of the love spoken of is Jacob, the church, or the entire world (Galatians 2:20; Ephesians 5:25; John 3:16). If it is the world, then it is but a short step to put this in light of the New

Testament. This special celebration of God's glory will find its ultimate fulfillment in the reign of Jesus Christ on earth.

Christians would later apply this psalm prophetically as Jesus came to earth, collected the inheritance and men and has gone up (4) to heaven. The *inheritance* as it is spoken of here does not necessarily mean land or goods, but the promises given to Abraham. Among the promises to Abraham is the gospel of Jesus (Galatians 3:16-18).

The psalmist instructs us (7) to sing with understanding. While exuberant praise is glorious, *understanding* implies the idea of consciousness and caution, which links praise to wisdom and prosperity. In Proverbs 21:16, a man who wanders away from understanding rests as if dead. When praise is sung with understanding, it is literally a testimony of God's love reaching out to a fallen world.

The divine sovereignty of God, which was introduced in Psalm 46 climbs now to a pinnacle. The very first stanza establishes who God is and describes His incredible glory. God has and is supreme in all things. Regardless of the thoughts of man, He is inerrant in all His decisions. The words here are both messianic and prophetic, viewing what is yet to happen as if it were occurring today. The psalmist sees the nations subdued. He sees Israel standing in a special relationship to God because of God's special love for them. Praise! Clap your hands! Rejoice! He is God!

Note: Shout! Rejoice! Clap your hands! All peoples are commanded to shout triumphantly to God, rejoice and to clap their hands in His honor. God has filled His people with an instinctive urge to clap and shout when victory is experienced. Some modern religions discourage this kind of worship however.

PSALM 48

¹A Song [and] Psalm for the sons of Korah. Great [is] the LORD, and greatly to be praised in the city of our God, [in] the mountain of his holiness.
²Beautiful for situation, the joy of the whole earth, [is] mount Zion, [on] the sides of the north, the city of the great King.
³God is known in her palaces for a refuge.
⁴For, lo, the Kings were assembled, they passed by together.
⁵They saw [it, and] so they marvelled; they were troubled, [and] hasted away.
⁶Fear took hold upon them there [and] pain, as of a woman in travail.
⁷Thou breakest the ships of Tarshish with an east wind.
⁸As we have heard, so we have seen in the city of the LORD of hosts, in the city of our God: God will establish it forever.
⁹We have thought of thy lovingkindness, O God, in the midst of thy temple.

¹⁰According to thy name, O God, so [is] thy praise unto the ends of the earth: thy right hand is full of righteousness.
¹¹Let mount Zion rejoice, let the daughters of Judah be glad, because of thy judgments.
¹²Walk about Zion, and go round about her: tell the towers thereof.
¹³Mark ye well her bulwarks, consider her palaces; that ye may tell [it] to the generation following.
¹⁴For this God [is] our God for ever and ever: he will be our guide, [even] unto death.

PSALM 48
Title: Twelfth Messianic Psalm
Author: for the Sons of Korah
Superscription: a Song
Theme: God's Glory on Mount Zion

This psalm shares a common ground with Psalm 46 in that it celebrates a great deliverance. The occasion that immediately inspired the psalm may be the siege by Sennacherib in 701 BC that is being referred to in verses 4-8 (reference Isaiah 37:33-37). This psalm describes the apocalyptic Jerusalem as the center of the messianic kingdom that is being described, but an unwritten consciousness indicates that the setting is far greater.

The view of God as a refuge (Psalm 46) and of God as King (Psalm 46 and 47) are a part of this psalm as well. In verses 1-8, *the city of our God*, the glory of the city and the awesome power of God complement one another. The greatness of the Lord is not only in heaven and earth, but also on Mt. Zion, with its glorious temple located on the northeastern part of the mountain. The strong towering walls of the temple reminded the people of God's strength. The song of praise begins in the city of God and enlarges to encompass the entire earth (10). For the Christian singer of this psalm, it is important to realize that the church must be a community as strong and indestructible as the temple on Mt. Zion (Ephesians 2:12-22).

After worship concluded, the pilgrims joined in a procession around the city, singing, praising and shouting with joy. Looking back at the trilogy (46-48) this *Psalm of Zion* stands not only as a witness to God's greatness, but also to the goodness He will bring to those who love Him. As the Lord pointed out (Matthew 5:35), the city will only be perfect when all nations have come to God. The psalm portrays the literal Zion in terms of heavenly Zion for a more complete understanding. Once again, there is a glimpse of the coming Messiah. As the City of Zion, the Christian church must also be strong, praying and praising with the energy of the Israelites and seeking God as the ultimate refuge.

PSALM 49

¹To the chief Musician, A Psalm for the sons of Korah. Hear this, all [ye] people; give ear, all [ye] inhabitants of the world:
²Both low and high, rich and poor, together.

³My mouth shall speak of wisdom; and the meditation of my heart [shall be] of understanding.
⁴I will incline mine ear to a parable: I will open my dark saying upon the harp.
⁵Wherefore should I fear in the days of evil, [when] the iniquity of my heels shall compass me about?
⁶They that trust in their wealth, and boast themselves in the multitude of their riches;
⁷None [of them] can by any means redeem his brother, nor give to God a ransom for him:
⁸(For the redemption of their soul [is] precious, and it ceaseth for ever:)
⁹That he should still live for ever, [and] not see corruption.
¹⁰For he seeth [that] wise men die, likewise the fool and the brutish person perish, and leave their wealth to others.
¹¹Their inward thought [is, that] their houses [shall continue] for ever, [and] their dwelling places to all generations; they call [their] lands after their own names.
¹²Nevertheless man [being] in honor abideth not: he is like the beasts [that] perish.
¹³This their way [is] their folly: yet their prosperity approve their sayings.
¹⁴Like sheep they are laid in the grave; death shall feed on them; and the upright shall have dominion over them in the morning; and their beauty shall consume in the grave from their dwelling.
¹⁵But God will redeem my soul from the power of the grave: for he shall receive me.

¹⁶Be not thou afraid when one is made rich, when
the glory of his house is increased;
¹⁷For when he dieth he shall carry nothing away: his
glory shall not descend after him.
¹⁸Though while he lived he blessed his soul:
and [men] will praise thee,
when thou doest well to thyself.
¹⁹He shall go to the generation of his fathers; they
shall never see light.
²⁰Man [that is] in honor, and understandeth not, is
like the beasts [that] perish.

PSALM 49
Title: Sixth Psalm of Instruction
Author: for the Sons of Korah
Superscription: to the chief Musician
Theme: The Confidence of the Ungodly

This moral lesson is designed not just for Israel, but also for all people. This psalm is a warning to those who have no interest in the God of Israel or His Laws. The purpose is to present a meditation on one of the biggest riddles of life: why are some people given wealth, prosperity and others are destined to live in poverty. The Levitical author makes it clear that many are wealthy and godly at the same time; yet, it is unwise to choose wealth over goodness. The familiar pattern of the use of opposites such as rich and poor, weak and strong, evil and righteous is seen here. While less poetic, as an instructional tool, the rhythm of the opposites makes the words of the lesson easier to recall.

It is often seen that those with wealth use this money and/or power to take advantage of those who have less (5). The same problem is dealt with in Psalms 37 and 73. It is a warning that seeking after "things" will not only lead a man to sin in this life, but to death when his time is done. God is never called to account of the inequalities that appear to exist. Those who put their faith in Him are aware that He does as He chooses. The wealthy and prosperous ones who commit evil acts will be called to account by God for their behaviors.

The moral is similar to the one Jesus used as he spoke of the rich man in Luke 12:16-21, when He said that it is easier for a camel to go through the eye of a needle than for a rich man to wealth enter Heaven. Men are reluctant to release *visible wealth* in exchange for the *invisible wealth* that comes from a pure faith in God. It is verse 15 binds this theme together. In verse 7 God is demanding a ransom; in verse 15, we see the hope that God will ransom His people. The New Testament holds the outcome of this hope.

Note: The psalmist has no clear concept of life after death and verse 15 is therefore often taken as a reference to premature death. One must remember, however, that before Christ eternal life was a vague understanding at best. In the psalmist's mind, life's inequalities must be dealt with prior to death.

PSALM 50

¹A Psalm of Asaph. The mighty God, [even] the LORD, hath spoken, and called the earth from the rising of the sun unto the going down thereof.
²Out of Zion, the perfection of beauty, God, hath shined.
³Our God shall come, and shall not keep silence: a fire shall devour before him, and it shall be very tempestuous round about him.
⁴He shall call the heavens from above, and to the earth, that he may judge his people.
⁵Gather my saints together unto me; those that have made a covenant with me by sacrifice.
⁶And the heavens shall declare his righteousness: for God [is] judge himself.
⁷Hear, O my people, and I will speak; O Israel, and I will testify against thee: I [am] God, [even] thy God.
⁸I will not reprove thee for thy sacrifices or thy burnt offerings, [to have been] continually before me.
⁹I will take no bullock out of thy house, [nor] he goats out of thy folds.
¹⁰For every beast of the forest [is] mine, [and] the cattle upon a thousand hills.
¹¹I know all the fowls of the mountains: and the wild beasts of the field [are] mine.
¹²If I were hungry, I would not tell thee: for the world [is] mine, and the fullness thereof.
¹³Will I eat the flesh of bulls or drink the blood of goats?

¹⁴Offer unto God thanksgiving; and pay thy vows unto the most High:
¹⁵And call upon me in the day of trouble: I will deliver thee, and thou shalt glorify me.
¹⁶But unto the wicked God saith, What hast thou to do to declare my statutes, or [that] thou shouldest take my covenant in thy mouth?
¹⁷Seeing thou hatest instruction, and castest my words behind thee.
¹⁸When thou sawest a thief, then thou consentedst with him, and hast been a partaker with adulterers.
¹⁹Thou givest thy mouth do evil, and thy tongue frameth deceit.
²⁰Thou sittest [and] speakest against thy brother; thou slanderest thine own mother's son.
²¹These [things] hast thou done, and I kept silence; thou thoughtest that I was altogether [such an one] as thyself: [but] I will reprove thee, and set [them] in order before thine eyes.
²²Now consider this, ye that forget God, lest I tear [you] in pieces, and [there be] none to deliver.
²³Whoso offereth praise glorifieth me: and to him that ordereth [his] conversation [aright] will I show the salvation of God.

PSALM 50
Title: Psalm of Judgment
Author: a Psalm of Asaph
Superscription: none
Theme: God is the only Righteous Judge

Composed as a temple liturgy, this psalm of Israel reaffirms her commitment to God. The most probable use was at the Feast of Tabernacles. Clearly, there is an affinity with the prophecies of Amos, Micah and Isaiah and as such, the psalm may date from the late 8th and or early 7th century BC. Others find a closer relationship with the past ministry of Jeremiah. The psalm contains three parts: the announcement that Israel's covenant Lord will call His people to account, the Lord's words of correction for those of honest intent, ending with His sharp review of the wicked among men.

God appears in fire at Mount Sinai to summon Israel to His judgment seat. All eyes are upon Him and His eyes are upon Israel. His words address the covenant people, beginning with the unthinkingly religious, then to the hardened hypocrites. A warning is given to both of these groups. It is the thankful heart—stopping, listening and offering thanks—that matters. There are serious charges against those who simply mouth God's commands, mimicking with insincere words, rather than with the true spirit of worship. Acceptable worship and social morality represent the two divisions of the Ten Commandments: man's relation to God and man's relation to his neighbor.

The message to the worshiper (7-15) is for all men to hear. God is speaking to the formalistic worshiper and the ones who trust in ritual. The judgment is not upon sacrifices as such, but upon the wrong motives involved. It is clear that God is not dependent upon the sacrifices of His people. He desires heartfelt thanksgiving, proper payment of vows and sincere prayer. There will be special punishment for the hypocrites within Israel who keep the Law in outward observance, but use the Law as justification for their evil deeds. Even though God has kept silent and has delayed punishment, there is a time reserved for wrongdoers.

God's power, majesty and glory are obvious to all humanity. If God is left out, rebellion and destruction will follow. In contrast, simple road to success is set forth: offer praise to God and follow His instructions in *everything*. The result is personal revelation and understanding of God's plan of salvation.

PSALM 51

¹To the chief Musician, A Psalm of David, when Nathan the prophet came unto him, after he had gone into Bathsheba. Have mercy upon me, O God, according to thy lovingkindness: according unto the multitude of thy tender mercies blot out
my transgressions.
²Wash me thoroughly from mine iniquity,
and cleanse me from my sin.

³For I acknowledge my transgressions:
and my sin [is] ever before me.
⁴Against thee, thee only, have I sinned, and done
[this] evil in thy sight: that thou mightest
be justified when thou speakest,
[and] be clear when thou judgest.
⁵Behold, I was shapen in iniquity, and in sin did my
mother conceive me.
⁶Behold, thou desirest truth in the inward parts:
and in the hidden [part]
thou shalt make me to know wisdom.
⁷Purge me with hyssop, and I shall be clean: wash
me, and I shall be whiter than snow.
⁸Make me to hear joy and gladness; [that] the bones
[which] thou hast broken may rejoice.
⁹Hide thy face from my sins,
blot out all mine iniquities.
¹⁰Create in me a clean heart, O God;
and renew a right spirit within me.
¹¹Cast me not away from thy presence; and take not
thy Holy Spirit from me.
¹²Restore unto me the joy of thy salvation;
and uphold me [with thy] free spirit.
¹³[Then] will I teach transgressors thy ways;
and sinners shall be converted unto thee.
¹⁴Deliver me from blood guiltiness, O God, thou God
of my salvation: [and] my tongue shall sing aloud of
thy righteousness.
¹⁵O Lord, open thou my lips;
and my mouth shall show forth thy praise.

¹⁶For thou desirest not sacrifice; else would I give [it]: thou delightest not in burnt offering.
¹⁷The sacrifices of God [are] a broken spirit: a broken and a contrite heart, O God, thou wilt not despise.
¹⁸Do good in thy good pleasure unto Zion: build thou the walls of Jerusalem.
¹⁹Then shalt thou be pleased with the sacrifices of righteousness, with burnt offering and whole burnt offering: then shall they offer bullocks upon thine altar.

PSALM 51
Title: First Prayer Psalm
Author: a Psalm of David
Date: Nathan Approaches David Regarding Bathsheba
Superscription: to the chief Musician
Theme: Repentance

This psalm is both a confession of sin and a fervent prayer for forgiveness. David comes before God pleading for mercy when he knows his transgression was brought about by his own lust. He not only had thoughts of sin, he acted upon those thoughts. The depth of the individual experience, the sin involved and the plea for forgiveness is unsurpassed in any other psalm. To some, it has a corporate significance (the addition of verses 18 and 19 seem to adapt a plea from an individual to meet the requirements of corporate worship); this may have been added later. Verses 1-17, however, bear the pain of a man when he is confronted by the prophet regarding his adultery with Bathsheba and covering up this sin with the far greater one of the murder of Bathsheba's husband, Uriah.

"Have mercy upon me, O God," is his cry for forgiveness. The psalmist neither pleads innocence nor seeks to blame anyone else. He knows what he has done does not deserve forgiveness. Based solely on God's lovingkindness and in line with God's mercy, he asks that his transgressions and rebellion be wiped out and his iniquity be washed, cleansed. He emphasizes the fact that he knows and is constantly aware of his misdeeds, acknowledging that his sin is more than sin against a man—it is a sin against God. The depth of his confession and the anguish it carries show a bare soul completely open to God.

David, on his face before God, begs for both internal and external cleansing. This prayer of repentance is a tear-stained testimony of his pain and brokenness before God. On his knees, he humbles himself, seeking God's presence and the presence of the Holy Spirit. The fear of the angering of God and the possibility of punishment caused by his own disobedience to God does not dissuade him. Instead, he cries out—not just for pardon, not just forgiveness, but for a complete reunion of his spirit with the spirit of God. He is morally bankrupt and needs a total, complete cleansing, a removal of his internal impurities and a restoration of his soul.

In the midst of this heart-wrenching sorrow, a ray of sunlight comes as he begins to realize that he is still loved by the God of boundless and endless mercy.

He believes in his heart that he has been purged of his evil desires and sets his face forward once again serve God to his greatest ability. His greatest desire is that God will fill his soul and use him to teach other transgressors, giving evidence that he has been pardoned and that his very nature has been changed.

This prayer, although belonging to David, gives a reminder to all that even after the greatest of sins, God is still waiting with open arms.

PSALM 52

¹To the chief Musician, Maschil, [A Psalm] of David, when Doeg the Edomite came and told Saul, and said unto him, David is come to the house of Abimelech. Why boastest thou thyself in mischief, O mighty man? the goodness of God [endureth] continually.
²Thy tongue deviseth mischiefs; like a sharp razor, working deceitfully.
³Thou lovest evil more than good; [and] lying rather than to speak righteousness.
⁴Thou lovest all devouring words, O [thou] deceitful tongue.
⁵God shall likewise destroy thee for ever, he shall take thee away, and pluck thee out of [thy] dwelling place, and root thee out of the land of the living.
⁶The righteous also shall see, and fear, and shall laugh at him:

⁷Lo, [this is] the man [that] made not God, his strength; but trusted in the abundance of his riches, [and] strengthened himself in his wickedness.
⁸But I [am] like a green olive tree in the house of God: I trust in the mercy of God for ever and ever.
⁹I will praise thee for ever, because thou hast done [it]: and I will wait on thy name; for [it is] good before thy saints.

PSALM 52
Title: Seventh Psalm of Instruction
Author: a Psalm of David
Date: David comes to the House of Abimelech
Superscription: to the chief Musician *Maschil thoughtful or reflective*
Theme: Peace of the Godly-Destruction of Evildoers

This psalm is similar in its topic of the power of wealth contrasted with the power of godliness. Here it is shown how useless and futile is the seeking of material things and the belief that such things bring power, authority or righteousness in God's eyes. The fate of the arrogant sinner is exposed. Presented in a direct manner, there is no appeal for God's intervention, only an unspoken belief that God will remain true to Himself and bring to ruin those who defy Him.

Verses 1 through 4 outline the attributes of those who oppose God: 1) they love *treachery;* 2) they are *deceitful*; 3) they *assault people* with their speech; 4) they *take from the needy* and helpless; 5) they are *greedy;* 6) they are *liars;* 7) they are *arrogant*. All abhorrent behaviors are characteristic of this group of people. The psalmist shouts that God will soon destroy them. The destruction of those who turn against God is described in verse 5. Quite succinctly, God will wreak havoc upon them. He will snatch, carry away and uproot all of those who are wicked. Although these verbs sometimes appear within a prayer, here it is a confident statement that the righteous will know and possibly observe their destruction.

The final contrast comes when the psalmist reiterates his trust in God's mercy. The wicked may trust in any number of worldly things. The righteous, however, need only the security of complete trust in God. David shows a fearless confidence as he is attacked by his ungodly enemies. He hurls his accusatory condemnation straight in the face of his attackers. Confidence is, as David deduced, a priceless gift from God given to those who seek to do His will.

PSALM 53

¹To the chief Musician upon Mahalath, Maschil,
[A Psalm] of David. The fool hath said in his heart,
[There is] no God. Corrupt are they,
and have done abominable iniquity:
[there is] none that doeth good.
²God looked down from heaven upon the children of
men, to see if there were [any]
that did understand, that did seek God.

³Every one of them is gone back:
they are altogether become filthy; [there is]
none that doeth good, no, not one.
⁴Have the workers of iniquity no knowledge? who
eat up my people [as] they eat bread:
they have not called upon God.
⁵There were they in great fear, [where] no fear
was: for God hath scattered the bones of him that
encampeth [against] thee: thou hast put [them] to
shame, because God hath despised them.
⁶Oh that the salvation of Israel [were come] out of
Zion! When God bringeth back the captivity of his
people, Jacob shall rejoice, [and] Israel shall be glad.

PSALM 53
Title: Eighth Psalm of Instruction
Author: a Psalm of David
Superscription: to the chief Musician *Mahalath or melancholy tune*
Theme: Foolishness of Godless Men

Psalm 53 is a revision of Psalm 14, along with several others, giving a portrait of the godless man. The only real significant difference is that of the content of 14:5-6 where the description is strengthened and compressed into a single verse. It is highly possible that both of these psalms are different versions of an original poem, but as many of the psalms are reflective of one another, it is impossible to say. One significant difference is that Psalm 53 uses the word *Elohim* instead of *Yahweh* for the name of God. This is yet another sign that the psalms are an evolutionary collection.

The psalm begins with the words, "the fool has said in his heart, there is no God. They are corrupt and have done abominable iniquity; there is none that does good." These words form the basis of Christianity and carry the meaning that no one, either by works or deeds, is good enough to enter heaven without the salvation of Christ. Searching his mind, David recalls how, in the past, God has reduced the proud and haughty ones to a pile of rubble. In light of this memory, David feels confident that the future will be no different from the past and once again his God will chastise the godless and deliver due punishment.

It is interesting to note here that the word "corrupt" as it is used in this psalm is the same word used in Genesis 6:5 to describe the wickedness of mankind prior to the flood. This brings strength of meaning to the corrupt man of which the psalmist speaks. Also in verse 4, the term to "eat up" is an indicator that the evildoers are so confident in their ways that they literally devour anyone they choose.

PSALM 54

¹To the chief Musician on Neginoth, Maschil, [A Psalm] of David, when the Ziphims came and said to Saul, Doth not David hide himself with us? Save me, O God, by thy name, and judge me by thy strength.

²Hear my prayer, O God;
give ear to the words of my mouth.
³For strangers are risen up against me,
and oppressors seek after my soul:
they have not set God before them.
⁴Behold, God [is] mine helper:
the Lord [is] with them that uphold my soul.
⁵He shall reward evil unto mine enemies:
cut them off in thy truth.
⁶I will freely sacrifice unto thee:
I will praise thy name, O LORD; for [it is] good.
⁷For he hath delivered me out of all trouble: and
mind hath seen [his desire] upon mine enemies.

PSALM 54
Title: Ninth Psalm of Instruction
Author: a Psalm of David
Date: While David was Hiding from Saul
Superscription: to the chief musician, *on Neginoth/ Maschil reflective-played on a stringed instrument*
Theme: Answered Prayer and Deliverance

This short psalm was written by David during the time he was hiding from King Saul. It is at this time that the Ziphites (1 Samuel 26) revealed to Saul where David was hiding. The first half of the psalm pinpoints David's situation. People have risen up against him, oppressors have sought after his life; they much prefer to kill David rather than to listen to the word or direction of God.

The style of this psalm is the same as the typical prayers of David, which are found in the Psalter. The psalm begins with a plea for protection from his enemies, a remembrance of the past victories and wondrous deeds of God, followed by a statement of assurance that God will triumph over his enemies.

Though clearly this is an individual psalm and the appeal of a deeply troubled man, it also takes the appearance of a psalm of instruction. The language and content used here are so general that it is very adaptable to the needs of any individual or group who find themselves oppressed by godless men. David's plea for help is based on God's name (His character) and the power and strength He has revealed to man. He is so confident in the character of God that he makes a pledge to bring a free will offering to the temple and to continually sing and praise the glory of Yahweh.

PSALM 55

¹To the chief Musician on Neginoth, Maschil,
[A Psalm] of David. Give ear to my prayer, O God;
and hide not thyself from my supplication.
²Attend unto me, and hear me:
I mourn in my complaint and make a noise;
³Because of the voice of the enemy,
because of the oppression of the wicked:
for they cast iniquity upon me,
and in wrath, they hate me.
⁴My heart is sore pained within me:
and the terrors of death are fallen upon me.

⁵Fearfulness and trembling are come upon me,
and horror hath overwhelmed me.
⁶And I said, Oh, that I had wings like a dove!
[for then] I would fly away, and be at rest.
⁷Lo, [then] would I wonder far off, [and]
remain in the wilderness.
⁸I would hasten my escape from
the windy storm [and] tempest.
⁹Destroy, O Lord, [and] divide their tongues: for I
have seen violence and strife in the city.
¹⁰Day and night they go about it upon the walls
thereof: mischief also and sorrow
[are] in the midst of it.
¹¹Wickedness [is] in the midst, there of:
deceit and guile depart not from her streets.
¹²For [it was] not an enemy. [that] reproached me;
then I could have borne [it]: neither [was it] he that
hated me [that] did magnify [himself] against me;
then I would have it myself from him:
¹³But [it was] thou, a man mine equal, my guide,
and mine acquaintance.
¹⁴We took sweet counsel together, [and] walked
unto the house of God in company.
¹⁵Let death seize upon them, [and] let them go down
quick into hell: for wickedness [is] in their dwellings,
[and] among them.
¹⁶As for me, I will call upon God and the LORD
shall save me.
¹⁷Evening, and morning, and at noon, will I pray, and
cry aloud: and he shall hear my voice.

[18] He hath delivered my soul in peace from the battle [that was] against me for there were many with me.
[19] God shall hear, and afflict them, even he that abideth of old. Because they have no changes, therefore they fear not God.
[20] He has put forth his hands against such as be at peace with him: he hath broken his covenant.
[21] [The words] of his mouth were smoother than butter, but war [was] in his heart: his words were softer than oil, yet [were] they drawn swords.
[22] Cast thy burden upon the LORD, and he shall sustain thee: he shall never suffer the righteous to be moved.
[23] But thou, O God, shalt bring them down into the pit of destruction: bloody and deceitful men shall not live out half of their days; but I will trust in thee.

PSALM 55
Title: Tenth Psalm of Instruction
Author: a Psalm of David
Superscription: to the chief Musician *Neginoth/Maschil or music of a stringed instrument.*
Theme: Overcoming the Treachery of Friends

This psalm contains four requests and eight complaints against the wicked ones. David's health and perhaps his life are being threatened by a powerful conspiracy in Jerusalem. He describes strife, violence, sorrow and mischief that is rampant within the city. Sadly, the leader of this secretive plot is a man who was once one of David's closest friends. David feels the deep sting of betrayal. (See Jesus's attitude towards such a man in Mark 14:21). The city is in turmoil and there is no one who can be trusted. False reports, slanderous lies and unscrupulous rumors are everywhere around him. With words of exquisite musical beauty, he expresses his desire to fly away to the wilderness and escape all men and all persecution. The joy of peace, however, seems to be out of the question, so he gives his weariness and care to God.

The words of this psalm fit very well with the time of Absalom's rebellion (2 Samuel 5:17), when Antiphonel, one of David's closest friends turned on him and sided with the enemy. (This is a foreshadowing of when Jesus is betrayed by Judas.) This betrayal by a man whom David deemed to be righteous, has become the last straw (1-4, 9-11). He is full of conflicting emotions, not knowing whether he would prefer to simply avoid the entire situation (4-8); or to be still and watch as God devours his enemies (9, 15). Trust eventually takes center court (16-18, 22) and he stands solid in the faith that although human friends may be faithless, God is a friend who never deserts His people.

Note: David prays evening, morning and noontime. The Hebrew day started as the sun went down and continued through the afternoon of the following day—thus, this is the correct order for praying all day long.

PSALM 56

¹To the chief Musician upon Jonathelemrechokim, Michtam of David, when the Philistines took him in Gath. Be merciful unto me, O God: for a man would swallow me up; he fighting daily oppresseth me.
²Mine enemies would daily swallow [me] up: 4 [they be] many that fight against me, O thou most High.
³What time I am afraid, I will trust in thee.
⁶They gather themselves together,
they hide themselves, they mark my steps,
when they wait for my soul.
⁴In God I will praise his word, in God have I put my trust; I will not fear what flesh can do unto me.
⁵Every day they wrest my words: all their thoughts [are] against me for evil.
⁷Shall they escape by iniquity? in [thine] anger cast down the people, O God.
⁸Thou tellest my wanderings: for thou, my tears into thy bottle: [are they] not in thy book?
⁹When I cry [unto thee], then shall mine enemies turn back: this I know; for God [is] for me.
¹⁰In God will I praise [his] word:
in the LORD will I praise [his] word.
¹¹In God have I put my trust: I will not be afraid what man can do unto me.
¹²Thy vows [are] upon me, O God:
I will render praises unto thee.
¹³For thou hast delivered my soul from death: [wilt] not [thou deliver] my feet from falling, that I may walk before God in the light of the living?

PSALM 56
Title: Twelfth Prayer of Distress
Author: a Prayer of David
Date: David captured by Philistines in Gath
Superscription: to the chief Musician-*on Jonath-elem-rech (to the tune of an old melody)*
Theme: Relief from Enemies

When David fled from Saul to the city of Gath (6), the Philistines were underwhelmed by his presence and treated him quite poorly. The whole of the psalm is framed by an urgent appeal to God and the word of confident assurance. This confidence in God's defense and deliverance stands in sharp contrast to the failure of the wicked earthly rulers referred to in Psalm 58. David has used his own resources to the limit, even to the point of pretending to be insane. Nothing seems to have worked.

At the beginning of the psalm, David cries to the Lord, "Be merciful to me." This phrase is often found in the psalms and was frequently repeated by Israel's devout worshipers. David's enemies are warriors rather than religious heretics. They continually denounce him with evil words and he is in constant danger. David silently bears these attacks until verse 5, where there is a definite change in the tone. Verses 5-11 are filled with descriptions of his enemies and the treachery, schemes and plots they have put in his path. There is an appeal for vengeance and destruction of his enemies. Each time David has suffered,

God has conquered his *fear*; this time he knows that God must conquer his *oppressors*.

In his heart, David begins to feel God's comfort. With victory envisioned, he recalls his own obligations to God-that of giving praise and thanksgiving. He knows God will answer his prayers, which lead him to a repetition of the expression of trust found in verse 4. The message is: no matter *who*, *when*, *why* and *what* struggles to destroy man, there is no situation in which God cannot be trusted to bring victory.

Note: In verse 8, there is an indication that God keeps records of a man's life. This verse is uncharacteristic for the Book of Psalms, but the same thought is also found in Exodus 32:32 and in Luke 10:20.

PSALM 57

¹To the chief Musician, Altaschith, Michtam of David, when he fled from Saul in the cave. Be merciful unto me O God, be merciful unto me: for my soul trusteth in thee: yea, in the shadow of thy wings will I make my refuge, until [these] calamities be overpast.
²I will cry unto God most high; unto God that preformeth [all things] for me.
³He shall send from heaven, and save me [from] the reproach of him that would swallow me up. God shall send forth his mercy and his truth.
⁴My soul [is] among lions: [and] I lie [even among] them that are set on fire, [even] the sons of men,

whose teeth [are] spears and arrows,
and their tongue a sharp sword.
⁵Be thou exalted, O God, above the heavens;
[let] thy glory [be] above all the earth.
⁶They have prepared a net for my steps; my soul is bowed down: they have digged a pit before me, into the midst whereof they are fallen [themselves].
⁷My heart is fixed, O God, my heart is fixed:
I will sing and give praise.
⁸Awake up, my glory; awake, psaltery and harp:
I [myself] will awake early.
⁹I will praise thee, O Lord, among the people:
I will sing unto thee among the nations.
¹⁰For thy mercy [is] great unto the heavens, and thy truth unto the clouds.
¹¹Be thou exalted O God, above the heavens:
[let] thy glory [be] above all the earth.

PSALM 57
Title: Thirteenth Prayer of Distress
Author: a Psalm of David
Date: When David Fled from Saul
Superscription: to the chief Musician *Altaschith/ Michtam A tune, where the words are identified as a popular saying and used as the reassuring words of God*
Theme: David's Prayer of Distress

Once again, things look very, very dark for David. He is hiding from Saul and his soldiers in the cave of Adullam, (1 Samuel 22:1; 24:1; 26:21). This plea for

God's protection reads much like Psalm 56, as both have the same spirit, context and style and begin with the same appeal to God. Verses 7-11 of this psalm will be seen again in Psalm 108, in the form of a striking hymn. The refrain in verses 5 and 11 splits the psalm into two unique segments. The first part of the psalm shows David's heartfelt prayer for God's protection while praise fills the second half of the psalm.

In verses 1 through 5, David seems to bear little anger as he requests no destruction or annihilation of his enemies, but only for God to watch over him. He knows that in this situation, only his trust in God will see him through. Having the confidence that God's mercy and truth will suffice, he takes his refuge, knowing that God will fully protect him. The words that fill him are words of thanksgiving. "My heart is fixed; I will sing and give praise" is his promise to God.

After only a brief reminder of his current situation, the psalmist makes a steadfast resolution which is universal in tone, showing the competence of God's mercy and the pureness of His love. David has determined that even though he is surrounded by evildoers, living in caves and fleeing for his life, it will eventually end. The night of danger will be followed by a morning of salvation.

The final verse of the Psalm (11) "be exalted, above the heavens; let your glory be of above all the earth" is the hope, the prayer, the desire and ultimately the need of the Israelites, Christians and Jews in the world today.

PSALM 58

¹To the chief Musician, Altaschith, Michtam of David.
Do ye indeed speak righteousness, O congregation?
do ye judge uprightly, O ye sons of men?
²Yea, in heart you work wickedness; ye weigh the
violence of your hands in the earth.
³The wicked are estranged from the world: they go
astray as soon as they be born, speaking lies.
⁴Their poison [is] like the poison of a serpent: [they
are] like the deaf adder [that] stoppeth her ear;
⁵Which will not hearken to the voice of charmers,
charming never so wisely.
⁶Break their teeth, O God, in their mouth: break out
the great teeth of the young lions, O LORD.
⁷Let them melt away as waters [which] run continually: [when] he bendeth [his bow to shoot] his
arrows, let them be as cut in pieces.
⁸As a snail [which] melteth, let [every one of them]
pass away: [like] the untimely birth of a woman,
[that] they may not see the sun.
⁹Before your pots can feel the thorns,
he shall take them away as with a whirlwind,
both living, and in [his] wrath.
¹⁰The righteous shall rejoice when he seeth the
vengeance: he shall wash his feet in
the blood of the wicked.
¹¹So that a man shall say, Verily [there is] a reward
for the righteous: verily he is a God
that judgeth in the earth.

PSALM 58
Title: Fifth Prayer for Judgment
Author: a Psalm of David
Superscription: none
Theme: Promise of Judgment of the Wicked

With blistering language, this psalm calls for justice. David is calling down God's most horrific judgment on all of the corrupt, evil and ungodly men who hold power in the nation. More specifically, he is asking God to be the supreme judge over all of human affairs and to discipline or remove all of those who corrupt justice. Since Moses *penned* the book of Judges, judicial power has been very persuasive and authoritative. The judges hold the responsibility of protecting the innocent—usually the poor and powerless—against the assaults of those who would take advantage of them. The Israelite society continually dealt with this corruption from the days of Samuel through the time of David's kingdom and to the end of the monarchy.

Verses 1 through 5 show that the whole problem of justice is caused by man's natural inclination to unrighteousness. The sarcasm here is directed at the unjust judges. In describing them, he calls them *"snails, wasting away"*. Throughout the psalm is the ring of vengeance. He wants God to break their teeth, let them melt as running water and blow them away in a whirlwind.

Yet the anger of the psalmist is overshadowed in verses 10 and 11 as we see David's confidence in more realistic terms. He feels certain that those he represents (the righteous) will witness the complete destruction of those who now judge and accuse them falsely. Those who do not judge correctly by the word of God will indeed be judged by God Himself.

Note: This psalm was used by the early church in reference to the Lord's trial before the Sanhedrin.

PSALM 59

¹To the chief Musician, Altaschith, Michtam of David; when Saul sent, and they watched the house to kill him. Deliver me from mine enemies, O my God: defend me from them that rise up against me.
²Deliver me from the workers of iniquity, and save me from bloody men.
³For, lo, they lie in wait for my soul: the mighty are gathered against me; not [for] my transgression, nor [for] my sin, O LORD.
⁴They run and prepare themselves without [my] fault: awake to help me, and behold.
⁵Thou therefore, O LORD God of hosts, the God of Israel, awake to visit all the heathen: be not merciful to any wicked transgressors.
⁶They return at evening: they make a noise like a dog, and go round about the city.
⁷Behold, they belch out with their mouth: swords [are] in their lips: for [say they], doth hear?
⁸But thou, O LORD, shalt laugh at them; thou shalt have all the heathen in derision.

⁹[Because of] his strength I will wait upon thee:
for God [is] my defense.
¹⁰The God of my mercy shall prevent me: God shall
let me see [my desire] upon mine enemies.
¹¹Slay them not, lest my people forget:
scatter them by thy power;
and bring them down, O Lord our shield.
¹²[For] the sin of their mouth [and] the words of
their lips let them even be taken in their pride: and
for cursing and lying [which] they speak.
¹³Consume [them] in wrath, consume [them], that
they [may] not [be]: and let them know that God
ruleth in Jacob unto the ends of the earth.
¹⁴And at evening let them return; [and] let them
make a noise like a dog, and go round about the city.
¹⁵Let them wander up and down for meat, and
grudge if they be not satisfied.
¹⁶But I will sing of thy power; yea, I will sing aloud
of thy mercy in the morning: for thou hast been my
defense and refuge in the day of my trouble.
¹⁷Unto thee, O my strength, will I sing: for God [is]
my defense, [and] the God of my mercy.

PSALM 59
Title: Sixth prayer for Judgment
Author: a Psalm of David
Date: When Saul sent men to Spy on David
Superscription: to the chief Musician
Altaschith/Michtam
Theme: Assured Judgment of Evil-doers

When Saul sent his soldiers to entrap David at his home (1 Samuel 19:10-17), David offered up this petition for deliverance from the violent men. If originally this poem was composed by David under the circumstances noted, it must have been revised for the use of David's sons when Jerusalem was under siege. As when Hezekiah was besieged by the Assyrians, this enemy also was made up of many nations. While this is a physical battle, the most prominent weapon is the tongue, which attacks with slander and vile words.

The first portion of the psalm is predominantly a prayer for safety, while the second section focuses on the assurance of God's deliverance. Written as an individual lament, this psalm has indications that it was later adapted for national use. Psalms 55 and 58 share the vindictive attitude of the writer, coupled with a situation of overwhelming oppression. Verses 6 and 13 are not identical, yet work as a repeating thought. Verses 9 and 10 repeat the thought pattern of verse 17.

"Deliver me; defend me; save me" is the cry of the psalmist in the beginning of this psalm. Almost to the point of becoming repetitive, David once again describes his anguish and the fact that he is continually at odds with his enemies. He describes their activities against him, all the while pleading his own innocence. David asks God to rise up against the nations that pursue him. While David seems to speak in the singular, it is apparent that this psalm applies to a national emergency. The fate of David and Israel depend upon David and his ability (in God) to overcome those who desire to have him destroyed.

As the psalm wraps up, David is confident that God will eventually laugh at His enemies. It would be normal that David would want his enemies completely removed from the earth, but this is not the case. He does not want them destroyed, but prays for a gradual, painful punishment upon them. It is his hope that in this way he will make an example of them. While the *wicked dogs will wander around the city, searching yet not satisfied*, he will be singing his praises to God with a full voice when the sun arises. He has found a refuge in His high tower.

PSALM 60

¹To the chief Musician upon Shushaneduth, Michtam of David, to teach; when he strove with Aramnaharaim and with Aramzobah, when Joab returned, and smote of Edom in the Valley of salt twelve thousand. O God, thou hast cast us off, thou

hast scattered us, thou hast been displeased;
O turn thyself to us again.
²Thou hast made the earth to tremble; thou hast broken it: heal the breaches thereof; for it shaketh.
³Thou hast showed thy people hard things: thou hast made us to drink the wine of astonishment.
⁴Thou hast given a banner to them that fear thee, that it may be displayed because of the truth.
⁵That thy beloved may be delivered;
save [with] thy right hand, and hear me.
⁶God has spoken in his holiness; I will rejoice, I will divide Shechem, and mete out the Valley of Succoth.
⁷Gilead [is] mine, and Manasseh [is] mine;
Ephriam also [is] the strength of mine head;
Judah [is] my lawgiver.
⁸Moab, [is] my washpot; over Edom will I cast out my shoe: Philistia, triumph thou because of me.
⁹Who will bring me [into] the strong city?
who will lead me into Edom?
¹⁰[Wilt] not thou, O God, [which] hadst cast us off? and [thou], O God, [which] didst not go out with our armies?
¹¹Give us help from trouble:
for vain [is] the help of man.
¹²Through God we shall do valiantly:
for he [it is that] shall tread down our enemies.

PSALM 60
Title: Eleventh Psalm of Instruction
Author: a Psalm of David
Date: David's fight against Mesopotamia and Syria
Superscription: to the chief Musician *Shushaneduth Michtam or Golden poem/silent prayer*
Theme: Prayer for the Restoration of God's Favor

"Is it not you, O God, who has cast us off?" This is the feeling of the writer as he looks at his nation and sees it in ruins. They have suffered a near deathblow from their enemies, (2 Samuel 8:3-14). In this time of national humiliation and destruction, several other psalms took shape (7, 9, 44, 74 and 108). While this prayer was led by the King, it is much more personal than a military defeat. It is interpreted by the people to mean that God has forsaken them and will not go before them in battle. God has given them His banner (the banner was the rallying point for the defense of righteousness, which Israel possessed in the midst of a pagan world) then led them into defeat. David mourns that his people have been forced to drink *the wine of astonishment (confusion).*

This psalm is classified as a national lament. While public complaint is voiced at length in the beginning and the end of the psalm, it is broken up by an Oracle of God at its center. (These verses 6-12 are repeated in Psalm 108.) While God is displeased with their murmuring against Him and their supposition that he has abandoned them, He chooses to answer their complaints. In boundless geographical and cultural depictions, He shows Himself to be all-powerful.

The victorious words of faith in verse 12 and God's words in verse 8 are realized as the ultimate and eventual victory. With renewed faith, he goes forward to fight these enemies once again. Later, he receives praise and gifts from those he has now defeated (2 Samuel 8:3-14). God's power is over His people in Israel and in all of the surrounding areas. This naming of towns and tribes as seen in the psalm clearly shows that God is infinite in every direction. Although the process is slow, the people eventually give way to understanding and grow in agreement that they must proceed with their eyes focused on nothing but God. In Him alone can there be victory.

PSALM 61

¹To the chief Musician upon Neginah, [A Psalm] of David. Hear my cry, O God; attend unto my prayer.
²From the end of the earth will I cry unto thee,
when my heart is overwhelmed:
lead me to the rock, [that] is higher than I.
³For thou hast been a shelter for me,
[and] a strong tower from the enemy.
⁴I will abide in thy tabernacle for ever:
I will trust in the cover of thy wings.
⁵For thou, O God, hast heard my vows: thou hast given [me] the heritage of those that fear thy name.
⁶Thou wilt prolonging the king's life: [and]
his years as many generations.

⁷He shall abide before God for ever: O prepare mercy and truth, [which] may preserve him.
⁸So will I sing praise unto thy name for ever, that I may daily perform my vows.

PSALM 61
Title: Third Psalm of Trust
Author: a Psalm of David
Date: (Possibly) as David Fled from Absalom
Superscription: to the chief Musician *Neginoth or stringed instrument*
Theme: Assurance of God's Protection

Similar to the situations referenced in Psalm 42 and 43, this psalm recounts both the national and the individual promise of God's protection. It is dissimilar in that it shows the involvement of the King. If David was the author, he may have composed this prayer at the time he was fleeing from his son, Absalom. David, moving like the wind, is journeying either to his home or on his way to a distant land. The psalm is the earnest lament of one who is a great distance from home. Used here, *"the end of the earth"* does not necessarily refer to a remote area, as distances are frequently magnified in the psalms. Although this phrase *may* indicate a forced exile, it is not mandatory to the psalm.

Personal restoration is the prayer of the author as he cries, "Hear my cry, O God." Lost in a deep well full of despair, frustration and anguish, he begs for the ability to feel God's presence surrounding him. His one desire is to experience the safety of a rock that is too high for him to climb and can only be accessed by God Himself. While meditating on the safety of the rock, he thinks of the power and might of God's past blessings. It is here that he finds assurance for the present and hope for the future.

The psalmist prays for three things: *a prolonged life, extended reign* and for the continuance of *God's blessings* of mercy. While these prayers are for the King, they can easily be extended to cover all of humanity. In the colorful and picturesque metaphors used to describe God, He is seen as a shelter, a high rock, a fortified tower, a pitched tent and a mother hen with outstretched wings. These metaphors all bear the same theme of solidness and safety. In the end, the psalmist is so confident that God will answer his prayers that he vows to give thanks daily to the God who is that *higher rock*.

PSALM 62

¹To the chief Musician, to Jeduthun, A Psalm of David. Truly my soul waited upon God: from him [cometh] my salvation.
²He only [is] my rock and my salvation; [he is] my defense; I shall not be greatly moved.
³How long will ye imagine mischief against a man? ye shall be slain all of you: as a bowing wall [shall you be, and as] a tottering fence.
⁴They only consult to cast [him] down from his excellency: they delight in lies: they bless with their mouth, but they curse inwardly.

⁵My soul, wait thou only upon God; for my expectation [is] from him.
⁶He only [is] my rock and my salvation: [he is] my defense; I shall not be moved.
⁷In God [is] my salvation and my glory: the rock of my strength, [and] my refuge, [is] in God.
⁸Trust in him at all times; [ye] people, pour out your heart before him: God [is] a refuge for us.
⁹Surely men of low degree [are] vanity, [and] men of high degree [are] a lie: to be laid in the balance, they [are] altogether [lighter] than vanity.
¹⁰Trust not in oppression, and become not in vain in robbery: if riches increase, set not your heart [upon them].
¹¹God hath spoken once; twice have I heard this; that power [belongeth] unto God.
¹²Also unto thee, O Lord, [belongeth] mercy: for thou renderest to every man according to his work.

PSALM 62
Title: Fourth Psalm of Trust
Author: a Psalm of David
Superscription: to the chief Musician-*to Jeduthun (a choir director)*
Theme: Waiting on God's Salvation

The author of this psalm is assumed to be David. The circumstances could well have been the efforts of the family of Saul to topple David's kingdom. Verse 3 shows a time of weakness and may indicate that David is in his advanced years of life. Implicitly, however, the psalm is an appeal to God to be the power which upholds him and the kingdom. A warning is given to those who are conspiring against him, using their schemes to get what they want, placing no trust in the sustenance of God. There is an element of lamentation in both the opening and closing verses, but the center focuses on the primary theme of trust and confidence that God will fulfill every need.

Beginning with verse 6, the psalmist describes the God to which he clings. He boldly proclaims that God is my rock and my salvation; he is my defense; in God is my salvation and my glory; the rock of my strength and my refuge. Having used these words, it becomes obvious to the reader that as the psalmist himself says, "I shall not be moved."

The psalm takes a turn at verse 9, where it changes from praising God to an admonishment to all men. He first notes that men of low degree are little more than a *vapor*; men of high degree are a *lie*. To both of these groups of men he has a warning. Men should not trust in their perceived power, nor should they gain wealth by taking advantage of other people. For all the power and all the wealth belongs to God.

Note: In Matthew 6:13 Jesus adds, "the kingdom and the glory" to the list of things that belong to God. The serene confidence found in this psalm is probably tied up with the Hebrew particle 'ak, which occurs six times in this brief psalm. (Three times this particle is used as the first word of the stanza.) The translation of the particle 'ak is generally translated to mean "surely", but standing alone, perhaps a better translation would be "only". Truly God is the only rock and it is His salvation and defends the righteous from persecution.

PSALM 63

¹A Psalm of David, when he was in the wilderness of Judah. O God, thou [art] my God; early will I seek thee: my soul thirsteth for thee, my flesh longeth for thee in a dry and thirsty land, where no water is;
²To see thy power, and thy glory, so [as] I have seen thee in the sanctuary.
³Because thy lovingkindness [is] better than life, my lips shall praise thee.
⁴Thus will I bless thee, while I live: I will lift up my hands in thy name.
⁵My soul shall be satisfied as [with] marrow and fatness; and my mouth shall praise [thee] with joyful lips:
⁶When I remember thee upon my bed, [and] meditate on thee in the [night] watches.
⁷Because thou hast been my help, therefore, in the shadow of thy wings will I rejoice.
⁸My soul followeth hard after thee: thy right hand upholdeth me.
⁹But those [that] seek my soul, to destroy [it], shall go into the lower parts of the earth.
¹⁰They shall fall by the sword: they shall be a portion for foxes.

[11]But the King shall rejoice in God; everyone that sweareth by him shall glory: but the mouth of them that speak lies shall be stopped.

PSALM 63
Title: Fifth Psalm of Trust
Author: a Psalm of David
Date: In the Wilderness of Judah
Superscription: none
Theme: Fellowship with God

This song of trust is based on the beauty that comes in a close relationship with God. The psalmist appears to come from a time of exile, probably when David was in the wilderness of Engedi (1 Samuel 24) continuing to flee from his son. This psalm exhibits the highest and purest type of personal and spiritual worship for Israelites (and Christians as well). Like Psalm 62, this psalm is a very personal prayer, which was later prescribed as a daily public prayer. Psalm 62 brings forth the terms *seeing* and *hearing* as a part of communion with God. The vision of danger at night and joy in the morning, found frequently in the psalms, appears here once again.

The first nine verses of the psalm shows the psalmist's desire to have a very special fellowship with God. A series of metaphors indicate his commitment to God. His words *"you are my God"* affirm his relationship to the Almighty. *"I seek you"* indicates his priorities. *"I thirst for you"* shows his depth of intensity. *"I long for you"* expresses his yearning. *"I looked *for you"* acknowledges his need. *"To see your power"* indicates his desire to be involved. *"To see your glory"* shows his joy in righteousness. *"Better than life"* is comfort of knowing personal needs will be met. *"Praise you"* expresses his gratitude to God. *"Bless you"* is the overwhelming desire to please. *"Lift up my hands"* is a physical sign of praise. *"Be satisfied"*—he is at peace and content. *"Praise you"* is his way of giving all to God. *"Remember You"* is the acknowledgment that God is in all things. *"Meditate on you"* shows his willingness to ponder the Word. *"Rejoice"* shows how he plans to praise God. *"Follow you"* is his desire to go where God leads. He is very involved in worship as is seen by the use of his eyes, lips, hands, mouth and mind. This is an example of a true worshiper, totally consumed in the presence of God.

Very briefly (9-10) David makes mentions of his enemies. Yet even as he speaks of those who want to kill him, he does so in an almost lighthearted way. Through his praise, he has released the blessings of God. Those seeking to take his life will be destroyed and fall by the sword. He is content. The conflict has not been resolved, but it seems of little concern. His greater concern is his fellowship with God. The blessings that David speaks of are available to everyone. All are encouraged to take time to reaffirm their relationship with the Father, assess priorities and seek God with a desire to worship and praise Him.

PSALM 64

¹To the chief Musician, A Psalm of David. Hear my voice, O God, in my prayer: preserve my life from fear of the enemy.
²Hide me from the secret counsel of the wicked; from the insurrection of the workers of iniquity:
³Who whet their tongue like a sword, [and] bend the [their bows to shoot] their arrows, [even] bitter words:
⁴That they may shoot in secret at the perfect: suddenly do they shoot at him, and fear not.
⁵They encourage themselves [in] an evil matter: they commune of laying snares privily; they say, Who shall see them?
⁶They search out iniquities; they accomplish a diligent search: both the inward [thought] of every one [of them], and the heart, [is] deep.
⁷But God shall shoot at them [with] an arrow; suddenly they shall be wounded.
⁸So they shall make their own tongue to fall upon themselves: all that see them shall flee away.
⁹And all men shall fear, and shall declare the work of God; for they shall wisely consider of his doing.
¹⁰The righteous shall be glad in the LORD, and shall trust in him; and all the upright in heart shall glory.

PSALM 64
Title: Fifth Praise/Prayer Psalm
Author: a Psalm of David
Date: When Ahithophel turned against David
Superscription: to the chief Musician
Theme: Rejoicing in the Lord when under Oppression

This is David's cry to be protected from the plots of his enemies. The circumstances may be similar to those reflected in Psalm 62, where Saul sent his men to kill David. There is no indication of a physically weakened condition and it is unclear whether those in conspiracy against him are Israelites or powers of other nations. Quite likely, this problem arises when David's trusted friend and chief counselor, Ahithophel, betrayed him (9) and assisted in his capture. In a series of haunting metaphors, David compares his enemies to wild animals. They sharpen their tongues to use as a bow, the arrows are made from bitter and angry words. Again, the power of the tongue stands out as a dangerous weapon.

The appeal begins with the request that God come to his aid and give him protection. He cries out to God, "Hear my voice; preserve my life." Although not terrified, David is concerned that those who have conspired in the darkness will achieve their victory in the light of day. He knows that his enemy is *secretly* scheming and slandering him instead of facing them directly. He suspects that at least one and possibly several of his closest friends are members of the secretive circle. Thus, along with his fear, he now feels the sorrow of knowing that he has been betrayed.

Beginning in verse 7 the psalm turns abruptly from a prayer for protection to a statement of prophetic authority. He declares that the evil deeds of the enemies shall turn back upon them (8); what they have planned for David will be their own future. God will lead them to *stumble* over their own tongues. Their greatest weapon shall be their greatest defeat. It is only then that men will recognize the hand of God at work. In their defeat, the evildoers shall run away and instead, they will become fearful. The psalmist feels the sorrow in his heart turn to gladness when he considers their fate.

Note: The theme of evil being done in darkness while victory comes with the light will be seen again at Jesus's crucifixion.

PSALM 65

¹To the chief Musician, A Psalm [and] Song of David.
Praise waiteth for thee, O God, in Zion: and unto thee shall the vow be performed.
²O thou that hearest prayer,
unto thee shall all flesh come.
³Iniquities prevail against me: [as for] our transgressions, thou shalt purge them away.
⁴Blessed [is the man whom] thou choosest, and causest to approach [unto thee, that] he may dwell

in thy courts: we shall be satisfied with the goodness
of thy house, [even] of thy holy temple.
⁵[By] terrible things in righteousness wilt thou
answer us, O God of our salvation; [who art] the
confidence of all the ends of the earth, and of them
that are afar off [upon] the sea:
⁶Which by his strength setteth fast the mountains;
[being] girded with power:
⁷Which stilleth the noise of the seas, the noise of
their waves, and the tumult of the people.
⁸They also that dwell in the uttermost parts are
afraid at thy tokens: thou makest the outgoings of
the morning and evening to rejoice.
⁹Thou visitest the earth, and waterest it: thou
greatly enricheth it with the river of God, [which] is
full of water: thou preparest them corn,
when thou hast so provided for it.
¹⁰Thou waterest the ridges thereof abundantly: thou
settlest the furrows thereof: thou makest it soft with
showers: thou blessest the springing thereof.
¹¹Thou crownest the year with thy goodness;
and thy paths drop fatness.
¹²They drop [upon] the pastures of the wilderness:
and the little hills rejoice on every side.
¹³The pastures are clothed with flocks; the valleys
also are covered over with corn;
they shout for joy, they also sing.

PSALM 65
Title: Second Psalm of praise
Author: a Psalm of David
Superscription: to the chief Musician *A Song*
Theme: God's salvation and Provision

This is a glorious song of the totality of nature. The psalmist gives God glory and takes pleasure in the abundance of the earth. There is a universal feeling here unbounded by Jerusalem or the nationalism of Israel, but rather an expression of all of God's handiwork for mankind. God's deeds are pictured as awe-inspiring and righteous to the end of the earth. His domain is seen in all creation. He IS creation. His power goes beyond the ability to calm the storm. He is the creator of man and all of nature. His sovereignty reigns over this earth. This hymn is closely connected with the Thanksgiving Festival, which was held at the Temple in Jerusalem and may have been composed for or inspired by that occasion.

Verses 9 through 13 give praise to God for the current harvest. Responsible for all things, it is He who has watered the seed, caused them to grow and brought about such a successful harvest. So great is the happiness in the land that not only the people are singing and dancing in praise, but also it appears that the hills, pastures and valleys surrounding them join in the celebration. The psalm also recognizes how God nurtures man in divine fellowship and communion (4). He cares for all men in all nations (8) and takes responsibility to maintain the intricacies of nature (9-13). In all of this, God's existence is very clear and His sustaining role is quite evident.

Overall, this is a hymn to praise God's greatness. There are not enough words to describe God's greatness, yet the psalmist makes an attempt by listing some of God's virtues and blessings. In this public setting, the psalmist reminds the Israelites that they have been blessed by a God who: 1) pardons their sins so that they might have a good life and enjoy fellowship at the Temple; 2) establishes the vibrancy and order of creation. Additionally, He has ordered all the nations of the world so that Israel may feel secure in her land. He makes the Promised Land into a *Garden of Eden* for His people. In the way that He established order out of chaos in Genesis 1, He takes nature and humanity into His hand making something beautiful out of nothing.

PSALM 66

¹To the chief Musician, A Song [or] Psalm. Make a joyful noise unto God, all ye lands:
²Sing forth the honor of his name:
makes his praise glorious.
³Say unto God, How terrible [art thou in] thy works! through the greatness of thy power shall thine enemies submit themselves unto thee.
⁴All the earth shall worship thee, and shall sing unto thee; they shall sing [to] thy name.
⁵Come and see the works of God: [he is] terrible [in his] doing toward the children of men.

⁶He turned the sea into dry [land]:
they went through the flood on foot:
there did we rejoice in him.
⁷He ruleth by his power for ever; his eyes behold the
nations: let not the rebellious exalt themselves.
⁸O bless God, ye people, and make the voice
of his praises to be heard.
⁹Which holdeth our soul in life, and suffereth
not our feet to be moved.
¹⁰For thou, O God, hast proved us: thou hast
tried us, as silver is tried.
¹¹Thou broughtest us into the net; and laidst
affliction upon our loins.
¹²Thou hast caused men to ride over our heads;
we went through fire and through water: but thou
broughtest us out into a wealthy [place].
¹³I will go into thy house, with burnt offerings:
I will pay thee my vows.
¹⁴Which my lips have uttered, and my mouth hath
spoken, when I was in trouble.
¹⁵I will offer unto thee burnt sacrifices of fatlings,
with the incense of the rams;
I will offer bullocks with goats.
¹⁶Come [and] hear, all ye that fear God, and I will
declare what he hath done for my soul.
¹⁷I cried unto him with my mouth, and he was
extolled with my tongue.
¹⁸If I regard iniquity in my heart,
the Lord will not hear [me]:
¹⁹[But] verily God hath heard [me];
he hath attended to the voice of my prayer.

[20]Blessed [be] God, which hath not turned away my prayer, nor his mercy from me.

PSALM 66
Title: Third Psalm of Praise
Author: anonymous
Date: Judah's Deliverance from Assyria (?)
Superscription: to the chief Musician *a song*
Theme: Praise God for His Magnificent Works

Corporate worship fills the skies in verses 1-12. It has been suggested that the psalm speaks of Judah and her remarkable deliverance from the Assyrians. This may have been a private crisis as in verses 13-20 the praises are quiet and become those of a personal testimony. Some commentators believe that in light of this abrupt change, there are actually two distinct psalms here. There is nothing in the psalm which makes it mandatory either as single psalm or as an eloquent joining of two beautiful pieces.

The corporate experience of the nation, forms an excellent background for the individual experience of the author. This psalm, is God's answer to prayer. God's deeds are pictured as righteous, resulting in both personal and national protection. He cries out to the people, "Come and hear." The praises offered at the Temple begin this invitation to all peoples of all nations. In his public testimony, the power of God is brought into the larger context, such as God's answer to the prayer of Israel, as seen in the Exodus. Beginning with the recollection of God's deliverance at the Red Sea, he shows the signs of God's power to rule the nations.

The psalm starts with the deliverance of Israel to the deliverance of all mankind. The events of the Exodus from Egypt and Israel's early history were inspiring enough to call forth the praise of God. This praise was later *replaced* with the New Testament deliverance, also inspiring praise.

PSALM 67

¹To the chief Musician on Neginoth, A Psalm [or] Song. God be merciful unto us, and bless us; [and] cause his face to shine upon us;
²That thy way may be known upon earth,
thy saving health among all nations.
³Let the people praise thee, O God;
let all the people praise thee.
⁴O let the nations be glad, and sing for joy;
for thou shalt judge the people righteously,
and govern the nations upon earth.
⁵Let the people praise thee, O God;
let all the people praise thee.
⁶[Then] shall the earth yield her increase; [and] God, [even] our own God, shall bless us.
⁷God shall bless us; and all the ends of the earth shall fear him.

PSALM 67
Title: Sixth Praise/Prayer Psalm:
Author: anonymous
Superscription: to the chief Musician *on Neginoth (stringed instrument)*
Theme: Invocation and Doxology

This brief psalm of thanksgiving is remarkable for its beauty and simplicity. The usage of this psalm and the reason for its writing may be seen in verse 6 and its expression of the harvest. Based on that thought, this may well have been a psalm for either the Feast of Pentecost or the Feast of Tabernacles. The style and brevity suggest that it served as a liturgical prayer at the conclusion of worship, perhaps just prior to or immediately following the benediction. In the benediction the priest said, "and cause his face to shine upon us." His face *shining* upon man is reminiscent to Numbers 6:24-26, where the words equate to God's looking down on us with approval.

This prayer contains thanksgiving and a petition, which asks God to bless His people. The motivation of this psalm was to share God's blessings upon the Israelites in the hope that His mighty acts and deeds will catch the attention of all peoples and all nations and encourage them to praise their mighty God. By speaking worldwide praise, may His mercy be known to all the people of the world. It is evident in the psalm that although God has chosen Israel as His special people, it is His intent that all nations come to Him and enjoy His blessings and mercy. When this testimony is shared, it presents the basis of a greater mission.

This psalm of praise is based God's continuing deliverance and special care, which determines the future of the nations, thus giving the psalm its universalistic tone. And although subtle, there is a messianic message which is anticipatory of Jesus sending the apostles to share the good news of the gospel.

PSALM 68

¹To the chief Musician, A Psalm [or] Song of David. Let God arise, let his enemies be scattered: let them also that hate him flee before him.
ᴬs smoke is driven away, [so] drive [them] away: as wax melteth before the fire, [so] let the wicked perish at the presence of God.
³But let the righteous be glad; let them rejoice before God: yea, let them exceedingly rejoice.
⁴Sing unto God, sing praises to his name: extol him that rideth upon the heavens by his name JAH, and rejoice before him.
⁵ A father of the fatherless, and a judge of the widows, [is] God in his holy habitation.
⁶God setteth the solitary in families: he bringeth out those which are bound with chains: but the rebellious dwell in a dry [land].
⁷O God, when thou wentest forth before thy people, when thou didst march through the wilderness.

⁸The earth shook, the heavens also dropped at the presence of God: [even] Sinai itself [was moved] at the presence of God, the God of Israel.
⁹Thou, O God didst send a plentiful rain, whereby thou didst confirm thine inheritance,
when it was weary.
¹⁰Thy congregation hath dwelt therein: thou, O God hast prepared of thy goodness for the poor.
¹¹The Lord gave the word: great [was] the company of those published [it].
¹²Kings of armies did flee apace: and she that tarried at home divided the spoil.
¹³Though ye have lien among the pots, [yet shall ye be as] the wings of a dove covered with silver, and her feathers with yellow gold.
¹⁴ When the Almighty scatters kings in it,
it was [white] as snow in Salmon.
¹⁵The hill of God [is as] the hill of Bashan; an high hill [as] the hill of Bashan.
¹⁶Why leap ye, ye high hills? [this is] the hill [which] God desireth to dwell in; yea,
the LORD will dwell [in it] for ever.
¹⁷The chariots of God [are] twenty thousand [even] thousands of angels: the Lord [is] among them, [as in] Sinai, in the holy [place].
¹⁸Thou hast ascended on high, thou hast led captivity captive: thou hast received gifts for men; yea, [for] the rebellious also, that the LORD God might dwell [among them].
¹⁹Blessed [be] the Lord, [who] daily loadeth us [with benefits, even] the God of our salvation.

²⁰[He that is] our God [is] the God of salvation; and unto GOD the Lord [belong] the issues from death.
²¹But God shall wound, the head of his enemies, [and] the hairy scalp of such an one as goeth on still in his trespasses.
²²The Lord said, I will bring again from Bashan, I will bring [my people] again from the depths of the sea:
²³That thy foot may be dipped in the blood of [thine] enemies, [and] the tongue of thy dogs in the same.
²⁴They have seen thy goings, O God; [even] the goings of my God, my King, in the sanctuary.
²⁵The singers went before, the players on instruments [followed] after; among [them were] the damsels playing with timbrels.
²⁶ Bless ye God in the congregations, [even] the Lord, from the fountain of Israel.
²⁷There [is] little Benjamin [with] their ruler, the princes of Judah, [and] their council the princes of Zebulun, [and] the princes of Naphtali.
²⁸Thy God hath commanded thy strength: strengthen, O God, that which thou hast wrought for us.
²⁹Because of thy temple at Jerusalem shall Kings bring presents unto thee.
³⁰Rebuke the company of spearman, the multitude of the bulls, with the calves of the people, [till everyone] submit himself with pieces of silver: scatter thou that people [that] delight in war.
³¹Princes shall come out of Egypt; Ethiopia shall soon stretched out her hand unto God.

³²Sing unto God, ye kingdoms of the earth; O sing praises unto the Lord;
³³To him that rideth upon the heavens of heavens, [which were] of old; lo, he doth send out his voice, [and that] a mighty voice.
³⁴Ascribe ye strength unto God: his excellency [is] over Israel, and his strength [is] in the clouds.
³⁵O God, [thou art] terrible out of thy holy places: the God of Israel [is] he that giveth strength and power unto [his] people. Blessed [be] God.

PSALM 68
Title: Thirteenth Messianic Psalm
Author: a Psalm of David
Date: Placement of the Ark in Jerusalem
Superscription: to the chief Musician
Theme: God's Goodness to Israel

The psalm commemorates triumphal *march* of Israel's God from Mount Sinai to Mount Zion. Within the psalm is the prayer that this magnificent display of God's love will not perish until all of God's people are rescued and all the earth sings His praise. This *march* figuratively begins in Egypt and ends with God dwelling in Israel. The dominant theme is God's march as victor, both past, present and future. The background of the material is to be seen in the totality of Israel's history, rather than in a specific deliverance.

The psalm may have been a liturgical procession which was sung as the people climbed the up to the Temple in Jerusalem. The first half of the Psalm (1-18) refers to both the triumphal march *from* Mount Sinai by Moses and the Israelites and the same march of David *to* Mount Zion in triumph.

To the people, having the Ark of the Covenant was a symbol of God living among them in Jerusalem. It marked the beginning of God's kingdom among the nations. Jerusalem, as caretaker of the Ark, is considered the Royal city. While verses 1-8 speaks joyously of the Ark, verses 9-25 closely resemble a temple hymn. Most commentators willingly recognize a great number of forms and styles and agree to classify this as a medley of songs and hymns.

The second half of the Psalm (19-35) is energized by the cry, "Praise be to the Lord!" It looks toward God's continuing triumph and the redemption of all people. "Let God arise" is either asking for or referring to His *appearance* in the Temple (Numbers 10:35). The picture given is that of a leader, possibly a king out in front of the people, as the Ark is brought to its new home. The righteous rejoice in this event, believing that God's special acts of kindness and mercy will now reside in the midst of them.

God's glory as seen in verses 19-23 show God's presence as the performer of mighty acts in Israel's past. He is also shown as a God who will help those who bless Him daily. The miracle filled days of Moses and the present day of bringing the Ark to Jerusalem show God's consistency. There is never a time when He will not be with His people. Verses 24-27 celebrate the enthronement of God. (Benjamin and Judah refer to the southern tribes, while Zebulun and Naphtali represent the northern tribes). Verses 28-35 are filled with joyous exaltation toward the Lord. All of history points to the future triumph of God. Having asserted this ultimate victory, all of the nations are called upon to praise God as the only and all-powerful Lord.

Note: In verses 5 and 6, there is a reference to the word "father". This is a very simple word, generally the first words of baby. In Aramaic, the word is "Abba". In Mark 14:36 Jesus used this word to call out to His father. The Holy Spirit now teaches man to call God by this personal name, "Abba" (Romans 8:15). This does not s refer ta physical father, but primarily a spiritual father. The protection and care that one receives in a family is so critical to life that God will personally parent those who call upon Him. (Ephesians 4:8-13 understood this psalm to foreshadow the resurrection, the ascension and the rule of Christ for eternity).

PSALM 69

¹To the chief Musician upon Shoshannim,
[A Psalm] of David. Save me, O God;
for the waters are come in unto [my] soul.
²I sink in deep mire, where [there is] no standing:
I am come into deep waters,
where the floods overflow me.
³I am weary of my crying: my throat is dried:
mine eyes fail while I wait for my God.
⁴They that hate me without a cause are more than the hairs of mine head: they that would destroy me,

[being] mine enemies wrongfully, are mighty: then I
restored [that] which I took not away.
⁵O God, thou knowest my foolishness;
and my sins are not hid from thee.
⁶Let not them that wait on thee, O Lord GOD of
hosts, be ashamed for my sake: let not those that
seek thee be confounded, for my sake,
O God of Israel.
⁷Because for thy sake I have borne reproach;
shame hath covered my face.
⁸I am become a stranger unto my brethren,
and an alien unto my mother's children.
⁹For the zeal of thine house hath eaten me up;
and the reproaches of them that reproached
thee are fallen upon me.
¹⁰When I wept, [and chastened] my soul
with fasting, that was to my reproach.
¹¹I made sackcloth also my garment;
and I became a proverb to them.
¹²They that sit in the gate speak against me; and I
[was] the song of the drunkards.
¹³But as for me, my prayer [is] unto thee, O LORD,
[in] an acceptable time: O God, in the multitude of
thy mercy hear me, in the truth of thy salvation.
¹⁴Deliver me out of the mire, and let me not sink: let
me be delivered from them that hate me,
and out of the deep waters.
¹⁵Let not the waterflood overflow me, neither let the
deep swallow me up, and let not the pit
shut her mouth upon me.

¹⁶Hear me, O LORD; for thy lovingkindness [is] good:
turn unto me according to the multitude
of thy tender mercies.
¹⁷And hide not thy face from thy servant;
for I am in trouble: hear me speedily.
¹⁸Drawn nigh unto my soul, [and] redeem it:
deliver me, because of mine enemies.
¹⁹Thou hast known my reproach, and my shame, and
my dishonor: mine adversaries [are] all before thee.
²⁰Reproach hath broken my heart; and I am full of
heaviness: and I looked [for some]
to take pity, but [there was] none;
and for comforters, but I found none.
²¹They gave me also gall for my meat; and in my
thirst they gave me vinegar to drink.
²²Let their table become a snare before them: and
[that which should have been] for [their] welfare,
[let it become] a trap.
²³Let their eyes be darkened, that they see not; and
make their loins continually to shake.
⁴Pour out thine indignation upon them, and let thy
wrathful anger take hold of them.
²⁵Let their habitation be desolate;
[and] let none dwell in their tents.
²⁶For they persecute [him], whom thou hast smitten;
and they talk to the grief of those
whom thou hast wounded.
²⁷Add iniquity unto their iniquity:
and let them not come into thy righteousness.
²⁸Let them be blotted out of the book of the living,
and not be written with the righteous.

²⁹But I [am] poor and sorrowful: let thy salvation,
O God, set me up on high.
³⁰I will praise the name of God with a song,
and will magnify him with thanksgiving.
³¹[This] also shall please the LORD better than an ox
[or] bullocks that hath horns and hoofs.
³²The humble shall see [this, and] be glad:
and your heart shall live that seek God.
³³For the LORD, heareth the poor,
and despiseth not his prisoners.
³⁴Let the heaven and earth praise him, the seas,
and everything that moveth therein.
³⁵For God will save Zion, and will build the cities of
Judah: that they may dwell there,
and have it in possession.
³⁶The seed also of his servants shall inherit it: and
they that love his name shall dwell therein.

PSALM 69
Title: Fourteenth Messianic Psalm
Author: a Psalm of David
Superscription: to the chief Musician *Shoshannim to the tune of "Lilies"*
Theme: An Urgent Plea for God's Help

An individual in despair and agony here laments his case before God. His persecution is viewed as a result of his religious convictions. If, as traditionally believed David authored this psalm, it is impossible to pinpoint the exact time or location. This attack from his aggressors seems to come at the same time during which he was suffering the consequences of sin in his personal life. Verse 35 pinpoints the time following the total destruction of Judea, but before the fall of Jerusalem. It is also possible that this applies to a later son of David, perhaps Hezekiah, who ruled over the kingdom in the south of Judah. In any of these situations, the words are applicable, for this is truly a psalm of deep suffering.

After he cries out to God, "Save me; I sink in deep mire," the psalmist goes into great lengths describing his problems. Intense words like "deep waters" and "floods" are used to show the profound abyss he believes surrounds him. His enemies are many—hateful, powerful and angry. He had once been thought of as a man who was righteous and it is his deep hope that this singular event will not destroy that thought among the righteous. In verse 7, we see that he has angered many because of his loyalty, faithfulness and the belief he has in the name of God. He has fought against the liberal and popular forms of religious expression which were most common at the time. In doing so, he has become the laughingstock of the community.

The psalmist continues to plead with God, repeating his previous suffering, but now asking God to intervene on his behalf and give him deliverance immediately. According to the psalmist, God also should hold a bitter indignation against those who struggle to discredit him. The author gingerly acknowledges that he has not sinned against those who have become his enemies, while admitting that there may be some sin in his own life.

The psalmist's anger increases in the first climax in the psalm where he not only seeks retribution and punishment, but now he wants them to be completely obliterated from the book of the living (Exodus 32:32; Philippians 4:3; Revelation 13:8). The thanksgiving from the psalmist to God seems to presuppose an answer to this request. It is unclear whether he is thanking God for his own deliverance, or for the punishment of his enemies. The psalmist also prays for God's discipline (6-12) asking God to intervene and correct his behavior, lest he bring disgrace to those who praise God. The psalm closes with a heartfelt prayer and an invitation to heaven and earth to join in the chorus.

Note: The authors of the New Testament view this cry for intervention as a foreshadowing of the suffering of Christ. The term "zeal" described the passion Jesus felt when He cleansed the Temple (John 2:17). Judas Iscariot prophetically becomes the object of the curses in verse 25 of this Psalm (Acts 1-16).

PSALM 70

¹To the chief Musician, [A Psalm] of David, to bring to remembrance. [Make haste], O God, to deliver me; make haste to help me, O LORD.
²Let them be ashamed and confounded that seek after my soul: let them be turned backward, and put to confusion, that desire my hurt.

³Let them be turned back for a reward of their shame that say, Aha, aha.
⁴Let all those that seek thee rejoice and be glad in thee: and let such as love thy salvation say continually, Let God be magnified.
⁵But I [am] poor and needy: make haste unto me, O God: thou [art] my help and my deliverer; O LORD, make no tarrying.

PSALM 70
Title: Fourteenth Prayer of Distress
Author: a Psalm of David
Superscription: to the chief Musician *to bring to remembrance*
Theme: Relief from Enemies

While this psalm is an individual lament, it is also a prayer for those who are poor or needy, either in the physical or spiritual sense. If the lines seem somewhat familiar, it is because it occurs as a part of Psalm 40. It also has many links to that of Psalms 71. In this psalm, the name for God has been changed from Yahweh to Elohim and only slight variations in wording and tone are evident. Its presence here as a single psalm may indicate that it was found in two or more of the original collections, or that it was detached (and slightly altered) for liturgical use in the temple.

The words used here—*need*, *destitute* and *lacking*—appear nearly 60 times in the Old Testament. Under the Mosaic Law, God required that the poor be treated justly. Making a profit from a "brother" was strongly discouraged and there was punishment for those who crushed or repressed the needy. Crimes committed against the poor and needy were considered to be crimes against God. This prayer for the provision and protection of the needy is framed by urgent prayers that God come quickly to their aid. With His help—and only with His help—will complete and constant sustenance be provided.

The balance of the prayer focuses on the effects of God's saving grace upon people. The psalmist underscores that God willingly protects those who willingly seek Him. God's deliverance of His servant brings happiness, joy and protection to His people. It is the choice of the servant to give all of his trust to the Lord. If a man places his trust correctly, the servant will find joy and the assurance of his salvation. In every situation, the psalmist truly believes that God's saving help will ensure victory.

Note: Jesus noted that the poor must have the gospel preached to them (Matthew 11:15). In light of this, one of the earliest groups of Jewish converts to what would later be known as Christianity felt that being poor was a way to heaven. These groups believed that living in worldly poverty would prepare them to see the riches of the gospel and the treasure that is the Lord Jesus.

PSALM 71

¹In thee, O LORD, do I put my trust:
let me never be put to confusion.
²Deliver me in thy righteousness, and cause me to escape: incline thine ear unto me, and save me.
³Be thou my strong habitation, whereunto I may continually resort: thou hast given commandment to save me; for thou [art] my rock and my fortress.
⁴Deliver me, O my God, out of the hand of the wicked, out of the hand of the unrighteous and cruel man.
⁵For thou [art] my hope, O Lord GOD:
[thou art] my trust from my youth.
⁶By thee have I been holden up from the womb: thou art he that took me out of my mother's bowels: my praise [shall be] continually of thee.
⁷I am as a wonder unto many;
but thou [art] my strong refuge.
⁸Let my mouth be filled [with] thy praise [and with] thy honor all the day.
⁹Cast me not off in the time of old age; forsake me not, when my strength faileth.
¹⁰ For mine enemies speak against me; and they that lay wait for my soul take counsel together,
¹¹Saying, God has forsaken him: persecute and take him; for [there is] none to deliver [him].
¹²O God, be not far from me:
O my God, make haste for my help.

¹³Let them be confounded [and] consumed that our adversaries to my soul; let them be covered [with] reproach and dishonor that seek my hurt.
¹⁴But I will hope continually,
and will yet praise thee more and more.
¹⁵My mouth shall show forth thy righteousness [and] thy salvation all the day;
for I know not the numbers [there of].
¹⁶I will go in the strength of the Lord GOD: I will make mention of thy righteousness,
[even] of thine only.
¹⁷O God, thou hast taught me from my youth: and hitherto have I declared thy wondrous works.
¹⁸Now also when I am old and greyheaded, O God, forsake me not; until I have showed thy strength unto [this] generation, [and] thy power
to everyone [that] is to come.
¹⁹Thy righteousness also, O God, [is] very high, who hast done great things:
O God, who [is] like unto thee!
²⁰[Thou], which hast showed me great and sore troubles, shalt quicken me again, and shalt bring me up again from the depths of the earth.
²¹Thou shalt increase my greatness,
and comfort me on every side.
²²I will also praise thee with the psaltery, [even] thy truth, O my God: unto thee will I sing with the harp,
O thou Holy One of Israel.
²³My lips shall greatly rejoice when I sing unto thee; and my soul, which thou hast redeemed.

[24]My tongue also shall talk of thy righteousness all the day long: for they are confounded, for they are brought unto shame, that seek my hurt.

PSALM 71
Title: Seventh Praise/Prayer Psalm
Author: anonymous
Superscription: none
Theme: God is the Rock of Salvation

This psalm has no title, but it may be that Psalm 70 was viewed by the editors of the Psalms as an introduction to Psalm 71, in which case the psalm is ascribed to David. This is the third in a series of three prayers with a dominant theme of hope. The whole of this psalm is framed by an appeal for help and a vow to praise God in light of His deliverances. There are references to some of the troubles which he has experienced and four verses refer to his age. The psalm appears to contain an unusual amount of references to other psalms, making it a part of Psalm 70 (which in itself is a "conglomerate" of other psalms).

An old man faces the end of his years (9) and as is evident by his frequent quotations, he has memorized (and probably lived) the Scriptures. This psalm may have been an instruction psalm, as the elderly Saint speaks intensely and devoutly regarding prayer and praise to God. He stresses that praise has many parts and is not to be shared only within the congregation or only as a personal musing in a secret garden (4). Creative praise will be fresh and lively, bring joy to the singer and to God. The psalmist says, "I will praise you." In this wonderfully expressed idea, we find a beautiful way of saying that praise is not to be limited by time, place or number of people.

The psalmist instructs the younger generation with resounding emphasis saying that praise is to be everywhere and all the time. He does not say, "I will praise you in the closet." He does not say, "I will praise you in song." He does not say, "I will only praise you while I am walking." He does not say, "I will praise you while at the Temple." What he does say is that he will continually find fresh and new ways to express his praise towards God. This does not mean an abandonment of the old ways, but rather a praise that continues to grow and stay alive, dependent upon the root, but becoming glorious as spring buds. As God continually creates new experiences within a man, he will continually grow in his expressions of faith. By growing in praise, there is little fear of falling prey to careless praise, becoming dull and boring or merely mouthing meaningless phrases.

This aged man shares his retrospect of life. His has been a life of trust, filled with troubles and enemies all the way, yet his joy in God remains unchanged. As long as he is alive, he knows that God is with him and his future is full of hope. He has been through persecution, sickness, attacks and calamities. Yet, as his life comes to a close, he realizes that although his head is now gray, he has retained his close relationship with God since his childhood. His one desire is to live long enough to share with the present generation something of what life has taught him. Based on God's special teaching, he has been able to teach others (17-21). Now he asks for more time in order to show forth God's strength, power and righteousness.

The aged Saint who is besieged by his enemies knows that they are quick and willing to take advantage of the weaknesses of age. Yet God has sustained him since the day of his birth and his enemies who believe that God has forsaken him are quite wrong. They have the wrong interpretation regarding his affliction. He may be weak within himself, yet God has stayed with him all of his life. His enemies may attack him, but they will fail. Even at (or perhaps because of) his late stage in life, he states boldly that he will praise God with his voice, with instruments, with his lips, with his tongue and indeed with his entire being. In this he rests assured that he will be vindicated before the Lord and before man.

PSALM 72

^{1}[A Psalm] for Solomon. Give the King thy
judgments, O God, and thy righteousness
unto the king's son.
^{2}He shall judge thy people with righteousness,
and thy poor with judgment.
^{3}The mountains shall bring peace to the people,
and the little hills, by righteousness.
^{4}He shall judge the poor of the people,
he shall save the children of the needy,
and shall break in pieces the oppressor.

⁵They shall fear thee as long as the sun and moon
endure, throughout all generations.
⁶He shall come down like the rain upon the mown
grass: as showers [that] water the earth.
⁷In his days shall the righteous flourish; and abundance of peace so long as the moon endureth.
⁸He shall have dominion also from sea to sea, and
from the river unto the ends of the earth.
⁹They that dwell in the wilderness shall bow before
him; and his enemies shall lick the dust.
¹⁰The Kings of Tarshish and of the isles shall bring
presents: the kings of Sheba
and Seba shall offer gifts.
¹¹Yea, all kings shall fall down before him:
all nations shall serve him.
¹²For he shall deliver the needy when he crieth;
the poor also, and [him] that hath no helper.
¹³He shall spare the poor and needy,
and shall save the souls of the needy.
¹⁴He shall redeem their soul from deceit and violence: and precious shall their blood be in his sight.
¹⁵And he shall live, and to him shall be given of the
gold of Sheba: prayer also shall be made for him
continually; [and] daily shall he be praised.
¹⁶There shall be an hand full of corn in the earth
upon the top of the mountains; the fruit thereof
shall shake like Lebanon: and [they] of the city shall
flourish like grass of the earth.
¹⁷His name shall endure for ever: his name shall be
continued as long as the sun: and [men] shall be
blessed in him: all nations shall call him blessed.

¹⁸Blessed [be] the LORD God, the God of Israel,
who only doeth wondrous things.
¹⁹And blessed [be] his glorious name for ever:
and let the whole earth be filled [with] his glory;
Amen and Amen.
²⁰The prayers of David, the son of Jesse are ended.

PSALM 72
Title: Fifteenth Messianic Psalm
Author: a Song of Solomon
Superscription: none
Theme: The Messiah's Reign and Glory

1 Kings 4:32 indicates that Solomon wrote 1,005 psalms, yet only numbers 72 and 127 appear in the Psalter. This underscores the well-known truth that the Book of Psalms as it is known today are only a mere smattering of the total psalms which were written.

This psalm is a prayer for the king of Israel, a son of David who now sits on the throne after David's death. The "throne" is given as the earthly place in which the representative of God is seated. In its format and tone, this psalm was to be sung at the King's coronation celebration. It is a prayer that the King's reign will be one that is characterized with the attributes of God: justice and wisdom.

At first glance, this psalm looks to be a description of the Kingdom under Solomon's reign. Upon a deeper inspection, however, a number of statements as well as the general tone of the psalm it goes beyond the reign of Solomon and alludes to a kingdom of the

One who is much greater than the King of Israel. It looks beyond the perfect reign of Solomon to the perfect and eternal reign of the Son of God.

Note: a number of manuscripts do not include verse 20.

NOTES ON BOOK TWO
Themes from Psalms 42-72

- The ways to grow in godliness
- Steps to powerful worship
- Biblical forms of worship
- Personal conversation with God
- Acting in the spirit of God
- Being humble
- Need for personal cleansing

BOOK THREE

The Leviticus Psalms
PSALMS 73-89

The third book of the Psalter contains only 17 psalms. Asaph, one of the chief musicians, is given "credit" for the first eleven psalms. Other chief musicians, Hemen and Ethan, are also connected with the psalms in Book Three. The balance of psalms are attributed to the Sons of Korah, a portion of the Levitical Guild.

The sanctuary or Temple appears in almost every psalm in Book Three. The counsel of God is brought to light against the background of the sanctuary, which Book Three follows from its ruin to its restoration.

PSALM 73

¹A Psalm of Asaph. Truly God [is] good to Israel, and [even] to such as are of a clean heart.
²But as for me, my feet were almost gone; my steps had well-nigh slipped.

³For I was envious at the foolish,
[when] I saw the prosperity of the wicked.
⁴For [there are] no bands in their death:
but their strength [is] firm.
⁵They [are] not in trouble [as other] men; neither
are they plagued like [other] men.
⁶Therefore pride compasseth them about as a chain;
violence covereth them [as] a garment.
⁷Their eyes stand out with fatness: they have more
than a heart could wish.
⁸They are corrupt, and speak wickedly [concerning]
oppression: they speak loftily.
⁹They set their mouth against the heavens, and their
tongue walketh through the earth.
¹⁰Therefore his people return hither: and waters of a
full [cup] are wrung out to them.
¹¹And they say, How doth God, know? and is there
knowledge in the most high?
¹²Behold, these [are] the ungodly, who prosper in
the world; they increase [in] riches.
¹³Verily I have cleansed my heart [in] vain, and
washed my hands in innocency.
¹⁴For all the day long I have been plagued, and
chastened every morning.
¹⁵If I say, I will speak thus; behold, I should offend
[against] the generation of thy children.
¹⁶When I thought to know this,
it [was] too painful for me;
¹⁷Until I went into the sanctuary of God; [then]
understood I their end.

¹⁸Surely thou didst set them in slippery places: thou castedst them down into destruction.
¹⁹How are they [brought] into desolation, as in a moment! they are utterly consumed with terrors .
²⁰As a dream when [one] awaketh; [so], O Lord, when thou awakest, thou shalt despise their image.
²¹Thus my heart was grieved,
and I was pricked in my reins.
²²So foolish [was] I, and ignorant:
I was [as] a beast before thee.
²³Nevertheless I [am] continually with thee:
thou hast holden [me] by my right hand.
²⁴Thou shalt guide me with thy counsel,
and afterword, receive me [to] glory.
²⁵Whom have I in heaven. [but thee]? and [there is] none upon earth [that] I desire beside thee.
²⁶My flesh and my heart faileth: [but] God [is] the strength of my heart, and my portion for ever.
²⁷For, lo, they that are far from thee shall perish: thou hast destroyed all them that go
a whoring from thee.
²⁸But [it is] good for me to draw near to God:
I have put my trust in the Lord GOD,
that I may declare all thy works.

PSALM 73
Title: Twelfth Psalm of Instruction
Author: a Psalm of Asaph
Date: (possibly) as late as the Post-Exilic Period
Superscription: none
Theme: Do Not Envy the Wicked or their Possessions

Placed at the beginning of Book Three, this psalm tells of the faith confessed, tested and reaffirmed that undergirds the following collection. It serves in Book Three the same way as Psalms 1 and 2 serve in Book One. The psalmist addresses one of the most disturbing problems of the Old Testament saints: how is it that the wicked so often prosper while the godly suffer so much? Although the psalmist is troubled by his own suffering, he is more perplexed by the lack of punishment of the wicked. This psalm goes deeper into the problem than most do. It may be classified as a song of trust, with overtones that link it with the wisdom writers.

This psalm focuses on the writer's condition, which is sharply contrasted with the perceived condition of the wicked. In the third verse, the psalmist gives voice to his thoughts: "I was envious of the wicked." He begins to make a journey into the *Valley of Doubt*. Doubt encourages generalizations, many of which are very incorrect. He refers to all of these men as arrogant, prideful and continually mocking God. He walks briefly along the edge of apostasy. His anger toward those prosperous men is not godly.

In verses 13-22, the psalmist starts to wonder if cleansing his heart and following God has been in vain. His journey through the *Valley of Doubt* eventually leads to the Temple. It is there, as he humbles himself before God, that his faith returns and once again he is on even ground. While he has been very frank about his envy of the wealthy, he also sees them as ruthless, sinning by choice and in well-planned ways. He gives up his doubts and turns to God, knowing that he can experience His presence in any situation.

This psalm goes beyond what God can *do* for a man, focusing on what God can *be* to mankind. God is the source of a pure heart. Attitudes of the mind can be soured by selfishness or fleshly desires. "Pure" is the state of a heart that is committed totally to God. It is only in this state of heart that a man can experience God's goodness. An attitude of the mind places the man inside his circumstances and makes him question life.

The psalmist is called back to his responsibility as a follower of God. He acknowledges that he has been foolish in his *questioning* of God. He now believes that God will reveal the evil ones for who they truly are. Their future will unmake all that the past has accomplished. Judgment is not simply the logical end of evil, but it is ultimately God's personal rejection. If trust is placed firmly placed in God, men are called in, welcomed, received and acknowledged by the Holy One. Nothing is so blinding as envy, anger or grievance against another. Yet, as if to repeat verse 1, God is endlessly good to those who are pure in heart.

PSALM 74

¹Maschil of Asaph. O God, why hast thou cast [us] off for ever? [why] doth thine anger smoke against the sheep of thy pasture?
²Remember thy congregation, [which] thou hast purchased of old; the rod of thine inheritance, [which] thou hast redeemed; this mount Zion, wherein thou hast dwelt.
³Lift up thy feet unto the perpetual desolations; [even] all [that] the enemy hath done wickedly in the sanctuary.
⁴Thine enemies roar in the midst of thy congregations; they set up their ensigns [for] signs.
⁵[A man] was famous according as he had lifted up axes upon the thick trees.
⁶But now they break down the carved work thereof at once with axes and hammers.
⁷They have cast fire into thy sanctuary, they have defiled [by casting down] the dwelling place of thy name to the ground.
⁸They said in their hearts, Let us destroy them together: they have burned up all the synagogues of God in the land.
⁹We see not our signs: [there is] no more any prophet: neither [is there] among us any that knoweth how long.
¹⁰O God, how long shall the adversary reproach? shall the enemy blaspheme thy name for ever?
¹¹Why withdrawest thou thy hand, even thy right hand? Pluck [it] out of thy bosom.

¹²For God [is] my King of old, working salvation in
the midst of the earth.
¹³Thou didst divide the sea by thy strength: the thou
breakest the heads of the dragons in the waters.
¹⁴Thou brakest the heads of Leviathan in pieces,
[and] gavest him [to be] meat to the people inhab-
iting the wilderness.
¹⁵Thou didst cleave the fountain and the flood:
thou driedst up mighty rivers.
¹⁶The day [is] thine, the night also [is] thine:
thou hast prepared the light and the sun.
¹⁷Thou hast set all the borders of the earth:
thou hast made summer and winter.
¹⁸Remember this, [that] the enemy hath reproached,
O LORD, and [that] the foolish people have
blasphemed thy name.
¹⁹O deliver not the sole of thy turtledove unto
the multitude [of the wicked]: forget not the congregation of thy poor for ever.
²⁰Have respect unto the covenant: for the dark
places of the earth are full of
the habitations of cruelty.
²¹O let not the oppressed return ashamed:
let the poor and needy praise thy name.
²²Arise, O God, plead thine own cause: remember
how the foolish man reproacheth thee daily.
²³Forget not the voice of thine enemies: the
tumult of those that rise up against thee
increaseth continually.

PSALM 74
Title: Thirteenth Psalm of Instruction
Author: a Contemplation of Asaph
Date: Temple Destruction/Jewish Captivity
Superscription: a *Maschil (reflective poem)*
Theme: Protection from those who Destroyed the Temple

Although attributed to him, this psalm could not have been composed by Asaph as the subject matter belongs to a date beyond his lifetime. It is presumed that it was written in his name by those of the same Levitical group. The disaster relates to either the time of Shishrnak's invasion (1 Kings 14:25) or at the beginning of the Jewish exile in Babylon. Psalm 72 and 137, along with the Book of Lamentations, place this psalm within one lifetime of the destruction of the Temple (587 BC) by the Babylonians.

It seems to them that God has turned His face (1-2). The temple has been taken apart brick-by-brick (3-8) and yet God has not intervened on their behalf. The people are perplexed and angry. How could God allow this to happen? The nation appeals to God, reminding Him of His covenant relationship with His chosen people. They know that divine wrath is a part of God's character, but it is very incomprehensible that God would forsake His people. The power of God is remembered (12-17) with the plea (19-20) that God will remove their enemies (18).

Verses 4-11 envision the temple of God filled with Babylonians. The implements of worship have been stolen and replaced by the emblems of the invaders. It is faith more than doubt that precipitates the shower of questions which begins and ends this half of the psalm. The real questions here are not about God's punishment, but over the severity. No songs come from the Temple; no words come from the prophets; the Book of Law is not read; all is destruction and silence. With one voice they ask, "Is it forever?" We can see now that God was not neglecting them at all, He was preparing the Israelites to become a *church* rather than a mere group of individuals.

The psalmist's thoughts return to God's goodness. God is the creator and redeemer. Everything that happens to a man is in God's hands and will be accorded to man at His divine discretion. Looking beyond the immediate suffering, hasty conclusions are dissuaded much as in the closing chapter of Job to the totality of life which God coordinates in wisdom. The suffering remains and the psalm ends with a stream of urgent prayers. However, perhaps more significantly are the questions of verses 1-11: "Why? How long? Why?" have ceased to be spoken. In the silence, the echo of the songs of the temple can be heard.

PSALM 75

[1]To the chief Musician, Altaschith, A Psalm [or] Song of Asaph. Unto thee, O God, do we give thanks, [unto thee] do we give thanks: for [that] thy name is near thy wondrous works declare.

²When I shall receive the congregation
I will judge uprightly.
³The earth and all the inhabitants thereof
are dissolved: I bear up the pillars of it.
⁴I said unto the fools, Deal, not foolishly:
and to the wicked, Lift not up the horn:
⁵Lift not up your horn on high:
speak [not with] a stiff neck.
⁶For promotion [cometh] neither from the east,
nor from the west, nor from the south.
⁷But God [is] the judge: he putteth down one,
and setteth up another.
⁸For in the hand of the LORD, [there is] a cup,
and the wine is red; it is full of mixture; and he
poureth out of the same: but the dregs thereof, all
the wicked of the earth shall wring [them] out,
[and] drink [them].
⁹But I will declare for ever;
I will sing praises to the God of Jacob.
¹⁰All the horns of the wicked also will I cut off;
[but] the horns of the righteous shall be exalted.

PSALM 75
Title: Fourth Psalm of Praise
Author: a Psalm of Asaph
Superscription: to the chief Musician *Altaschith/ Michtam A tune, where the words are identified as a popular saying and used as the reassuring words of God*
Theme: Praise for God's Righteous Judgments

The theme of this psalm is exultation by way of humility. This theme runs throughout the Bible, from the mouth of Samuel's mother (1 Samuel 2:8) to the heart of Mary, the mother of Jesus (Luke 1:38). This psalm may date from the time of the Assyrian menace and is a song of reassurance when arrogant, worldly powers threaten Israel's security. The congregation speaks, perhaps lead in its praise by one of the descendants of Asaph. The psalm is framed by thanksgiving and praise. The first stanza contains a reassuring word from heaven; the second contains a triumphant response from Earth. Some commentators suggest that verse 1 has been added to an individual prayer for victory in order to adapt the psalm for public worship. Although this may have been the case, the psalm exhibits careful poetic arrangement as well as a definite progression of thought.

At the beginning of the psalm, we see the words "unto thee we give thanks". Although this is a terse statement of gratitude, there appears to be an actual historical deliverance. The reality of the recent manifestation of power gives confidence that God's revealed nature (His name) is nearby. God responds to His people by telling them that He will judge uprightly. There is an appointed time when God will take His place on the judgment seat. His control of the universe assures that judgments will be absolute.

Verse 7 is addressed to all humanity. *Forgive* and *bow down* are the two main examples of adoration and worship. *Forgive* enlists the mind, heart, hands and voice to declare the greatness of God. *Bowing down* is a willful action which humbles the worshiper. True worship, (Psalm 29:3) reflects the love in a person's heart going out towards God. The final verse may be a prayer, but more likely, it is the psalmist's vision of the future: the Lord will give; the Lord will bless.

The psalmist gives a warning to the wicked and the arrogant that the power to rise up is not found in the East, West, or South. God alone can lift up or put down the entire earth. It is he who executes judgment and causes the wicked to drink the cup of His wrath (Psalm 11:6; Revelation 14:10).

There will be the triumph of the righteous and speaking as Israel's representative, the psalmist vows to give- endless praise, keeping God continually in his memory. Memory is a retelling of the great things that God has done (Psalm 78:4; Deuteronomy 31:10-13). This was and is a critical part of worship (1 Corinthians 11:23-26) for His name comes through the reading, telling and hearing of His wonderful deeds.

Caught in the joy and beauty of his own memories, the psalmist pledges to fight God's battles; only

God will be the Judge. There will be a time for power without aggression and glory without pride.

Note: In verses 2-5, the set time is very important in both the Old and New Testaments. It is used the four seasons of the year with its dependable heartbeat (Genesis 1:14) for marking festival dates (Leviticus 23:2) and for setting a rhythmic pattern for worship. Although unknown to ancient Israel, the set time refers to when Christ would suffer, die and ascend to Heaven. The time, times and half a time mark the approaching end (Daniel 12:7). No word could better express His control. All that happens will happen in His set time.

PSALM 76

¹To the chief Musician on Neginoth, A Psalm [or] Song of Asaph. In Judah [is] God known:
his name [is] great in Israel.
²In Salem also is his tabernacle,
and his dwelling place in Zion.
³There brake he the arrows of the bow,
the shield, and the sword, and the battle.
⁴Thou [art] more glorious [and]
excellent than the mountains of prey.
⁵The stouthearted are spoiled, they have slept their sleep: and none of the men of might have
found their hands.

⁶At thy rebuke, O God of Jacob,
both the chariot and of course are cast
into a dead sleep.
⁷Thou, [even] thou, [art] to be feared: and who may
stand in thy sight when once thou art angry?
⁸Thou didst cause judgment to be heard from
heaven; the earth feared, and was still,
⁹When God arose to judgment,
to save all the meek of the earth.
¹⁰Surely the wrath of man shall praise thee:
the remainder of wrath shalt thou restrain.
¹¹Vow, and pay unto the LORD your God: let all that
be round about him bring presents unto him
that ought to be feared.
¹²He shall cut off the spirit of princes: [he is] terrible
to the kings of the earth.

PSALM 76
Title: Fourteenth Psalm of Instruction
Author: a Psalm of Asaph
Date: The Defeat of the Assyrians
Superscription: to the chief Musician *on Neginoth a stringed instrument*
Theme: The Majesty of God's Judgment

This song of victory is very similar to Psalms 46, 48 and 75 in that it is a song of triumph and God's righteous judgment upon the enemies of Israel. Technically a psalm of instruction, it carries the same tone and wording as a psalm of praise. The Lord God has proven Himself in battle after battle and His reputation has spread throughout the kingdoms of the world. He is glorious and majestic, more majestic than the mountains themselves.

The background for these four psalms appears to be the defeat of the Assyrian army in 701 BC. It is also possible that these psalms were written when Israel had defeated Sennacherib's army (2 Kings 19:35). While the occasion of the psalm may be unclear, its purpose is unquestionable. Used in temple worship, this is a testament to God's protection of the Israelites. The psalm looks forward to the judgments of God, not just for current circumstances, but forever.

In verses 10-12 the righteous see the value in prayer to the Lord. God has the power to turn every thought and deed into His glory. There is a great call for worship and praise recognizing all that He is able to perform. Regardless of the size or strength of the enemy, real or imagined, the outcome is certain, in Israel, throughout the world, for nations and individuals. God takes His seat in Heaven all of the earth is still and silent. He alone is the Judge to be feared by mankind. He destroys the evil ones and saves the oppressed.

PSALM 77

¹To the chief Musician, to Jeduthun, A Psalm of Asaph. I cried unto God with my voice, [even] unto God with my voice; and he gave ear unto me.
²In the day of my trouble I sought the Lord: My sore ran in the night, and ceased not:
my soul refused to be comforted.

³I remembered God, and was troubled: I complained, and my spirit was overwhelmed.
⁴Thou holdest mine eyes waking:
I am so troubled that I cannot speak.
⁵I have considered the days of old,
the years of ancient times.
⁶I call to remembrance my song in the night:
I commune with mine own heart:
and my spirit made diligent search.
⁷Will the Lord cast off forever?
and will he be favorable no more?
⁸Is his mercy clean gone for ever? doth
[his] promise fail for evermore?
⁹Hath God for gotten to be gracious? hath he in anger shut up his tender mercies?
¹⁰And I said, This [is] my infirmity:
[but I will remember] the years of
the right hand of the most High.
¹¹I will remember the works of the LORD:
surely I will remember thy wonders of old.
¹²I will meditate also all of thy work,
and talk of thy doings.
¹³Thy way, O God, [is] in the sanctuary:
who [is so] great a God as [our] God?
¹⁴Thou [art] the God that doest wonders:
thou hast declared thy strength among the people.
¹⁵Thou hast with [thine] arm redeemed thy people;
the sons of Jacob and Joseph.
¹⁶The waters saw thee, O God, the waters saw thee;
they were afraid: the depths also were troubled.

¹⁷The clouds poured out water: the skies sent out a
sound: thine arrows also went abroad.
¹⁸The voice of thy thunder [was] in the heaven: the
lightnings lightened the world:
the earth trembled and shook.
¹⁹Thy way [is] in the sea, and thy path in the great
waters, and thy footsteps are not known.
²⁰Thou leddest thy people like a flock by
the hand of Moses and Aaron.

PSALM 77
Title: Fifteenth Psalm of Instruction
Author: a Psalm of Asaph
Superscription: to the chief Musician, *to Jeduthun*
Theme: Deliverance from Troubles through Remembrance

The psalm begins with the psalmist struggling to understand God's actions. It appears that God no longer listens to his prayers. This psalm gives no hint to the cause or time in Israel's history. The psalmist speaks of his symptoms of sleeplessness and confusion (4), but chiefly his focus is God's abandonment and his state of doubt. "I cried unto the Lord; my spirit was overwhelmed." In the following nine verses the questioning of God's love and assistance continues. The psalmist has seen the glory and the majesty of God's deliverance. God listens no more and the psalmist reaches a point where he fails to believe. He has sought God and after receiving no response the psalmist wonders if God has forsaken and him and his kingdom forever.

Although God would prefer unwavering trust, he completely understands man's frustration in times of trouble. It is not unholy or unrighteous to cry out to God in painful frustration. One need only remember when Jesus Himself cried out to God with loud tears and God heard Him (Hebrews 5:7). Having confessed his doubts, the psalmist begins to wonder if his God would *really* abandon him. Memory begins to invade his thoughts and invigorates reminders of the power and majesty displayed by God from the beginning of time. God is the one who dwells in the unapproachable light and in Him is a love beyond comprehension.

The poetic description of God colorfully displays His power and His majesty. The Israelites believed the power of God was hidden within the thunderstorms and earthquakes. The Book of Exodus speaks of God in the cloud and the fire, while verses 15-20 include the depths of the water and the voice of thunder and lightning that shook the world. Hebrew poets associated thunderstorms and earthquakes to mean that the Lord is coming to bring either his redemption or judgment. For today's Christians, the display of God's power as he brought His children out of Israel now includes the resurrection of Jesus Christ from the dead, thus ensuring that He will bring His people through this life and regardless of insecurity and questions, Jesus will take us back to Him.

The candor of the psalmist shows the wisdom of expressing his fears and frustrations to God. Greater still, however, are the thoughts which once brought torment led him to memories of the past, have forced him to reexamine the light and the love of God. His thoughts become void of despair. His openness with God takes him to a place where his faith is once again strong. Though still feeling overwhelmed and frustrated on a worldly sense, his spirit rejoices, knowing that God will never forget him. As God was with Moses and Aaron, so He will be with all men. Nothing happens by chance.

PSALM 78

¹Maschil of Asaph. Give ear, O my people,
[to] my law: incline your ears to the words
of my mouth.
²I will open my mouth in a parable:
I will utter dark sayings of old:
³Which we have heard and known,
and our fathers have told us.
⁴We will not hide [them] from their children,
showing to the generation to come the praises of
the LORD, and his strength,
and his wonderful works that he hath done.
⁵For he established a testimony in Jacob, and
appointed a law in Israel, which he commanded
our fathers, that they should make
them known to their children:
⁶That the generation to come might know [them,
even] the children [which] should be born; [who]
should arise, and declare [them] to their children:

⁷That they might set their hope in God,
and not forget the works of God,
but keep his commandments:
⁸And might not be as their fathers, a stubborn and
rebellious generation; a generation [that]
set not their heart aright,
and his spirit was not steadfast with God.
⁹The children of Ephriam, [being] armed, [and]
carrying bows, turned back in the day of battle.
¹⁰They kept not the covenant of God,
and refused to walk in his law;
¹¹And forgat his works, and his wonders
that he had showed them.
¹²Marvelous things did He in the sight of their
fathers, in the land of Egypt, [in] the field of Zoan.
¹³He divided the sea, and caused them to pass
through; and he made the waters
to stand as an heap.
¹⁴In the daytime, he led them with the cloud,
and all the night with a light of fire.
¹⁵He clave of the rocks in the wilderness,
and gave [them] drink as [out of] the great depths.
¹⁶And He brought streams also out of the rock, and
caused waters to run down like rivers.
¹⁷And they sinned yet more against him by provoking
the most High in the wilderness.
¹⁸And they tempted God in their heart
by asking meat for their lust.
¹⁹Yea, they spake against God; they said, Can God
furnish a table in the wilderness?

²⁰Behold, he smote the rock, that the waters gushed
out, and the streams overflowed; can he give bread
also? can he provide flesh for his people?
²¹Therefore the LORD heard [this], and was wroth,
so a fire was kindled against Jacob,
and anger also came up against Israel;
²²Because they believed not in God,
and trusted not in his salvation:
²³Though he had commanded the clouds from
above, and open the doors of heaven,
²⁴And had rained down manna upon them to eat,
and had given them of the corn of heaven.
²⁵Man did eat angel's food:
he sent them meat to the full.
²⁶He caused an east wind to blow in the heaven:
and by his power he brought in the south wind.
²⁷He rained flesh also upon them as dust,
and feathered fowls like as the sand of the sea:
²⁸And he let [it] fall in the midst of their camp,
round about their habitations.
²⁹So they did eat, and were well filled:
for he gave them their own desire;
³⁰They were not estranged from their lust.
But while there meat [was] yet in their mouths,
³¹The wrath of God came upon them,
and slew the fattest of them,
and smote down the chosen [men] of Israel.
³²For all this they sinned still,
and believed not for his wondrous works.
³³Therefore their days did he consume in vanity,
and their years in trouble.

³⁴When he slew them, then they sought him: and
they returned and inquired early after God.
³⁵And they remembered that God [was] their rock,
and the high God their redeemer.
³⁶Nevertheless they did flatter him with their mouth,
and they lied unto him with their tongues.
³⁷For their heart was not right with him, neither
were they steadfast in his covenant.
³⁸But he [being] full of compassion,
forgave [their] iniquity, and destroyed [them] not:
yea, many a time, turned he his anger away,
and did not stir up all his wrath.
³⁹For he remembered that they [were but] flesh; a
wind that passes away, and cometh not again.
⁴⁰How oft did they provoke him in the wilderness,
[and] grieve him in the desert!
⁴¹Yea, they turned back and tempted God, and
limited the Holy One of Israel.
⁴²They remembered not his hand, [nor] the day
when he delivered them from the enemy.
⁴³How he had wrought his signs in Egypt, and his
wonders in the field of Zoan:
⁴⁴And had turned their rivers into blood; and their
floods, that they could not drink.
⁴⁵He sent divers sorts of flies among them, which
devoured them; and frogs, which destroyed them.
⁴⁶He gave also their increase unto the caterpillar, and
their labor unto the locust.
⁴⁷He destroyed their vines with hail, and the syca-
more trees with frost.

⁴⁸He gave up their cattle also to the hail,
and their flocks to hot thunderbolts.
⁴⁹He cast upon them the fierceness of his anger,
wrath, and indignation, and trouble,
by sending evil angels [among them].
⁵⁰He made a way to his anger;
he spared not their soul from death,
but gave their life over to the pestilence;
⁵¹And smote all of the firstborn in Egypt; the chief of
[their] strength in the Tabernacles of Ham.
⁵²But made his own people to go forth like a sheep,
and guided them in the wilderness like a flock.
⁵³And he led them on safely, so that they feared not:
but the sea overwhelmed their enemies.
⁵⁴And he brought them to the border of his sanctuary, [even to] this mountain,
[which] his right hand had purchased.
⁵⁵He cast out the heathen also before them, and
divided them, and inheritance by line, and made the
tribes of Israel to dwell in their tents.
⁵⁶Yet they tempted and provoked the most high God,
and kept not his testimonies:
⁵⁷But turned back, and dealt unfaithfully like their
fathers: they were turned aside like a deceitful bow.
⁵⁸For they provoked him to anger with
their high places, and moved him
to jealousy with their graven images.
⁵⁹When God heard [this], he was wroth,
and greatly abhorred Israel:
⁶⁰So that he forsook the tabernacle of Shiloh,
the tent [which] he placed among men;

⁶¹And delivered his strength into captivity,
and his glory into the enemies' hand.
⁶²He gave his people over also unto the sword; and
he was wroth with his inheritance.
⁶³The fire consumed their young men; and their
maidens were not given to marriage.
⁶⁴Their priests fell by the sword;
and their widows made no lamentation.
⁶⁵Then the Lord awaked as one out of sleep, [and]
like a mighty man that shouteth by reason of wine.
⁶⁶And he smote his enemies in the hinder parts: he
put them to a perpetual reproach.
⁶⁷Moreover he refused the tabernacle of Joseph, and
chose not the tribes of Ephriam:
⁶⁸But chose the tribe of Judah,
the Mt. Zion which he loved.
⁶⁹And he built his sanctuary like high [palaces],
like the Earth which he hath established for ever.
⁷⁰He chose David also his servant,
and took him from the sheepfolds:
⁷¹From following the ewes great with young he
brought him to feed Jacob his people,
and Israel, his inheritance.
⁷²So he fed them according to the integrity of his
heart; and guided them by the
skillfulness of his hands.

PSALM 78
Title: Sixteenth Psalm of Instruction
Author: a Psalm of Asaph
Date: Choosing the Site of the Temple
Superscription: *Maschil-(reflective)*
Theme: God's Grace upon a Rebellious Israel

Isaiah and Hosea speak of the two kingdoms, Ephraim to the north and Judah, the foremost tribe of the south. This indicates that the psalm was written after the kingdom of Israel had divided into two parts by Jeroboam's rebellion. The purpose of this psalm was to encourage each man to search his own conscience. Meant to warm the heart and recount the tales of great miracles, it tells of the grace that persists through all judgments. It also serves as a warning that the rebellion of the past must not repeat itself.

Sadly, this cycle of praise, rebellion, chastening and forgiveness and back to praise is the legacy not only of those who traveled in the wilderness, but the Israelites as a whole. As in Deuteronomy 31, the people receive instruction to repeat the stories of old and to tell the stories of the past. Here, God also tells Moses that the people will continue to repeat their miserable and misguided ways. The psalmist retells the story of how God brought them out of Egypt, loved them, fed them and gave them water, yet it never seemed to be enough. Almost immediately, they provoke God by demanding something more or by their turning to worship the idols of the pagans. In both the Old and New Testament, countless stories emphasize this tragic sequence of events. It was only the hand of God that awoke them to their sins.

The psalm begins in the style of the wisdom writings: "I will open my mouth in a parable." The word *"parable"* comes from the same root word that gives title to the Book of Proverbs. In the Book of Proverbs, comparisons are used. Parables are much the same. The use of this method makes the lesson much easier to retain. Jesus would teach in this way (Matthew 13:35), although His lessons were frequently more vague than they appear here. Jesus would use a common story from history and encourage listeners to come to their own conclusions.

In this psalm and in Deuteronomy 31, a father is reminded of his responsibility to teach his children the marvelous works of God and the history of the Israelite people. The generation that dwelt in the wilderness insulted and grieved God by continually testing Him and asking for more. *"Testing"* used here means giving someone a task and continually checking their response. God tested Abraham. David asked God to test his heart. It is God's right to test man; it is never man's right to test God. The response Jesus gave to Satan after His 40 days in the wilderness: "Thou shall not test the Lord thy God." Israel's record is her shame; God's endless goodness is her hope. This hope in God is Israel's confidence for what is yet an unfinished story.

Note: The rhythm of the psalm is positive and negative terms. The three phrases of verse 7 show a threefold cord of faith made up of obedience, informed and humble thinking and trust.

PSALM 79

¹A Psalm of Asaph. O God, the heathen are come into thine inheritance; thy holy temple have they defiled; they have laid Jerusalem on heaps.
²The dead bodies of thy servants have they given [to be] meat unto the fowls of the heaven, the flesh of thy saints unto the beast of the earth.
³Their blood have they shed like water roundabout Jerusalem; and [there was] none to bury [them].
⁴We are become a reproach to our neighbors, a scorn and derision to them that are round about us.
⁵How long, LORD? wilt thou be angry for ever? shall thy jealousy burn like fire?
⁶Pour out thy wrath upon the heathen that have not known thee, and upon the kingdoms
that have not called upon thy name.
⁷For they have devoured Jacob,
and laid waste to his dwelling place.
⁸O remember not against us, former iniquities: but thy tender mercies speedily prevent us:
for we are brought very low.
⁹Help us, O God of our salvation,
for the glory of thy name: and deliver us,
and purged away our sins, for thy name's sake.
¹⁰Wherefore should the heathen say, Where [is] their God? let him be known among the heathen

in our sight [by] the revenging of the blood of thy servants [which is] shed.
¹¹Let the sighings of the prisoner come before thee; according to the greatness of thy power preserve thou those that are appointed to die.
¹²And render unto our neighbors, sevenfold into their bosom their reproach,
wherewith they have reproached thee, O Lord.
¹³So we thy people and sheep of thy pasture will give thee thanks for ever: we will show forth thy praise to all generations.

PSALM 79
Title: Fourth Prayer for Judgment
Author: a Psalm of Asaph
Date: After the Destruction of the Temple
597-587 BC
Superscription: (none given)
Theme: Anguish over Destruction/Abandonment by God

This psalm is a lament for the destruction and bloodshed following the fall and desecration of the Holy Temple in Jerusalem. The entire contents of the Temple had been stolen when invaders destroyed its walls. Unburied bodies of the Israelite warriors cover the ground. The smell of death and defeat lingers in the air. The destruction of the temple dates this psalm to the Babylonian conquest. This psalm and Psalm 74 center upon the same event. These psalms are historically connected and were used as single song on a day of fasting. The psalms joined to commemorate the two destructions of the Temple; the first in 586 BC and the second in 70 AD.

This psalm is an eyewitness account from the survivors left in Jerusalem escaping the exile in Psalm 137. Their gloom, anger and depression seem to be unending, yet it never quite reaches despair. In verse 11, the Israelites stand in confusion and wonder why God is withholding His help from His people. It is not a cry that indicates a lack of favor, but rather one that screams with perplexity. The question asked is why God's anger burns against them and God fails to remember His covenant with Israel.

The psalmist is begging God to wreak vengeance on the godless, even before he asks Him to extend His tender mercies to His own people. He uses the words *"help"*, *"deliverance"* and *"for His namesake"*. The psalmist not only recognizes his ancestor's sin, but also confesses sin of his own generation. He makes no pretense of innocence (the word used for *"jealous wrath"* here is far too similar to that of the Second Commandment found in Exodus 20:5). Israel willing accepts their punishment by other nations because of her sin, but also realizes that the nations acted out of hostility and distaste for God's people. On these grounds, they ask God to place His judgment upon the heads of the invaders. Those who destroyed His holy temple have abused the name of God. If God will but answer this prayer of His people, they vow to give continual praise to God and to act as witnesses of His Holy presence.

The tone here is one of indignation and an appeal to God's honor. The people have two options: they can either accept their fate because of sin or indignantly reject it, thus accusing God of great injustice. The humility seen in the people is in itself a plea for compassion, yet it is followed by a vigorous demand for punishment upon the invaders.

Note: Every tongue must confess the Lord (Isaiah 43)) and every drop of innocent blood will be demanded (Matthew 23:35; Luke 18:7). God will give recompense for suffering. This is something unknown until the coming of Christ and the power of His blood, which flows upon sinner who is seeking forgiveness and vengeance for those who persecute the godly.

PSALM 80

¹To the chief Musician upon Shoshannimeduth, A Psalm of Asaph. Give ear, O Shepherd of Israel, thou that leadest Joseph like a flock; thou that dwellest [between] the cherubims, shine forth.
²Before Ephriam and Benjamin and Manasseh stir up thy strength, and come [and] save us.
³Turn us again, O God, and cause thy face to shine; and we shall be saved.
⁴OLORD God of hosts, how long wilt thou be angry against the prayer of thy people?
⁵Thou feedest them with the bread of tears; and givest them tears to drink in great measure.

⁶Thou makest us a strife unto our neighbors: and our enemies laugh among themselves.

⁷Turn us again, O God of hosts, and cause thy face to shine; and we shall be saved.

⁸Thou hast brought a vine out of Egypt: thou hast cast out the heathen, and planted it.

⁹Thou preparest [room] before it, and didst cause it to take deep root, and it filled the land.

¹⁰The hills were covered with the shadow of it, and the boughs thereof [were like] the goodly cedars.

¹¹She sent out her boughs unto the sea, and her branches unto the river.

¹²Why hast thou [then] broken down her hedges, so that all they which pass by the way do pluck her?

¹³The boar out of the wood doth waste it, and the wild beast of the field doth devour it.

¹⁴Return, we beseech thee, O God of hosts: looked down from heaven, and behold, and visit this vine;

¹⁵And the vineyard which thy right hand hath planted, and the branch [that] thou made us strong for thyself.

¹⁶[It is] burned with fire, [it is] cut down: they perish at the rebuke of thy countenance.

¹⁷Let thy hand be upon the man of thy right hand, upon the son of man [whom] thou madest strong for thyself.

¹⁸So will not we go back from thee: quicken us and we will call upon thy name.

¹⁹Turn us again, O LORD God of hosts, cause thy face to shine; and we shall be saved.

PSALM 80
Title: Fifteenth Prayer of Distress
Author: a Psalm of Asaph
Date: Near the time of the Northern Kingdom Exile
Superscription: to the chief Musician *Shoshannim-eduth to the tune of "Lilies"*
Theme: Plea for Restoration

The 80th prayer is yet another prayer for the restoration of Israel. The occasion for the psalm is after the exile of the northern kingdom (2 Kings 18), but before the fall of the city of Jerusalem (2 Kings 25). Ten of the northern tribes were destroyed between 734 and 722 BC, leaving the border of Judah exposed on the north to the Assyrians. The three tribes of Ephraim, Benjamin and Manasseh appear to be the only tribes remaining. The psalmist has been exiled from the north, as his recent experiences indicate. Archaeological surveys of the holy land have shown that Jerusalem and the surrounding countryside experienced a dramatic increase of population at this time, no doubt the result of a massive influx (verse 2) of those dispersed from the north.

The occurrences of a refrain in verses 3, 7 and 19 are an abbreviated form of the plea found in verse 14. This refrain reinforces the fact that Israel is in shock at the destruction of Jerusalem and the destruction of most of the tribes of Israel. The 19 verses of this psalm seem to follow and often-used pattern: the suffering of Israel, the questioning of God and ending with a reassuring confidence of His love.

Israel is pictured as a grapevine (8-16), stretching out in all directions. The psalmist speaks of the nurturing of the vine, which God has brought forth from Egypt. In doing so, he reflects how God has cared for His people and, after taking them from Egypt to Canaan, the Lord planted them in a new land. Verse 12 compares this past with what he now believes to be God's rejection. He pleads that God will come and tend once again to this *vine*. The people believe that God's anger has caused the vine to whither and that they are now in danger of death. If God will but revive His people, they will worship Him.

The psalmist is hoping here that God will not only restore Israel, but will place a penalty upon those who defile her. Justice plays a large part in God's economy and it is certain that He will return Israel to her former glory. It does appear that God prefers boldness in prayer as long as the boldness is something more than continual babbling and repetition (Ecclesiastes 5:2; Matthew 6:7). It is imperative that He is acknowledged as the Father of the Israelite children, not a Father of street beggars hoping for His goodness. He is the one who created man, He is the one who separated out Israel and He is not one to begin a good thing and then simply lose interest in it.

The psalmist prays for God's help for Israel, as it has been chosen as God's right hand. In the context of this psalm, the term "son of man" may sound messianic, but here it points to Israel as being God's firstborn. Ultimately, the Messiah became the fulfillment of this prayer. The Son of Man as seen in the

Gospels references Christ as being at the right hand of God (Hebrews 1:3; 8:1; 10:12; Acts 7:56).

Note: In other passages, both Jews and Christians will focus on a single figure who will become the true vine and the literal Son of Man.

PSALM 81

¹To the chief Musician upon Gittith, [A Psalm] of Asaph. Sing aloud unto God our strength: make a joyful noise unto the God of Jacob.
²Take a Psalm, and bring hither the timbrel, the pleasant harp with the psaltery.
³Blow up the trumpet in the new moon, in the time appointed, on our solemn feast day.
⁴For this [was] a statute for Israel, [and] a law of the God of Jacob.
⁵This he ordained in Joseph [for] a testimony, when he went out through the land of Egypt: [where] I heard a language [that] I understood not.
⁶I removed his shoulder from the burden: his hands were delivered from the pots.
⁷Thou calledst in trouble, and I delivered thee; I answered thee in the secret place of thunder: I proved thee at the waters of Meribah.
⁸Hear, O my people, and I will testify unto thee: O Israel, if thou wilt hearken unto me;
⁹There shall no strange god be in thee; neither shalt thou worship any strange god.

¹⁰ I [am] the LORD thy God,
which brought thee out of the land of Egypt:
open thy mouth wide, and I will fill it.
¹¹But my people would not hearken to my voice;
and Israel would none of me.
¹²So I gave them up unto their own heart's lust:
[and] they walked in their own counsels.
¹³Oh that my people had hearkened unto me, [and]
Israel had walked in my ways!
¹⁴I should soon have subdued their enemies, and
turned my hand against their adversaries.
¹⁵The haters of the LORD should have submitted
themselves unto him: but their time should
have endured for ever.
¹⁶He should have fed them also with the finest of the
wheat: and with honey out of the rock should
I have satisfied thee.

PSALM 81
Title: Seventeenth Psalm of Instruction
Author: a Psalm of Asaph
Superscription: to the chief Musician *upon Gittith-(instrument of Gath)*
Theme: Israel's Repentance

A hymn of praise opens the psalm and a prophetic utterance concludes it. The abrupt change at the end of verse 5 suggests that fragments of two psalms have been joined to create this psalm. This view is not imperative, however. In the Jewish text, the word *"solemn"* is replaced with the words *"festival day"*.

Such gatherings would be a time for remembering God's relation to His people. The use of the trumpet (*shofar*) indicates a *joyous*, not *solemn* celebration. This Feast of Tabernacles or the Passover Feast are the two most likely candidates for the usage of this psalm. The *new moon* was a sign to begin the festival (the first day of the month) and the *full moon* (the 15th day of the month) indicated the termination of the celebration.

The psalm cannot be defined as either pre-exilic or post-exilic, but what it can do is show the intense significance of Israel's gathering together to remember God's mercy. This "coming together" served as a great time of recommitment for the Israelites. The lessons of the 40 years in the wilderness will not be forgotten. The term *"sing aloud"* came from the song of Moses (Deuteronomy 32:14) and set the tone for active rejoicing. The word *"song"* as it is used here is more likely referring to an instrument which is played (probably the tambourine), celebrating the tune to which Mariam danced.

The first five verses introduce an oration where God speaks personally to His people. In the following verses God promises that He will never change; He will always take care of Israel, if only they will trust Him. Man's actions choose God's response (Romans 1:24-32). In the past (and probably in the future), the Israelites did not listen to the voice of God. The cry in verse 13 shows the aching in God's heart—how different things would have been if only Israel had trusted Him. He had offered them constant victory and blessings, but by their disobedience they had chosen misery.

This psalm was written for a joyous occasion, yet, there are no criteria as to *how* one is required to *express* their feelings. There is no *perfect* form of praise. One only needs to follow the spirit to find a valid means of praising and of sharing that rejoicing with others (Ephesians 5:19). Music is recommended as a central part of worship, but there is a firm warning that we should not become individualistic or neglect to meet with other believers (Hebrews 10:25). While God is always ready to meet man one-on-one with His children, it is also important that the children make the effort to meet with one another.

The psalm ends with a strong reminder of God's grace and ability. God does not change; He gives the best and brings goodness out of devastation.

PSALM 82

¹A Psalm of Asaph. God standeth in the congregation of the mighty; he judgeth among the gods.
² How long will you judge unjustly,
and accept the persons of the wicked?
³Defend the poor and fatherless:
do justice to the afflicted and needy.
⁴Deliver the poor and needy:
rid [them] out of the hand of the wicked.
⁵They know not, neither will they understand; they walk on in darkness: all the foundations of the earth are out of course.
⁶I have said, Ye [are] gods;
and all of you [are] children of the most High.

⁷But ye shall die like men,
and fall like one of the princes.
⁸Arise, O God, judge the earth:
for thou shall inherit all nations.

PSALM 82
Title: Eighth Prayer for Judgment
Author: a Psalm of Asaph
Superscription: none
Theme: Corrupt and Vindictive Judges

The Levitical author of this psalm envisions the rulers and judges gathered before the great King to give an account of their administration of justice. God can easily see that the judges are using their positions to take advantage of the oppressed. It is important to notice the repeated reference to gods (small G) to determine exactly who these judges are. The New Testament reference in the Book of John 10:34 leaves their identity unclear. The term *"gods"* in Canaanite culture refers to the heads of clans or tribes. Exodus 22:8 speaks of those given the task of settling disputes based on the Laws of Moses.

Confusion comes from Exodus 22:28, which states, "You shall not revile God nor curse the ruler of your people." If taken in this sense, God and the local magistrates seem to be synonymous. This reference does not forbid a synonym, nor does it require one. The human judges have no right to be more than what Moses spoke of himself, saying that *the people come to me* to inquire of God and *I shall make known* to them the statutes of God and His decision* (Exodus 18:15). Yet another possibility is that these *gods* refer to unseen powers and principalities which govern the darkness (Ephesians 6:12). There are also a few references in the Old Testament to rulers, both good and bad (Isaiah 24:21; Daniel 10:13, 20), which the New Testament refers to as angels (Revelation 12:7) A final interpretation lies within polytheism: these are gods of the heathen being brought to account before the true God.

God's words, "how long", are directed to those chosen as judges. The New Testament Book of Ecclesiastes 5:8 indicates that these corrupt judges are only a small part of Israel's missteps. There are higher judges and the highest judge of all has no patience with misrule and wickedness. Scripture, from the very beginning, shows the patience of God, which is oriented to perfecting salvation, not towards condoning corruption, which offends Him and abuses His world.

The psalm closes with an appeal to God to complete His work as the sovereign judge of all nations. He alone must pass judgment before true justice can be found.

PSALM 83

¹A Song [or] Psalm of Asaph. Keep not thou silence, O God: hold not thy peace, and be not still, O God.
²For, lo, thine enemies make a tumult: and they that hate thee have lifted up the head.

³They have taken crafty counsel against thy people,
and consulted against thy hidden ones.
⁴They have said, Come, and let us cut them off from
[being] a nation; that the name of Israel may be no
more in remembrance.
⁵For they have consulted together with one consent:
they are confederate against thee:
⁶The Tabernacles of Edom, and the Ishmaelites; of
Moab, and the Hagarenes;
⁷Gebal, and Ammon, and Amalek;
the Philistines with the inhabitants of Tyre;
⁸Assur also is joined with them:
they have holpen the children of Lot.
⁹Do unto them as [unto] the Midianites; as [to]
Sisera, as [to] Jabin, at the brook of Kison:
¹⁰[Which] perished at Endor:
they became [as] dung for the earth.
¹¹Make their nobles like Oreb, and like Zeeb:
yea, all their princes as Zebab, and as Zalmunna:
¹²Who said, Let us take to ourselves
the houses of God in possession.
¹³O my God, make them like a wheel;
as the stubble before the wind.
¹⁴As the fire burneth wood,
and as the flame setteth the mountains on fire;
¹⁵So persecute them with thy tempest,
and make them afraid with thy storm.
¹⁶Fill their faces with shame;
that they may seek thy name, O LORD.
¹⁷Let them be confounded and troubled for ever;
yea, let them be put to shame, and perish.

¹⁸That [men] may know that thou,
whose name alone [is] JEHOVAH,
[art] the most high over all the earth.

PSALM 83
Title: Ninth Prayer for Judgment
Author: a Psalm of Asaph
Superscription: none
Theme: God's Judgment upon those who Scheme Against Israel

Psalm 83 has the earmarks of *demanding* that God intervene on behalf of His people. All of Israel's past enemies are wagging their tongues about what they are going to do to blot out the inhabitants of Israel. The majority of the nations listed are nomadic, dwelling south and e3ast of Israel. Edom and Amalek were to the east, Philistia located to the southwest and Tyre to the northwest. It is unclear which of these tribes plan aggressive attack and which are merely standing in alliance with the attackers. While the date is not discernible, 2 Chronicles 21 tells the story of Moab, Ammon and other troops invading Judah. Without a doubt, the psalmist would like to see the enemy battered or destroyed altogether, yet there is a hint of a desire that his enemies would turn and seek the Lord.

In an appeal for action against their foes, the plea is spoken again as if to remind God that those who attack Israel have attacked God Himself. The psalmist begs for the destruction of his foes by saying, "Do unto *them*. . ." He asks that God defeat these conspirators as He defeated both the Canaanites and the Midianites. The psalmist recalls past victories that God has performed for Israel and for the past victories as recorded in the book of Judges (4, 5, 7, 8) in the battles of Gideon and Deborah. Verses 9 through 12 list the names of those defeated in the first two campaigns in the Book of Judges.

Their many past victories have made it clear that Israel is God's chosen people. God has made covenant with both the land and with the people of His pasture. God's protective care for what is His may be seen in New Testament terms: *my church* (Matthew 16:18), *my sheep* (John 10:27-29) and *my temple* (1 Corinthians 3:17). There are more references that can be found in both the Old and New Testaments which reinforce and support this *ownership* God has over His people.

The true reason for this psalm lies in the very last verse, "That [men] may know that thou, whose name alone [is] JEHOVAH, [art] the most high over all the earth."

PSALM 84

¹To the chief Musician upon Gittith, A Psalm for the sons of Korah. How amiable [are] thy tabernacles, O LORD of hosts!
²My soul longeth, yea, even the fainteth for the courts of the LORD: my heart and my flesh crieth out for the living God.

³Yea, the sparrow hath found an house, and the swallow a nest for herself, where she may lay her young, [even] thine altars, O LORD of hosts, my King, and my God.
⁴Blessed [are] they that dwell in thy house: they will still be praising thee.
⁵Blessed [is] the man whose strength [is] in thee; in whose heart [are] the ways [of them].
⁶[Who] passing through the valley of Baca make it a well; the rain also filleth the pools.
⁷They go from strength to strength, [every one of them] in Zion appeareth before God.
⁸O LORD God of hosts, hear my prayer: give ear, O God of Jacob.
⁹Behold, O God our shield, and look upon the face of thine anointed.
¹⁰For a day in thy courts [is] better than a thousand. I had rather be a doorkeeper in the house of my God, than to dwell in the tents of wickedness.
¹¹For the LORD God [is] a sun and shield: the LORD will give grace and glory: no good [thing] will he withhold from them that walk uprightly.
¹²O LORD of hosts, blessed [is] the man that trusteth in thee.

PSALM 84
Title: Third Psalm of the Righteous
Author: a Psalm for the sons of Korah
Superscription: to the chief Musician *upon Gittith (an instrument or melody of Gath)*
Theme: The Joy of Being in the House of God

There is joy in the heart of the pilgrim as he comes to worship at the Temple. Although he comes to the Temple as often as possible, he wishes that he were like the sparrow that comes and goes from the house of God as often as it pleases. There is no indication whether the psalmist speaks of a physical entrance into the Temple, or the prayer of a worshiper who is not near the temple, but longs to be in the house of God. In color and style this psalm is similar to Psalm 42 and may reflect a similar circumstance. If so, the author would be a Levite who normally functioned as a priest of the Temple, now barred from access to God's house (perhaps when Seneca was pillaging Judah). This circumstance would clarify his longing for the precious closeness to God which he found there. Whatever the roots of this psalm, it exhibits complete and utter devotion to God.

The words *"how amiable are thy tabernacles"* may be translated as *"how dear"* or *"how well loved"*. The Christian equivalent to this term is *"love of the brethren"* who have become individually and corporately God's Church (1 Corinthians 3:16, 6:19). Being in the presence of the living God is the true focus of man's longing and no longer are people required to attach themselves to a *place* such as the Temple in Jerusalem. The psalmist points out that if you cannot physically be in the Temple, you can still be with God. From anywhere in the world a man can *journey* to God's presence.

"For a day in thy courts is better than a thousand" (verse 10) begs the question of which a person will choose: a thousand days out in the *world,* or one day in the *House of God.* Whether a literal journey is taking place or if traveling only in spirit, the pilgrims press on, seemingly more eager than when they began. In terms of a personal pilgrimage, the psalmist states that a man should seek God and the church body as often as possible, but when impossible, the pilgrimage may be made within the heart. However God is reached, He bestows grace in this life and glory in the life to come.

The New Testament phrase "from glory to glory" (2 Corinthians 3:18) is spoken here as "from strength to strength" indicating a focus on seeing and knowing God. God is sun and shield—all that is outgoing and positive, as well as the defender of His people. *Favor* and *honor* are *grace* and *glory.* Grace already held a meaning similar to the *smile of God,* but as the apostles walked the earth, the benefits of His passion became known to the world. As he writes, the psalmist wraps himself in the blessing of those who have not seen, yet still believe. (Note the comparison to the Apostle Thomas in John 20:29).

Note: The message is to treat one's present state, be it joy and happiness, weakness and longings as the psalmist did, by choosing to be with God in spirit. God delights in a person of faith who, like the Israelites, have not seen yet believe. For today's Christians, the foot of the cross is a beautiful place to begin this journey.

PSALM 85

¹To the chief Musician, A Psalm for the sons of Korah. LORD, thou hast been favorable unto thy land: thou hast brought back the captivity of Jacob.
²Thou hast forgiven the iniquity of thy people, thou hast covered all their sin.
³Thou hast taken away all thy wrath: thou hast turned [thyself] from the fierceness of thine anger.
⁴Turn us, O God of our salvation, and cause thine anger toward us to cease.
⁵Wilt thou be angry with us for ever? wilt thou draw out thine anger to all generations?
⁶Wilt thou not receive us again: that thy people may rejoice in thee?
⁷Show us thy I mercy, O LORD, and grant us thy salvation.
⁸I will hear what God the LORD will speak: for he will speak peace unto his people, and to his saints: but let them not turn again to folly.
⁹Surely his salvation [is] nigh them that fear him; that glory may dwell in our land.
¹⁰Mercy and truth are met together; righteousness and peace have kissed [each other].

¹¹Truth shall spring out of the earth; and righteousness shall look down from heaven.
¹²Yea, the LORD shall give [that which is] good; and our land shall yield her increase.
¹³ Righteousness shall go before him; and shall set [us] in the way of his steps.

PSALM 85
Title: Second Prayer Psalm
Author: a Psalm for the Sons of Korah
Superscription: to the Chief Musician
Theme: Prayer for Restoration of the Land

Although this psalm bears a strong prophetic element, it is a prayer for revival. It is most probable that this prayer of gratitude was written after the Babylonian exile, yet prior to the restoration of the land and the rebuilding of the Temple. Those returned from exile and the trouble which still lingers are those alluded to by both Nehemiah and Malachi. In verse 12 there is the suggestion of the drought that ravaged the land during the time of Haggai. The drought was a chastening came upon Israel, a result of turning away from the Lord. The first of these occasions is more likely, but either may be the cause of the psalmist's writing.

The first three verses find the Israelites thanking God for bringing them out of captivity and for the forgiveness that it indicates. In verse 4, there is a united plea for God to restore His people and to support them as they move forward. Then, in a somewhat backward motion, verses 5 and 6 ask the question, "Wilt thou be angry with us for ever?" The returning exiles have already thanked God for His favor and forgiveness and are now (7) asking Him to quiet His anger against them and bring salvation. Although grateful that they are home, they are aware that the punishment given them was one of just consequence. Once His "holy anger" lifts from them, they can feel assured and confident that they will never again face exile.

"I will hear what God the Lord will speak" indicates that although unseen, he has received a favorable answer to prayer from God. Deep in his heart, the psalmist knows that he has heard directly from God. Beyond the rebuilding and reoccupying the land, there is found a request which is perhaps the one most needed: that God will not let them return to their previous folly, evilness, wicked ways and all "fleshly" deeds which they are so prone to get caught up in. When such temptations creep into life, it is good to remember that as in John 14:27, God both listens and speaks to His own. There may be a natural consequence, as with the Israelites, but His love will never fail to redeem anyone, even from their own folly.

In the eyes of the psalmist, the Lord has laid up their future before them. The psalmist receives God's message as an answer to prayer and is certain that peace will follow their time of sorrow. He will revive and restore them and grant them peace. The union of God's covenant love and their faithfulness, His righteousness will bring unity to them and the peace of heart, found in God, will bring each worshiper to the heavens with God. God's promise is to guide men, to sustain and provide for them if they chose to walk in His ways.

PSALM 86

¹A prayer of David. Bow down thine ear, O LORD,
hear me: for I [am] poor and needy.
²Preserve my soul; for I [am] holy: O thou my God,
save thy servant that trusteth in thee.
³Be merciful unto me, O Lord:
for I cry unto thee daily.
⁴Rejoice the soul of thy servant: for unto thee, O
Lord, do I lift up my soul.
⁵For thou, Lord, [art] good, and ready to forgive;
and plenteous in mercy unto
all them that call upon thee.
⁶Give ear, O LORD, unto my prayer;
and attend to the voice of my supplications.
⁷In the day of my trouble I will call upon thee:
for thou wilt answer me.
⁸Among the gods [there is] none like unto thee,
O Lord; neither [are there any works]
like unto thy works.
⁹All nations whom thou hast made shall come
and worship before thee, O Lord;
and shall glorify thy name.
¹⁰For thou [art] great, and doest wondrous things:
thou [art] God alone.

¹¹Teach me thy way, O LORD; I will walk in thy truth:
unite my heart to fear thy name.
¹²I will praise thee, O Lord my God, with all my heart:
and I will glorify thy name for ever more.
¹³For great [is] thy mercy toward me: and thou hast
delivered my soul from the lowest hell.
¹⁴O God, the proud are risen against me, and the
assemblies of violent [men] have sought after my
soul; and have not set thee before them.
¹⁵But thou, O Lord, [art] a God full of compassion,
and gracious, long-suffering,
and plenteous in mercy and truth.
¹⁶O turn unto me, and have mercy upon me;
give thy strength unto thy servant,
and save the son of thine handmaid.
¹⁷Show me a token for good; that they which hate
me may see [it], and be ashamed: because thou,
LORD, hast holpen me, and comforted me.

PSALM 86
Title: Eighth Prayer/Praise Psalm
Author: a prayer of David
Superscription: none
Theme: Meditation on the Excellence of the Lord

This is the only psalm in Book Three identified with David. This psalm is very simple in its form, with an opening and closing supplication emphasized by what the psalmist proposes will be his future. In general terms, the psalmist goes before God and spells out his needs. He gives God the reason why God should respond to his pleas. God should respond to him because of his weakened condition, his continual prayer and his dedication to God. His greatest reason is the fact that God is generous, with abundant mercy and forgiveness.

David asks for God's merciful protection and requests God to give him a sign. God has the option of doing this (Judges 6:36), but David must be cautious, lest he *put God to the test.* His prayer is for guidance and protection. *"Teach me; unite my heart"* shows his awareness that only God's teaching will enable him to walk in truth. He desires unity of purpose that he may worthily praise and glorify the name of the Lord with the humility of a slave.

David's praise as seen in verses 8-10 indicates more of a statement of fact rather than joyous celebration. Along with the prayers for pitying comfort, this psalm carries the plea for strength. David is also spirited enough to want to play the part of a man (not a sick man) in driving back the enemy. The comfort he desires is less to ease his mind than to prove his point and clear his name. This is a world away from self-pity; it is an awareness of weakness and an overwhelming desire to be one with God.

The impact of this psalm can be life changing. It is a prayer about forming right habits, rather than simply making right decisions. *"Unite my heart to fear thy name"* is a highly penetrating confession. Love and kindness should be given to others freely and with joy, just as they are received from God. Two virtues, goodness and forgiveness, are given by God and planted by faith in the spirit of a man. He wants man to be like Him—to stand ready to forgive others in the same abundance and with a spirit of willingness.

PSALM 87

¹A Psalm [or] Song for the sons of Korah. His foundation [is] in the holy mountains.
²The LORD lovest the gates of Zion more
than all the dwellings of Jacob.
³Glorious things are spoken of thee, O city of God.
⁴I will make mention of Rahab and Babylon to them
that know me: behold Philistia, and Tyre, with
Ethiopia; this [man] was born there.
⁵And of Zion it shall be said,
This and that man was born in her:
and the highest himself shall establish her.
⁶The LORD shall count, when he writeth up to the
people, [that] this [man], was born there.
⁷As well the singers as the players on instruments
[shall be there]: all my springs [are] in thee.

PSALM 87
Title: First Psalm of Zion
Author: a Psalm for the Sons of Korah
Superscription: none
Theme: The Wonder of God's Holy City

The City of Zion is the mother of all nations. This is a prophecy of the Holy City's glorious future. The Old Testament sees this largely in physical and geographic terms, while the New Testament holds it to be purely spiritual in nature (Revelation 21:1-22:5). In verse 4, *Rahab* is a poetic synonym for Egypt. *Zion* is the city of God, the special object of God's love and center of His earthly kingdom. In this psalm, God is writing the names of those who acknowledge Him as Lord (Hosea 6:3). Ominously, He warns the nations that He has written the names of His people and will hold other nations accountable for how they treat Israel. The concept of the future Jerusalem as the mother of all people is developed in Isaiah 60, 66:7-23) and is also referred to in Galatians 4:26 and Hebrews 12:22.

It is a constant source of delight that Zion, of all places, is God's Holy Mount. None can understand just why God would choose Zion (of all places) as "special". Why God chose Jerusalem as His home is just as unknown as why He chose tiny Bethlehem to be the birthplace of Jesus. God chose these places simply because He loved them—a reason that is sufficient. Israel is keeping the oath which He gave to their fathers and it is made clear that Zion is the name of a group of people, not only the place of the Temple. There is solid comparison here to the modern body of the church in Christianity.

There is solid indication that the Gentile world is in the house of the firstborn. The initiation of the Gentiles as described has two meanings: towards God, they will be counted as those who knew Him and towards the people of God, they are not merely proselytes. Just as Paul claimed his rights as a Roman citizen (Acts 22:28), Gentiles are invited to claim their rights and responsibility of the household of God.

PSALM 88

¹A Song [or] Psalm for the sons of Korah, to the chief Musician upon Mahalath Leannoth, Maschil of Heman the Ezrahite. O LORD God of my salvation, I have cried day [and] night before thee:
²Let my prayer come before thee:
incline thine ear unto my cry;
³For my soul is full of troubles:
and my life draweth nigh unto the grave.
⁴I am counted with them that go down into the pit: I am as a man [that hath] no strength:
⁵Free among the dead, like the slain that lie in the grave, whom thou rememberest no more: and they are cut off from thy hand.
⁶Thou hast laid me in the lowest pit,
in darkness, in the deeps.
⁷Thy wrath lieth hard upon me, and thou hast afflicted [me] with all thy waves.
⁸Thou hast put away mine acquaintance far from me; thou hast made me an abomination unto them:
[I am] shut up, and I cannot come forth.
⁹Mine eye mourneth by reason of affliction: LORD, I have called daily upon thee,
I have stretched out my hands unto thee.
¹⁰Wilt thou show wonders to the dead? Shall the dead arise, [and] praise thee?

¹¹Shall thy lovingkindness be declared in the grave?
[or] thy faithfulness in destruction?
¹²Shall thy wonders be known in the dark? and thy
righteousness in the land of forgetfulness?
¹³But unto thee have I cried, O LORD; and in the
morning shall my prayer prevent thee.
¹⁴LORD, why castest thou off my soul? [why] hidest
thou thy face from me?
¹⁵I [am] afflicted and ready to die from [my] youth
up: [while] I suffer thy terrors I am distracted.
¹⁶Thy fierce wrath goeth over me;
thy terrors have cut me off.
¹⁷They came round about me daily like water; they
compassed me about together.
¹⁸Lover and friend hast thou put far from me, [and]
mine acquaintance into darkness.

PSALM 88
Title: Eighteenth Psalm of Instruction
Author: for the Sons of Korah
Superscription: to the chief Musician *upon Mahalath-lean-noth-(humble song of affliction)*
Theme: Instruction in Distress

This psalm has the questionable honor of being the most melancholy song of the Psalter. This is possibly a song written for Heman (1 Kings 4:31), who was gravely ill with leprosy. Others suggest that this psalm is a corporate sequel to the Book of Lamentations, but this seems unlikely as the depth and personal aspects do not seem suitable for a group setting.

However, this does not exclude the reader from walking in companionship with those who share this type of sadness or sorrow.

His depression makes him feel certain that he is well beyond the reach of God. He speaks of Sheol in verse 4, where God is never present and the dead are literally *cut off* from the living. He feels that the Lord no longer remembers him and he is counted among the dead. Surrounded by the dark shadows of death, the psalmist feels totally abandoned and rejected by God. Though still upon the earth, he feels as if he is isolated in the narrow prison of himself (8).

He has no one to turn to but God, that being peculiar as he believes that God who is *punishing* him with trial after trial (7-8, 13-18). In the dark, in a hole, in desperation, in anguish, in frustration, alone, bitter and lonely, he feels the life being crushed from within him. The blackest despair has him in its grip, coiled around him and threatening his life. The psalmist ends with a bewildered question, the repeated question, "Why?" in verse 14. The only response appears to be more anguish. Looking back, this man can remember nothing but pain. Looking forward, he sees nothing and as he calls upon God, there is only silence.

Note: There is no proof that God is the cause of the psalmist's pain. However, it is a sharp reminder that one must, regardless of circumstances, turn towards God and seek the redemption of our bodies (Romans 8:22). Like Job, this psalmist must hang on to his faith. Though still in silence, the psalmist takes notice that his existence is no mistake—there is a divine plan and he has a place in it.

PSALM 89

¹Maschil of Ethan the Ezrahite. I will sing of the mercies of the LORD for ever: with my mouth will I make known thy faithfulness to all generations.
²For I have said, Mercy shall be built up forever: thy faithfulness shalt thou establish in the very heavens.
³I have made a covenant with my chosen, I have sworn unto David my servant,
⁴Thy seed will I establish for ever, and build up thy throne to all generations.
⁵And the heavens shall praise thy wonders, O LORD: thy faithfulness also in the congregation of the saints.
⁶For who in the heaven can be compared unto the LORD? [who] among the sons of the mighty can be likened unto the LORD can be likened unto the LORD?
⁷God is greatly to be feared in the assembly of the saints, and to be had in reverence of all [them that are] about him.
⁸O LORD God of hosts, who [is] a strong LORD like unto thee? or to thy faithfulness round about thee?
⁹Thou rulest the raging of the sea: when the waves thereof arise, thou stillest them.
¹⁰Thou hast broken Rahab in pieces, as one that is slain; thou hast scattered thine enemies with thy strong arm.

¹¹The heavens [are] thine, the earth also [is] thine:
[as for] the world and the fullness thereof,
thou hast founded them.
¹²The north and the south thou hast created them:
Tabor and Hermon shall rejoice in thy name.
¹³Thou hast a mighty arm: strong is thy hand, [and]
high is thy right hand.
¹⁴Justice and judgment [are] the habitation of thy
throne: mercy and truth shall go before thy face.
¹⁵Blessed [is] the people that know the joyful sound:
they shall walk, O LORD,
in the light of thy countenance.
¹⁶In thy name shall they rejoice all the day: and in
thy righteousness shall they be exalted.
¹⁷For thou [art] the glory of their strength: and in thy
favor our horn shall be exalted.
¹⁸For the LORD [is] our defense;
and the Holy One of Israel [is] our king.
¹⁹Then thou spakest in vision to thy holy one, and
saidst, I have laid help upon [one that is] mighty; I
have exalted [one] chosen out of the people.
²⁰I have found David my servant;
with my holy oil have I anointed him:
²¹With whom my hand shall be established: mine
arm also shall strengthen him.
²²The enemy shall not exact upon him; nor the son
of wickedness afflict him.
²³And I will beat down his foes before his face, and
plagued them that hate him.
²⁴But my faithfulness and my mercy [shall be] with
him: and in my name shall his horn be exalted.

²⁵I will set his hand also in the sea,
and his right hand in the rivers.
²⁶He shall cry unto me, Thou [art] my father,
my God, and the rock of my salvation.
²⁷Also I will make him [my] firstborn,
higher than the kings of the earth.
²⁸My mercy will I keep for him for evermore,
and my covenant shall stand fast with him.
²⁹His seed also will I make [to endure] for ever,
and his throne as the days of heaven.
³⁰If his children forsake my law,
and walk not in my judgments;
³¹If they break my statutes,
and keep not my commandments;
³²Then I will visit their transgression with the rod,
and their iniquity with stripes.
³³Nevertheless, my loving kindness will I not utterly
take from him, nor suffer my faithfulness to fail.
³⁴My covenant I will not break,
nor alter the thing that is gone out of my lips.
³⁵Once I have sworn by my holiness that
I will not lie unto David.
³⁶His seed shall endure for ever,
and his throne as the sun before me.
³⁷It shall be established for ever, as the moon,
and [as] a faithful witness in heaven.
³⁸But thou hast cast off and abhorred, thou hast
been wroth with thine anointed.
³⁹Thou hast made void the covenant of thy servant:
thou hast profaned his crown [by casting it]
to the ground.

⁴⁰Thou hast broken down all his hedges;
thou hast brought his strong holds to ruin.
⁴¹All that pass by the way spoil him:
he is a reproach to his neighbors.
⁴²Thou hast set up the right hand of his adversaries;
thou hast made all his enemies to rejoice.
⁴³Thou hast also turned the edge of his sword, and
hast not made him to stand in the battle.
⁴⁴Thou hast made his glory to cease, and cast his
throne down to the ground.
⁴⁵The days of his youth hast thou shortened: thou
hast covered him with shame.
⁴⁶How long, LORD? wilt thou hide thyself for ever?
Shall thy wrath burn like fire?
⁴⁷Remember how short my time is: wherefore hast
thou made all men in vain?
⁴⁸What man [is he that] liveth, and shall not see
death? Shall he deliver his soul
from the hand of the grave?
⁴⁹Lord, where [are] thy former lovingkindnesses,
[which] thou swarest unto David in thy truth?
⁵⁰Remember, Lord, the reproach of thy servants;
[how] do I bear in my bosom [the reproach of]
all the mighty people;
⁵¹Wherewith thine enemies have reproached, O
LORD; wherewith they have reproached the footsteps of thine anointed.
⁵²Blessed [be] the LORD for evermore.
Amen, and Amen.

PSALM 89
Title: Sixteenth Messianic Psalm
Author: of Ethan the Ezrahite
Date: The Attack of Jerusalem by Nebuchadnezzar 597 BC
Superscription: to the chief Musician *on Maschil-(reflective melody)*
Theme: Remembering God's Covenant; Grief over Lost Blessings

The psalmist sings the story of God's faithful love of Israel, His covenant and His promises to the line of David. The psalm is a lament by an individual who speaks for the nation. The psalm consists of both elated praise and a deep feeling of lament. These divergent elements suggest to some commentators that this piece is a composite of two or three original poems. Even if this is the case, the psalm possesses a very logical order. God's apparent withdrawal of His Covenant Promise is the beginning of the psalmist's lament. The events of his life lead him to believe that God, the faithful Almighty, seems to have abandoned His anointed one. Though sincere and filled with pain, this brings forward a lament that leans toward reproach.

The foundation of this psalm is the great prophecy of 2 Samuel 7:4-17 and the promise to David and his ancestors that the throne will be theirs forever. This promise is His guarantee of His love forever for David and his family. As in 2 Samuel 7:13, God has made a promise saying, "I will establish; I will be his father and he shall be my son." The psalmist struggles with the word *"forever"*, which the turn of events later seems to contradict. His question, "How long O Lord?" gives a slight indication that he is not quite sure that God is doing what He has promised. Yet, the psalmist remains humble, depending on the prophecy given to David in 2 Samuel 7:12.

Yet who in heaven can be compared unto the Lord? There are many allusions used here to show God's power in creation, His victory over all opposition and His dominion over heaven and earth. In the center of the psalm, the psalmist deals with the divine promise to David. The former promise to the nation as God's firstborn, in his estimation (Exodus 4:22), is now focused on the King and is extended to all the Davidic succession, culminating in Jesus, God's anointed one. Then the emphasis has shifted in verse 29 to the working account of the promise through the seed of David. While he appeals to God's sworn testimony that the covenant will stand, he recognizes that punishment must come upon David's seed for their unfaithfulness.

The psalm changes to a pointed reminder that as God can make promises, He is also able to unmake kings. As praise dwindles, we see the assertion that as God can make man great, so he is able to destroy those who "cast off" His anointed. Verse 41 brings a foreshadowing of the relationship of the life of Christ to mankind. Verse 47 cries for an answer to questions and doubts that have arisen about the anointed. The prayer brings the psalmist to the place where he begins to understand the combination of servant (50) and Messiah (the anointed one). The intertwining of God's promises and the bitter and insulting things one lives through lead only to an unanswerable question.

The doxology contains the blessing and the double amen (like those of 41:13 and 72:19) and ends the Third Book of the Psalter. This book is filled with both national and personal suffering from Israel. Yet, for all its anguish, Book Three never lets go of its firm foundation and dedication to the praise of God.

NOTES ON BOOK THREE
Major Themes

- Take care of the unfortunate
- Be completely devoted to God
- God must be first in one's life
- Humility invites continual growth
- Wisdom is the application of God's word
- Willingly accept the mercy of God
- Trust in God, not in man
- Personal testimony is powerful
- Avoid pride, arrogance and temptation

BOOK FOUR

PSALMS 90-106
Referred to as the Numbers Psalms

The fourth major division in the Psalter is actually a part of a larger collection, which embraces Psalms 90-150. The break at Psalm 106 seems to be for convenience, since the dominant thought continues with Psalm 107. While the Psalms in Book One centered mainly upon personal issues and those in Books Two and Three revolved around events and upsets in the kingdom, Books Four and Five focus on worship. These psalms were written in such a way that they might be used as individual songs or as songs for public worship.

In Book Four Yahweh is the name used for God. Yahweh occurs in every psalm in Book Four with the exception to three Psalms in Book Five. The majority of these psalms are anonymous. Psalm 90 is attributed to Moses and Psalms 101 and 103 bear the name of David.

PSALM 90

¹A prayer of Moses the man of God. LORD, thou hast been our dwelling place in all generations.
²Before the mountains were brought forth, or ever thou hadst formed the earth and the world, even from everlasting to everlasting, thou [art] God.
³Thou turnest man to destruction; and sayest, return, ye children of men.
⁴For a thousand years in thy sight [are but] as yesterday when it is past, and [as] a watch in the night.
⁵Thou carriest them away as with a flood; they are [as] a sleep: in the morning [they are] like grass, [which] groweth up.
⁶In the morning it flourisheth, and groweth up; in the evening it is cut down, and withereth.
⁷For we are consumed by thine anger, and by thy wrath we are troubled.
⁸Thou hast set our iniquities before thee, our secret [sins] in the light of thy countenance.
⁹For all our days are passed away in thy wrath: we spend our years as a tale [that is told].
¹⁰The days of our years [are] threescore years and ten; and if by reason of strength [they be] fourscore years, yet [is] their strength labor and sorrow; for it is soon cut off, and we fly away.
¹¹Who knoweth the power of thine anger? even according to thy fear, [so is] thy wrath.
¹²So teach [us] to number our days, that we may apply [our] hearts unto wisdom.

¹³Return, O LORD, how long?
and let it repent thee concerning thy servants .
¹⁴O satisfy us early with thy mercy; that we may rejoice and be glad all our days.
¹⁵Make us glad according to the days [wherein] thou hast afflicted us, [and] the years [wherein] we have seen evil.
¹⁶Let thy work appear unto thy servants, and thy glory unto their children.
¹⁷And let the beauty of the LORD our God be upon us; and establish thou the work of our hands upon us; yea, the work of our hands establish thou it.

PSALM 90
Title: Third Prayer Psalm
Author: a prayer of Moses the man of God
Superscription: none
Theme: The Eternity of God; the Brevity of Man

This is the only psalm attributed to Moses, who clearly was one of the wisest men in history. Moses lived 400 years before David and it may be that this is the first psalm ever written. Isaiah 40 gives a wonderful presentation of God's eternity as it tells of the limited amount of time a man has in the mortal world. This psalm echoes various portions of Isaiah 40. Acting as a companion to this psalm is the Book of Exodus, where Moses became known as *"Moses, the man of God"* and received the word that while he would not live forever, his sons, his nation and his God would continue. Isaiah brings comfort, this psalm brings discipline. The Book of Ecclesiastes in the New Testament carries a similar theme.

This is a personal meditation, yet it speaks for all of the people in the wilderness. Remembering the 40 years of wandering, Moses seems to understand the reason for God's discipline. Moses is aware that God (1-4) is the creator of all and that He existed in the time before creation. Man will be swept away like the flood (5) and like grass, will wither in one day. In the sixth verse, Moses states that the days of man are limited due to their sinful nature. This idea is similar to that in Romans 6:23, reaffirming that the New Testament rests upon the foundation of days of old. A man's life must be worked out under God's judgment (7-10) and the psalmist appeals to God (13-17) to forgive man's sins and prays that even though he is standing in God's wrath, that God will teach him true wisdom that he may enjoy happiness.

The psalmist has seen God, remembers that His face is brighter than the sun and can search even the darkest parts of a man. A man's limited life span is pitifully short in comparison to the eternity of God. Moses has suffered a great deal in his life and has watched the pain and sorrow of the Israelites as they traveled from Egypt to the Promised Land. Through these experiences, he has learned to lean on God, yet he also strives to understand the meaning and value of such a short life. This psalm presents an opportunity to reflect on mortality and judgment. Along with the Law of Moses, this psalm was considered to be *required reading.* Used with 1 Corinthians 15, this verse is often present at the burial of the dead.

The first verse shows man's relationship with God, while the rest of the psalm pleads for a reversal of the life Moses has lived up to this point. He prays that all of the bitterness and wrath will now turn into to joy. He is weary of rebuke and now asks for mercy. The New Testament goes beyond the simple words of verse 15 by asking happiness to balance the sorrows of life based on the promise of a *light of glory* beyond all comparison in 2 Corinthians 4:17. Man is transitory, but God's work will endure forever. In light of the unwelcome thought of a man's mortality, a life spent with God makes its own *balance.*

PSALM 91

¹He that dwelleth in the in the secret place of
the most High shall abide under
the shadow of the Almighty.
²I will say of the LORD, [He is] my refuge and my
fortress: my God; in him will I trust.
³Surely he shall deliver thee from the snare of the
fowler, [and] from the noisome pestilence.
⁴He shall cover thee with his feathers,
and under his wings shalt thou trust: his truth
[shall be thy] shield and buckler.
⁵Thou shalt not be afraid for the terror by night;
[nor] for the arrow [that] flieth by day;
⁶[Nor] for the pestilence [that] walketh in darkness;
[nor] for the destruction [that] wasteth at noonday.

⁷A thousand shall fall at thy side, and ten thousand at thy right hand; [but] it shall not come nigh thee. ⁸Only with thine eyes shalt thou behold
and see the reward of the wicked.
⁹Because thou hast made the LORD, [which is] my refuge, [even] the most High, thy habitation;
¹⁰There shall no evil befall thee, neither shall any plague come nigh thy dwelling.
¹¹For he shall give his angels charge over thee,
to keep thee in all thy ways.
¹²They shall bear thee up in [their] hands,
lest thou dash thy foot against a stone.
¹³Thou shalt tread upon the lion and the adder:
the young lion and the dragon shalt
thou trample under feet.
¹⁴Because he hath set his love upon me,
therefore will I deliver him: I will set him on high,
because he hath known my name.
¹⁵He shall call upon me, and I will answer him:
I [will be] with him in trouble;
I will deliver him, and honor him.
¹⁶With long life will I satisfy him,
and show him my salvation.

PSALM 91
Title: Five things in Which to Trust
Author: anonymous
Superscription: none
Theme: Safety in the Presence of God

Psalm 91 is a companion psalm to the previous psalm and opens in much the same manner. The depth of trust and confidence in God suggests that this was most likely an individual meditation. At the same time, the subject matter indicates that it could have been created for congregational use. While this psalm is similar to Psalm 90 and reminiscent of many of the Davidic Psalms, it is both anonymous and timeless. It is this special trait that makes the heart of the psalmist available to all.

Verses 3 through 8 focus on God's divine providence and show many of the attributes of God. The Creator is the One who *delivers* from the snare, provides *protection* beneath His wings, *removes fear and terror* and gives a *promise of victory*. The *terror by night* refers to the night demon known as Lilith, while the *arrow by day* is reference to the wickedness of Satan's minions. The pestilence *that walketh in darkness* may have an affinity with the demon Namtar, while the *destruction that wasteth at noonday* refers to a one-eyed demon also mentioned in rabbinical tradition. (Even if the demons were absent from the writer's thoughts, they are an integral part of the psalm in its Jewish use.)

God's people are saved only because of God's divine promises of deliverance. They have a virtual guarantee that God will send ministering angels to stand beside the believer to protect him from stumbling. Verse 12 appears again in the New Testament as Satan struggles to tempt Jesus in the wilderness. This story can be seen in Matthew 4:6 and Luke 4:10.

In its completeness, this psalm is a story of the helper and the helpless. It is all about grace. The man who is totally devoted and faithful to God will walk closely with Him every day, seeking His counsel and resting in His love. Nothing can touch the man of God-neither man nor beast, in darkness or in the brightness of day. Not all will be perfect and simple (15), but protection will remain as eternal as God Himself. These amazing promises of God to those who believe in Him are a daily reminder that regardless of circumstance, in the depth of all things, God may be found.

Note: Elyon, means the Most High; El Shaddai refers to the Almighty; and Elohim as it is used here means "the Sublime God". Each of these references from the Hebrew text give insight into the ways in which God takes care of His people.

PSALM 92

¹A Psalm [or] Song for the Sabbath day. [It is a] good [thing] to give thanks unto the LORD, and to sing praises unto thy name, O most High:

²To show forth thy lovingkindness in the morning,
and thy faithfulness every night,
³Upon an instrument of ten strings, and upon the
psaltery; upon the harp with a solemn sound.
⁴For thou, LORD, hast made me glad through thy
work: I will triumph in the works of thy hands.
⁵O LORD, how great are thy works!
[and] thy thoughts are very deep.
⁶A brutish man knoweth not;
neither doth a fool understand this.
⁷When the wicked spring as the grass, and when all
the workers of iniquity do flourish; [it is] that they
shall be destroyed for ever:
⁸But thou, LORD, [art most] high for evermore.
⁹For, lo, thine enemies, O LORD,
for, lo, thine enemies shall perish;
all the workers of iniquity shall be scattered.
¹⁰But my horn shalt thou exalt like [the horn of] an
unicorn: I shall be anointed with fresh oil.
¹¹Mine eye also shall see [my desire] upon mine
enemies, [and] mine ears shall hear [my desire] of
the wicked that rise up against me.
¹²The righteous shall flourish like a palm tree: he
shall grow like a cedar in Lebanon.
¹³Those that be planted in the house of the LORD
shall flourish in the courts of our God.
¹⁴They shall still bring forth fruit in old age; they shall
be fat and flourishing;
¹⁵To show that the LORD [is] upright: [he is] my rock,
and [there is] no unrighteousness in him.

PSALM 92
Title: Fifth Psalm of the Righteous
Author: anonymous
Superscription: a Psalm for the Sabbath
Theme: Praise for God's Love

This glorious Thanksgiving song recalls the wondrous things that God has done for Israel and its inhabitants. This hymn is a song of great gratitude and great confidence in the righteousness of God and His judgments. This confidence goes beyond theory or formal training, as it is obviously from personal experience. Jewish historians record that this psalm was sung weekly on the Sabbath. The psalms show that the Sabbath day was a day of rest and a day of corporate worship as seen in Genesis, Exodus, Leviticus and many other places in the Books of Moses. This day is to be a day of joy, not a burden. The test here for the individual is the conflict of faith and loyalty as it fights against the will of self-interest.

To *look up* in true worship as in verses 1-4, carries a meaning far greater than its words convey. Looking up is to be not only thoughtful, but also glad, joyous and inspired by all that God has created. The unfortunate soul who is blind to the wonderment of God (6) is a senseless fool with no understanding. In further description, verse 7 introduces the gloom and doom of the wicked and the eternal victory of God. In verse 9 we see the words *"be scattered"* which refers to those who do not see the ways of God. Evil, by its own basic nature, will disintegrate everything around it. Evil carries too many weaknesses to survive and eventually it will self-destruct.

The singer takes delight in the Lord's exploits as seen in the narratives of verses 10 through 15. If God is on high forever (8), He will give a new anointing and dedication to serve Him (10) and He will strengthen my horn. *Horn* is used here is a symbol of strength and power, a power that is greater than that of man alone, but the power of God infused into man. God's enemies are doomed (9); then man's enemies are doomed as well (11).

In the final verse the psalm has come full circle- the beginning with a call for man to praise God by the words of his lips. The beginning calls for man to bring glory to God by his actions, the ending is a call to glorify God by the way a man thinks and acts.

Note: In the Old Testament, the fool is one who is well known as a decadent sinner. It has nothing to do with one's capabilities or abilities, but rather the choices one makes.

PSALM 93

¹The LORD reigneth, he is clothed with majesty; the
LORD is clothed with strength, [wherewith] he hath
girded himself: the world also is established,
that it cannot be moved.
²Thy throne [is] established of old:
thou [art] from everlasting.

³The floods have lifted up, O LORD, the floods have lifted up their voice; the floods lift up their waves.
⁴The LORD on high [is] mightier than
the noise of many waters,
[yea, than] the mighty waves of the sea.
⁵Thy testimonies are very sure: holiness becometh thine house, O LORD, for ever.

PSALM 93
Title: Second Psalm of God
Author: anonymous
Date: Post-exilic
Superscription: Five Attributes of God
Theme: The Lord's Eternal Reign

During this time, the power of the Israelite God was frequently held in contrast to the claims of all other gods. God is the great King above all men and above creation itself. The central thought in this poem is that after all things have been washed away by floods of adversity, the Lord steadfastly remains. The psalmist states that the Lord's Kingship has been forever; it is not a new thing. God is the one who shares the permanence and perfection of His rule with mankind.

He is mightier than the sound of crashing waters. Raging storms and crushing waves cannot cause His everlasting throne to tremble. These statements refer to God's ultimate power in nature, His power also extends over those who are Israel's enemies. Regardless of what circumstances befall a man, God has established His world and what He has put in place will never move.

God reigns: He is clothed with majesty and strength, He hath girded Himself (prepared for battle), He has established His throne and it cannot and will not be moved. God is mighty and speaks only truth. He is the essence of holiness.

PSALM 94

¹O LORD God, to whom then just belongeth; O God, to whom vengeance belongeth; show thyself.
²Lift up thyself, thou judge of the earth:
render a reward to the proud.
³LORD, how long shall the wicked,
how long shall the wicked triumph?
⁴ [How long] shall they utter [and] speak hard things? [and] all the workers of
iniquity boast themselves?
⁵They break in pieces thy people, O LORD,
and afflict thine heritage.
⁶They slay the widow and the stranger,
and murder the fatherless.
⁷Yet they say, The LORD shall not see,
neither shall the God of Jacob regard [it].
⁸Understand, ye prudish among the people:
and [ye] fools, when will ye be wise?
⁹He that planted the ear, shall he not hear?
He that formed the eye, shall he not see?
¹⁰He that chastiseth the heathen, shall not he correct? He that teaches man knowledge,
[shall not he know]?

¹¹The LORD knoweth the thoughts of man,
that they [are] vanity.
¹²Blessed [is] the man whom thou chastenest,
O LORD, and teachest him out of thy law;
¹³That thou mayest give him rest from the days of
adversity, until the pit be digged for the wicked.
¹⁴For the LORD will not cast off his people, neither
will he forsake his inheritance.
¹⁵But judgment shall return unto righteousness: and
all the upright in heart shall follow it.
¹⁶Who will rise up for me against the evildoers?
[or] who will stand up for me against
the workers of iniquity?
¹⁷Unless the LORD [had been] my help,
my soul had almost dwelt in silence.
¹⁸When I said, My foot slippeth;
thy mercy O LORD, held me up.
¹⁹In the multitude of my thoughts within me thy
comforts delight my soul.
²⁰Shall the throne of iniquity have fellowship with
thee, which frameth mischief by a law?
²¹They gather themselves together against the soul
of the righteous, and condemn the innocent blood.
²²But the LORD is my defense;
and my God [is] the rock of my refuge.
²³And he shall bring upon them their own iniquity,
and shall cut them off in their own wickedness;
[yea], the LORD our God shall cut them off.

PSALM 94
Title: Tenth Prayer for Judgment
Author: anonymous
Superscription: none
Theme: The Refuge of Righteousness

This psalm carries a tone of urgency, yet lying beneath the urgency is a spirit which is content in and confident in God. Similar to the Book of Proverbs and Psalm 37 it is certain that the writer is one who knows of God's faithfulness first hand. Although embracing the community, there is an obvious personal element. Some commentators consider this psalm to be a composite, but there is little justification for this. While positioned between two much more joyous poems, the focus here is the injustices that have prevailed in Israel. The psalmist asks God to take vengeance upon earthly judges who oppress the weak and needy simply because they have the power to do so.

In the appeal to the judge of the earth, the writer knows that God uses His own criteria to bring justice. The logic used in this psalm is inescapable if one accepts the fact that God is the Supreme Creator. The bigger question here is not whether God can avenge wrongs done, but how long it will be before He brings about His justice. Either way, justice delayed is not justice denied.

In verses 4-7, the characteristics of the "unrighteous judges" are exposed. They *speak* insolent things; they *work* iniquity; they *slay* the widow;

murder the fatherless and worst of all, they have *convinced* themselves that "the God of Jacob" neither sees nor understands the evilness of their ways. They have no idea that the Lord God sees everything and their misdeeds will come with a great penalty.

Verses 12-15 would be well at home with in the Book of Proverbs as they stress the role of character building in the school of wisdom. The words are a triumph of faith, a positive reaction to the present trouble (1-7) and a personal acknowledgement of a general truth, which applies to both nations (10) and to man. The use of the word *rest* represents an inward quietness in the face of trouble. The wicked dig their pit deeper day by day through lies and evil deeds. They have earned their punishment. God does not waver, for one only goes back on a pledge out of insincerity or inability, neither which apply to God.

As the psalm reaches its close, the psalmist addresses his personal concerns. Here the mood is both somber and thankful. His life has not always been easy, but he has learned to cling to God in all situations. He knows that God will stand up against iniquity (16); He is the lifter of those who slip in life (18) and a delight to the soul (19). It is only through his personal experiences that he can understand these things of God. The end of the psalm is calmness in the knowledge that God will protect the righteous and that God is greater than anything the enemy can send.

PSALMS 90-106 Referred to as the Numbers Psalms

PSALM 95

¹O come, let us sing unto the LORD: let us make a joyful noise to the rock of our salvation.
²Let us come before his presence with thanksgiving, and make a joyful noise unto him with psalms.
³For the LORD [is] a great God,
and a great King, above all gods.
⁴In his hand [are] the deep places of the earth:
the strength of the hills [is] his also.
⁵The sea, [is] his, and he made it:
and his hands formed the dry [land].
⁶O come, let us worship and bow down:
let us kneel before the LORD, our maker.
⁷For he [is] our God; and we [are] the people of his pasture, and the sheep of his hand.
Today if ye hear his voice,
⁸Harden not your heart, as in the provocation, [and] as [in] the day of temptation in the wilderness:
⁹When your fathers tempted me,
proved me, and saw my work.
¹⁰Forty years long I was grieved with [this] generation, and said, It [is] a people that do err in their heart, and they have not known my ways:
¹¹Unto whom I sware in my wrath that they should not enter into my rest.

PSALM 95
Title: Fifth Psalm of Praise
Author: a Psalm of David
Date: post-exilic-second temple
Superscription: none
Theme: Worship of and Obedience to God

Almost a continuation of Psalm 93, these theocratic passages relate to the sovereignty of God, with vague hints of the coming Messiah. A change in tone occurs in the latter half of the psalm, which some commentators believe indicates that this is made up of fragments of two or more unrelated psalms. The psalm begins as the Levites call the people to worship at the Feast of Tabernacles.

In the call to worship, which the Levite priests speak, is a reminder that Israel's security begins with their praise, prayers and obedience to Yahweh. As the summons rings through the land, the procession begins. Worshipers begin to praise as the march toward the Temple starts. The worship and joy spoken of here are not merely for the sake of tradition, but for a reason larger than all creation. The *greater reason* for their joy is realized in Paul's Epistles as he describes heaven and earth. All things are created by God and for the Son of God to whom every knee must bow.

Verses 6-7 repeat the Levite's call to worship. The singing gives way to the more solemn acts of worship, such as bowing down and kneeling before God. The emphasis on God's sovereignty serves to remind the worshipers of His special relationship to Israel. The worshipers are reminded not to *harden their hearts,* as did their ancestors in the wilderness, lest they be tempted and fall into rebellion. God's rest historically refers to Israel's claim to enter the Promised Land. Yet this rest would never be available to those who doubted the power of God. The worshipers were admonished to keep their hearts gentle and to accept the laws and decrees of the Lord God.

Although this psalm comes to us from Israel, it would be a waste to confine it to Israel alone. Hebrews 4:1-13 agrees that this psalm still offers us an unimaginable rest, peace and contentment beyond anything one could imagine. Man has a share in God's own Sabbath rest-to enjoy the pleasure of a task come to completion. While God's first task was creation, He has given humanity a task as well. The quitters will turn back and in doing so, are turning their backs on the great inheritance of God.

The psalm closes with the reminder that if willing, man's heart and will can blend with the heart and will of God. Only in this way can each man make his personal pilgrimage. A man may choose to refuse or deny God, but God will never deny His children. Nothing can separate a man from His love-not time, not death and thankfully not rebellion. We belong to Christ and He is of God (1 Corinthians 3:22-23), making the bond eternal. The New Testament expounds upon what the psalm implies: praise God because He is above all; there is no corner of the earth that is not within His hands.

PSALM 96

^{1}O sing unto the LORD a new song:
sing unto the LORD, all the earth.
^{2}Sing unto the LORD, bless his name;
show forth his salvation from day to day.
^{3}Declare his glory among the heathen,
his wonders among all people.
^{4}For the LORD [is] great, and greatly to be praised:
he [is] to be feared above all gods.
^{5}For all the gods of the nations [are] idols:
but the LORD made the heavens.
^{6}Honor and majesty [are] before him:
strength and beauty [are] in his sanctuary.
^{7}Give unto the LORD, O ye kindreds of the people,
give unto the LORD glory and strength.
^{8}Give unto the LORD the glory [due unto] his name:
bring an offering, and come into his courts.
^{9}O worship the LORD in the beauty of holiness: fear
before him, all the earth.
^{10}Say among the heathen [that] the LORD reigneth:
the world also shall be established that it shall not
be moved: he shall judge the people righteously.
^{11}Let the heavens rejoice, and let the earth be glad;
let the sea roar, and the fullness thereof.
^{12}Let the field be joyful, and all that [is] therein: then
shall all the trees of the wood rejoice
^{13}Before the LORD: for he cometh, for he cometh
to judge the earth: he shall judge the world with
righteousness, and the people with his truth.

PSALM 96
Title: Sixth Psalm of Praise
Author: anonymous
Date: Post-exilic
Superscription: none
Theme: God Coming in Judgment

Psalm 96 sees those exiled in Babylon returning to their homeland. The Septuagint (the Greek translation) states that this occasion was the rebuilding of the Temple after captivity. The psalm included the praise which King David offered when he brought the Ark of the Covenant back to Jerusalem (1 Chronicles 16:23-37). This psalm joins with parts of Psalms 105 and 106, celebrating the greatness of God.

The psalm opens with the familiar words, "O sing to the Lord a new song! Sing to the Lord, all the earth. Sing to the Lord, bless His name; proclaim the good news of His salvation from day to day."

This opening verse sets the tone for the psalm, encouraging the people to greet each day with a new outburst of praise. The *new song* is not merely a composition (33:3), but a fresh way to worship in accordance with His mercy, which is new every day. The people are encouraged to bring offerings and enter His sacred presence to worship and to praise God simply because He is God.

Perhaps more than in any other psalm, one can see the methods of praise as well the reasons for this praise.

How to Praise	Reasons to Praise
Sing to the lord	He is great
Bless His name	He is to be feared
Proclaim the good news	He made the heavens
Declare His glory	He has beauty and strength
Fear Him	He reigns above all
Give glory to the Lord	He established the world
Bring an offering	He judges righteously
Tremble before Him	All things are His

The cry "the Lord reigns" is the same message heard in Psalm 93:1 and Isaiah 52:7. This vibrant response points to a belief in God's sovereignty and not merely a theological truth.

God is welcomed into the midst of His people. This welcome has its Christian counterpart on Palm Sunday where Jesus reminds the people that if they did not praise Him, the very rocks would sing His glory. It implies that the most humble people, regardless of how flawed they may be, are welcome to come before God with a *new song*. This psalm shows the effect of God's presence, even upon those who, through a glass darkly, already see His face.

PSALM 97

¹The LORD reigneth; let the earth rejoice; let the multitude of isles be glad [there of].
²Clouds and darkness [are] round about him: righteousness and judgment [are] the habitation of his throne.
³A fire goeth before him, and burneth up his enemies round about.
⁴His lightnings enlightened the world: the earth saw, and trembled.
⁵The hills melted like wax at the presence of the LORD, at the presence of the Lord of the whole earth.
⁶The heavens declare his righteousness, and all the people see his glory.
⁷Confounded be all they that serve graven images, that boast themselves of idols: worship him, all [ye] gods.
⁸Zion heard, and was glad; and the daughters of Judah rejoiced because of thy judgments, O LORD.
⁹For thou, LORD, [art] high above all the earth: thou art exalted far above all gods.
¹⁰Ye that love the LORD, hate evil: he preserveth the souls of the saints; he delivereth them out of the hand of the wicked.
¹¹Light is sown for the righteous, and gladness for the upright in heart.
¹²Rejoice in the LORD, ye righteous; and give thanks at the remembrance of his holiness.

PSALM 97
Title: Seventh Psalm of Praise
Author: anonymous
Superscription: none
Theme: Praise for God's Sovereignty

Among the many psalms of praise, this one carries a unique difference in that it does not praise God for deliverance, forgiveness or victory in battle. This song simply praises God for Who He is in relationship to the world in general and to the Israelites specifically. The psalm is broken into two major divisions, the first of which begin with 42 Hebrew words, praising God and His creation of earth and mankind. The second portion contains 43 Hebrew words and refers to the sovereignty of God as He cares for Israel. The hymn appears has a close relationship to the preceding psalm.

The theme is that Yahweh is King. Those who receive benefit under His kingship are destined to rejoice in His endless glory. His worshipers will always remain in His care. Majesty has characterized His coming and His creation testifies to His power. The worshipers of idols in the end are put to shame. With this thought in mind, it follows that Israel has a specific duty to God. Those who love the King and await His return must spend their time loving the Lord, hating evil, rejoicing and giving thanks.

In verse 2, the reference to *dark storm clouds* is a visual reminder of tremendous brightness of God's glory. It was for this reason that the *holy of holies* was separate from the main temple, leaving it in solitude. The Hebrew Temple was God's throne on earth. It is from there that His rule and justice extend outward across the nations. Founded upon His righteousness the heavens proclaim that it will be a day of rejoicing and a day of triumph for God's people when He returns to judge the world.

There is a blending of delight and dismay here as the Old Testament makes allusions to the coming of Christ. The tribes of the earth are those who worship false gods, idols, or nothing at all. They will be in anguish and mourning when the Lord returns for His people as in Matthew 24:30 and Revelation 1:7. Believers, however, look forward to this day with great anticipation and joy. Yahweh reigns supreme over the created world, the angels and mankind. There is nothing that exists which is beyond His supremacy.

The psalm ends on a joyous note: ". . .Give thanks at the remembrance of His holy name." We are not to wait anxiously or excitedly for the "new morning of the Lord", but rather to look at the final victory, as if already completed.

Note: verse 97:10 the Hebrew word "ahab" is very similar to the English word "love" in that it covers a variety of feelings. It can refer to romantic love, love for God, love for children and so forth. A second word, "oheb", refers specifically to a friend or lover. This describes man's love for the Lord. An example of this love is in Genesis 22:2, when Abraham speaks of his love for Isaac.

PSALM 98

¹A Psalm. O sing unto the LORD a new song; for he hath done marvelous things: his right hand, and his holy arm, has gotten him the victory.
²The LORD hath made known his salvation: his righteousness hath he openly showed in the sight of the heathen.
³He hath remembered his mercy and his truth toward the house of Israel: all the ends of the earth have seen the salvation of our God.
⁴Make a joyful noise unto the LORD, all the earth: make a loud noise, and rejoice, and sing praise.
⁵Sing unto the LORD with the harp; with the harp, and the voice of the psalm.
⁶With trumpets and sound of cornet make a joyful noise before the LORD, the King.
⁷Let the sea roar, and the fullness thereof; the world, and they that dwell therein.
⁸Let the floods clap [their] hands: let the hills be joyful together.
⁹Before the LORD; for he cometh to judge the earth: with righteousness shall he judge the world, and the people with equity.

PSALM 98
Title: The Eighth Psalm of Praise
Author: anonymous
Superscription: a Meditation
Theme: Praise to the Lord for His Salvation

Psalm 98 begins the same as Psalm 96: "Sing unto the Lord a new song!" This psalm is also in the Book of Common Prayer between the Old Testament readings and their fulfillment in the New Testament. Psalm 98 is often called the Cantate Domino. Here there are no instructions of worship, no mention of evil, only praise and joy. This psalm celebrates God's restoration of the Israelites to their homeland. Beginning in Israel, the three stanzas gradually extend to a worldwide call to praise.

This *new song,* although drawn from previous sources, speaks of a recent event. The God of Israel has done tremendous things. He has brought deliverance, given salvation and forgiven their misdeeds. The entire earth has seen God's great acts on behalf of His people; all nations should join in praising Him. This is a call for universal participation in keeping with the broad outlook of Isaiah 40:8-11.

The *joyful noise* of verses 4 and 6 are a spontaneous and exuberant shout that comes when there is victory. Such an outburst of praise is too great to be contained. All victories are complete and total-victories given to them by the Lord. The supernatural aspect is in the words *"marvelous things"*—more than a superlative, but the type of the interventions of God, such as in Exodus when Moses encountered Pharoah. The New Testament will later give a razor-sharp definition of the Savior, His salvation and His final victory as described in Revelation 19:11.

There are two primary streams of thought woven into this psalm. The first thought is the great and glorious power, seen when He comes to earth. The second thought is that even though man is able to hear the *song of heaven* through the voice of nature, it is only a prelude to the sounds of the heavenly choir. The entire earth belongs to Him and He has filled it with His glory. It makes the point upon which Romans 8:18 expounds: that nature will not come into its own until man is its proper master, ruling the earth in righteousness. This is the truth which modern man is slowly learning, primarily by default and with increasing alarm.

PSALM 99

¹The LORD reigneth; let the people tremble: he
sitteth [between] the cherubims;
let the earth be moved.
²The Lord [is] great in Zion;
and he [is] high above the people.
³Let them praise thy great and terrible name;
[for] it [is] holy.
⁴The king's strength also lovest judgment;
thou dost establish equity, thou executest judgment,
and righteousness in Jacob.

⁵Exalt ye the LORD our God, and worship at his footstool; [for] he [is] holy.
⁶Moses and Aaron among his priests, and Samuel among them that call upon his name; they called upon the LORD, and he answered them.
⁷He spake unto them in the cloudy pillar: they His testimonies, and the ordinance [that] he gave them.
⁸Thou answeredest them, O LORD our God: thou wast a God that forgavest them, though thou tookest vengeance of their inventions.
⁹Exalt the LORD our God, and worship at his holy hill; for the LORD our God [is] holy.

PSALM 99
Title: Ninth Psalm of Praise
Author: anonymous
Superscription: none
Theme: Three Admonitions to Praise the Lord

This psalm opens with a picture of God sitting upon the mercy seat between the cherubim. Here, after the lighthearted delight of Psalm 98, comes the solemn reminder of the reverence that man owes to God. This psalm begins on a positive note with strengthening examples of prayers heard and answered. Verse 8 is a reminder that all men, in spite of their efforts, are limited by the frailty of humanity.

The mood alternates between highly festive and chastened-for God is all that stirs and brings shame to man. Moses and Aaron are mentioned here as examples of man's weaknesses. Tragic lapses in walking with God are forgiven, but, as in Numbers 20:12, they cannot be undone. There is a clear distinction between the healing of relationships and the consequences of one's actions. Not only is God sovereign in His rule, but He is righteous in His judgment of humanity. A man must remember that there will be consequences of sin, lest a man forget how he offends God when he harms mankind. He does not wield His power in an arbitrary way, but according to His Holiness.

While this kingly portrait is true, it is primarily a proclamation of God's final advent. His grandeur is not the totality of His personality. Yes, He is great and terrible, but above all, He is righteous and a fair and impartial judge. Thus, the negative will always strengthen the positive. The psalm ends on a note of intimacy: "Exalt the Lord our God and worship at His holy hill; for the Lord Our God is holy." He *is* holy, yet He not ashamed to be called Israel's God.

Note: Worship or "shachah" in Hebrew literally means to bow, to stoop; to bow down as an act of submission or reverence; to fall down when paying homage to God. In this psalm it is used in contrast to exultation: exalt the Lord, lift Him up high and worship; thou yourselves be low before Him at the place of His feet.

Cherubim are not the chubby smiling creatures of religious art, but mighty beings whose forms summed up the whole kingdom of earthly creatures. This is the place where God spoke to Moses and the high priest (Exodus 25:18-22).

PSALM 100

¹A Psalm of praise. Make a joyful
noise unto the LORD, all ye lands.
²Serve the LORD with gladness:
come before his presence with singing.
³Know ye that the LORD, he [is] God: [it is] he [that]
hath made us, and not we ourselves; [we are] his
people, and the sheep of his pastor.
⁴Enter into his gates with thanksgiving,
[and] into his courts with praise:
be thankful unto him, [and] bless his name.
⁵For the LORD [is] good; his mercy [is] everlasting;
and his truth [endureth] to all generations.

PSALM 100
Title: Tenth Psalm of Praise
Author: anonymous
Superscription: none
Theme: Praise for the Lord's Faithfulness to Israel

This psalm was written and used as a hymn to usher the Israelites into the Temple. Known as the *Jubilate,* this psalm begins with two calls to worship. Verse 1 instructs the worshipers to "make a joyful shout to the Lord" followed by the "come before His presence" found in verse 2. The first call to worship was sung by the choir outside the Temple courts and the second came from inside the Temple as an invitation to come and worship. Within the Temple courts, His praise is to be sung for the reasons listed in verse

5: "for the Lord is good; His mercy is everlasting, and His truth endureth to all generations."

The *joyful noise* is not a special contribution of the tone deaf, but similar to the homage one would pay to a Royal King as in 98:6. This thought-provoking song claims the entire world for God and sets forth the key to entering God's presence by means of heartfelt praise, which includes singing, thanksgiving and devoted worship. The servants are responsible for doing the bidding of God and the King. A previous hint to this type of *king* is in Isaiah, where a veiled reference is made to Jesus as a powerful Master. God, the King, cares about the complete lives of His people, thus barging arrogantly into His court is well beyond being inappropriate.

Entering God's presence in worship is an act of service. The greater extent of worship will be shown in Romans 12:10-21, where a living sacrifice of a person's life is considered as *appropriate* worship. Both prayer and praise will go stale when practiced only in private. Worshipping with gladness and singing out praise implies the singing of *many* voices as seen in Isaiah 40. The prerequisite of praise is to know Him and to realize the firmness of the ground He has provided for man to stand upon. God is revealed by His holy name and gives insight to His character by *degrees*. By answering the call to praise, a man comes into communion with God.

Note: "Jubilate" is the Hebrew word for joyful.

PSALM 101

ᴷ¹A Psalm of David. I will sing of mercy and judgment: unto thee, O LORD, will I sing.
²I will behave myself wisely in a perfect way. O when wilt thou come unto me? I will walk within my house with a perfect heart.
³I will set no wicked thing before mine eyes: I hate the work of them that turn aside; [it] shall not cleave to me.
⁴A froward heart shall depart from me: I will not know a wicked [person].
⁵Whoso privily slandereth his neighbor, him will I cut off: him that hath an high look and a proud heart will not I suffer.
⁶Mine eyes [shall be] upon the faithful of the land, that they may dwell with me: he that walketh in a perfect way, he shall serve me.
⁷He that work is deceit shall not dwell with in my house: he that tell it lies shall not tarry in my site.
⁸I will early destroy all the wicked of the land; that I may cut off all wicked doers from the city of the LORD.

PSALM 101
Title: Sixth Psalm of the Righteous
Author: a Psalm of David
Superscription: none
Theme: Faithfulness to the Lord

This is a firm statement of how King David intends to rule his kingdom. The King speaks directly to God, although the general congregation is encouraged to listen. No specific king is actually named in the psalm, but the expressions and determination seem to refer to David. He pledges to remove sin from all public and private lives, not only from his presence, but also from the presence of God. Verse 5 refers to his official intentions. He will deny favor to the proud, to the deceitful and to the liars. He will accept no interaction with evil men or any who practice iniquity or refuse to acknowledge Yahweh as King. This declaration does not spring from pride, but rather from his commitment that his kingdom will be pleasing to God. He had no way of knowing how far short he would fall in his own actions.

The success of the kingdom will depend upon the choice of its officials. It is important here to look beyond the words with the anticipation of the Messiah and His eternal Kingdom. Loyalty and justice concern the King greatly, as loyalty will draw attention to the Covenant to which both the King and his people are bound. The loyalty to God is vertical; the loyalty between men is horizontal. Even in David's kingdom, the need was for the affirmation of values, not selfish desires. Swerving from the right course as in (2 Timothy 2:18) and yielding to the will of another against the knowledge of truth is a sin. A man must persevere and stand against the twisted mind and will, which hate the truth and the straight path. He cannot afford to be selfish or prideful, but must lead his kingdom with a spiritual attitude.

Note: Happily, however, the last word is not with David, nor with his subjects, but with Jesus. Standing in the light of Jesus, there will be no shadow.

PSALM 102

¹A Prayer of the afflicted, when he is overwhelmed,
and poureth out his complaint before the LORD.
Hear my prayer, O LORD,
and let my cry come unto thee.
²Hide not thy face from me in the day [when] I am in
trouble; incline thine ear unto me: in the day
[when] I call answer me speedily.
³For my days are consumed like smoke,
and my bones are burned as an hearth.
⁴My heart is smitten, and withered like grass;
so that I forget to eat my bread.
⁵By reason of the voice of my groaning
my bones cleave to my skin.
⁶I am like a pelican of the wilderness;
I am like an owl of the desert.
⁷I watch and am as a sparrow alone upon
the house top.

⁸Mine enemies reproach me all the day; [and] they
that are mad against me are sworn against me.
⁹For I have eaten ashes like bread,
and mingled my drink with weeping.
¹⁰Because of thine indignation and thy wrath: for
thou hast lifted me up, and cast me down.
¹¹My days [are] like a shadow that declineth;
and I am withered like grass.
¹²But thou, O LORD, shall endure for ever;
and thy remembrance unto all generations.
¹³Thou shalt arise, [and] have mercy upon Zion: for
the time to favor her, yea, the set time, is come.
¹⁴For thy servants take pleasure in her stones,
and favor the dust thereof.
¹⁵So the heathen shall fear the name of the LORD,
and all the kings of the earth thy glory.
¹⁶When the LORD shall build up Zion,
he shall appear in his glory.
¹⁷He will regard the prayer of the destitute,
and not despise their prayer.
¹⁸This shall be written for the generation to come:
and the people which shall be
created shall praise the LORD.
¹⁹For he hath looked down from the height of his
sanctuary; from heaven did the LORD,
behold the earth;
²⁰To hear the groaning of the prisoner; to loose
those that are appointed to death;
²¹To declare the name of the LORD in Zion,
and his praise in Jerusalem;

²²When the people are gathered together, and the kingdoms, to serve the LORD.
²³He weakened my strength in the way;
he shortened my days.
²⁴I said, O my God, take me not away in the midst of my days: thy years [are] throughout all generations.
²⁵Of old hast thou laid the foundation of the earth: and the heavens [are] the work of thy hands.
²⁶They shall perish, but thou shalt endure: yea, all of them shall wax old like a garment;
as a vesture shalt thou change them,
and they shall be changed:
²⁷But thou [art] the same,
and thy years shall have no end.
²⁸The children of thy servants shall continue, and their seed shall be established before thee.

PSALM 102
Title: Seventeenth Messianic Psalm
Author: anonymous
Date: Probably during the Babylonian exile
Superscription: a Prayer of the Afflicted
Theme: The Lord's Endless Love

The title of this psalm identifies the type of life situation in which this prayer is used. Israel has had many times of affliction, yet no circumstance or date is known although it is obviously exilic. The descriptions used here suggest a personal affliction, caused by an international disaster, such as the exile, which binds the King to the nation. This prayer was originally composed for a Davidic King or one who was a member of the Royal House during the Babylonian exile. The lament bears a corporate element, although several phrases use the terms "*I*" and "*we*", as found in Psalm 90. Verses 1-11 and 23-24 are definitely corporate, but the center of the psalm is a distinct personal appeal.

While in the form of a penitential psalm, this is the cry of one who, like Job, bears suffering beyond explanation. Nearing the end of his endurance, the psalmist finds words that lead into a larger place than his own life. Personal traumas and troubles fade and they are gradually replaced by a concern for society whose destiny is glorious, yet painfully slow in coming to fulfillment. A sense of urgency is in the cry, "Hear my prayer O Lord." Both he and the nation are suffering and he believes that the suffering is a sign of God's wrath against them.

The transition in verse 11 suggests that the psalmist has turned his face toward the well-being of the nation. The solutions of the speaker's personal problems are intimately linked to the well-being of his nation. He begins to realize that God looks beyond the battle and is more concerned with final victory. Man's urgency is insistent, while God's measured pace is immovable. Yet both agree that the fullness of time is quickly approaching.

As the psalm gazes toward the distant future when this deliverance will be a current event. Revelation 15:3 calls it the *Song of the Lamb.* Verse 24 recites again the contrast between man's frailty and God's eternity as spoken in verses 1-11. The human timescale blends artfully with the Lord's eternity, closing the psalm with a majestic conclusion that is later quoted in praise of Jesus. Suffering brings hope, the hope seen in Psalm 22 and in the salvation of Christ.

PSALM 103

¹[A Psalm] of David. Bless the LORD, O my soul: and
all that is with in me, [bless] his holy name.
²Bless the LORD, O my soul,
and forget not all his benefits:
³Who forgiveth all thine iniquities;
who healeth all thy diseases;
⁴Who redeemeth thy life from destruction;
who crowneth thee with lovingkindness
and tender mercies;
⁵Who satisfieth thy mouth with good [things;
so that] thy youth is renewed like the eagle's.
⁶The LORD executeth righteousness and judgment
for all that are oppressed.
⁷He made known his ways unto Moses,
his acts unto the children of Israel.
⁸The LORD [is] merciful and gracious,
slow to anger, and plenteous in mercy.
⁹He will not always chide: neither will he keep
[his anger] for ever.
¹⁰He hath not dealt with us after our sins; nor
rewarded us according to our iniquities.
¹¹For as heaven is high above the earth, [so] great is
his mercy toward them that fear him.

¹²As far as the east is from the west, [so] far hath he removed our transgressions from us.
¹³Like as a father pitieth [is] children, [so] the LORD pitieth them that fear him.
¹⁴For he knowest our frame; he remembereth that we [are] dust.
¹⁵[As for] man, his days [are] as grass: as a flower of the field, so he flourisheth.
¹⁶For the wind passeth over it, and it is gone; and the place thereof shall know it no more.
¹⁷But the mercy of the LORD [is] from everlasting to everlasting upon them that fear him, and his righteousness unto children's children;
¹⁸To such as keep his covenant, and to those that remember his commandments to do them.
¹⁹The LORD hath prepared his throne in the heavens; and his kingdom ruleth over all.
²⁰Bless the LORD, ye his angels, that excel in strength, that do his commandments, hearkening unto the voice of his word.
²¹Bless ye the LORD, all [ye] hosts; [ye] ministers of his, that do his pleasure.
²²Bless ye the LORD, all his works in all places of his dominion: bless the LORD, O my soul.

PSALM 103
Title: The Eleventh Psalm of Praise
Author: a Psalm of David
Superscription: none
Theme: Praise God's Mercy

This hymn of praise is without peer in all of scripture. It appears to be the voice of an individual, although a corporate voice seems to break through in places. Psalm 104 gives praise to God, the Savior and creator, Father and sustainer, the One who is mighty and merciful. Echoes of this psalm appear in both Isaiah and Jeremiah, giving a vague hint to its timeline. Humbly, the psalmist gives thanks to God, not just for His goodness, but also for His unchangeable love and mercy. He glorifies God for what He has done and for what he believes that God will do in the future. The recital of thanksgiving falls into two unequal parts: one part celebrates God's glory as shown to individuals, the second, what God has done for His people, Israel.

"Bless the Lord, O my soul" is more than exultation. The word which is translated as soul and the parallel expression of "all that is within me", signifies that he is praising with his entire being. As he counts his many blessings, the Great Exodus is a wonderful record of the journey of man. Grace abounds and Israel is forgiven for its many failures. The psalmist uses many illustrations to convey a picture of God's loving-kindness. He does not know how far it is from earth to heaven, but he knows that even that vastness could not contain all of God's love and mercy. The most beautiful and intimate illustration is that of God as the Father who has compassion upon a man in his weaknesses, his frailty and his failures.

The Old Testament promise of bodily healing is based solely upon the character of Yahweh. It is clear that the dimension of healing promised here is *specifically* to include physical wholeness. The Hebrew word *tachawloo* means "disease" and comes from the same root word *chawlah* the word for disease found in Exodus 15:26. Several books of the Old Testament state that "healing" is both physical and spiritual; that God will heal both infirmities as well as iniquities. In the New Testament there can be found many instances where Jesus healed a "sinner" and in doing so forgave his sins and cured his well as the physical ailments.

Almost as a sidebar, the fivefold ministry of God's angels is in Verses 20-21. Angels exist solely to serve God. Their service includes: blessing the Lord in worship, doing His will on earth, listening to the voice of God's word, to minister on God's behalf as described in Hebrews 1:14 and finally to please God, as all things are at His direction.

The word *"redeemed"* may mean rescue from an earthly death, but more likely, it refers to a questions of man's *ransom* from death, that he should live forever. This concept is explored elsewhere (Psalm 49:7-9, 13-15) and suggests that verse 4 should be taken in its full meaning-a resurrection to eternal life. Conscious or not, the use of these phrases speak to eternal life, paving the way for the atoning work of Jesus. David's song is not a solo-all of creation is singing or will at some point in the future sing with him.

PSALM 104

¹Blessed the LORD, O my soul.
O LORD my God, thou art very is great; thou art clothed with honor and majesty.
²Who coverest [thyself] with light as [with] a garment: who stretches out the heavens like a curtain:
³Who layeth the beams of his chambers in the waters: who maketh the clouds his chariot: who walketh upon the wings of the wind:
⁴Who maketh his angels spirits;
his ministers a flaming fire:
⁵[Who] laid the foundations of the earth, [that] it should not be removed for ever.
⁶Thou coveredst it with the deep as [with] a garment: the waters stood above the mountains.
⁷At thy rebuke, they fled;
at the voice of thy thunder they hasted away.
⁸They go up by the mountains; they go down by the valleys unto the place which thou hast founded for them.
⁹Thou hast set a bound that they may not pass over; that they turn not again to cover the earth.
¹⁰He sendeth the springs into the valleys, [which] run among the hills.
¹¹They give drink to every beast of the field: the wild asses quench their thirst.

¹²By them shall the fowls of the heaven have their habitation, [which] sing among the branches.
¹³He watereth the hills from his chambers: the earth is satisfied with the fruit of thy works.
¹⁴He causeth the grass to grow for the cattle, and herb for the service of man: that he may bring forth food out of the earth;
¹⁵And wine [that] maketh glad the heart of man, [and] oil to make [his] face to shine, and bread [which] strengtheneth man's heart.
¹⁶The trees of the LORD are full [of]; the cedars of Lebanon, which he hath planted;
¹⁷Where the birds make their nests: [as for] the stork, the fir trees [are] her house.
¹⁸The high hills [are] a refuge for the wild goats; [and] the rocks for the conies.
¹⁹He appointed the moon for seasons: the sun knoweth his going down.
²⁰Thou makest darkness, and it is night: wherein all the beasts of the forest do creep [forth].
²¹The young lions roar after their prey, and seek their meat from God.
²²The sun ariseth, they gather themselves together, and lay them down in their dens.
²³Man goeth forth unto his work and to his labor until the evening.
²⁴O LORD, how manifold are thy works! in wisdom hast thou made them all: the earth is full of thy riches.
²⁵[So is] this great and wide sea, wherein [are] things creeping innumerable, both small and great beasts.

²⁶There go the ships: [there is] that Leviathan, [whom] thou hast made to play therein.
²⁷These wait all upon thee; that thou mayest give [them] their meat in due season.
²⁸[That] Thou givest them they gather: thou openest thine hand, they are filled with good.
²⁹Thou hidest thy face, they are troubled: thou takest away their breath, they die, and return to their dust.
³⁰Thou sendest forth thy spirit, they are created: and thou renewest the face of the earth.
³¹The glory of the LORD shall endure for ever: the LORD shall rejoice in his works.
³²He looketh on the earth, and it trembleth: he toucheth the hills, and they smoke.
³³I will sing unto the LORD as long as I live: I will sing praise to my God while I have my being.
³⁴My meditation of him shall be sweet: I will be glad in the LORD.
³⁵Let the sinners be consumed out of the earth, and let the wicked be no more. Bless thou the LORD, O my soul. Praise ye the LORD.

PSALM 104
Title: Twelfth Psalm of Praise
Author: anonymous
Date: Probably before the Babylonian Exile
Superscription: none
Theme: Praise to the Creator

This psalm names no author, yet continues to take praise beyond the blessings of what God has done for Israel onward to praise for all created things. Along with the bounty of praise, there are also parallels to Persian, Babylonian and Egyptian thought. The pre-exilic author has *adapted* Genesis 1 to his own unique purpose and has altered the sequence to support his own design. The poet here views the created world, taking the liberty of using each stage of creation as a starting point for praise. As each theme evolves, it tends to anticipate the later scenes of the creation drama. The *days* described in Genesis may overlap and mingle within this psalm, but the mutual support of Genesis to the Psalms is undeniably present.

Day one: Genesis 1:3-5-the light as seen in Psalm 104:2.

Day two: Genesis 1:6-8-the firmament and the division of the waters; Psalm 104:2-4

Day three: Genesis 1:9-10-the waters and land become distinct; Psalm 104:5-9

PSALMS 90-106 Referred to as the Numbers Psalms

Also Day three: Genesis 1:11-13-creation of vegetation and trees; Psalm 104:14-17

Day four: Genesis 1:14-19-the luminaries created as timekeepers; Psalm 104:19-23

Day five: Genesis 1:20-23-the creatures of the sea and the air; Psalm 104:25-26

Day six: Genesis 1:24-28-creation of animals and man; anticipated; Psalm 104:21-24

Also Day six: Genesis 1:29-31 food appointed for all creatures; Psalm 104:27,28

After calling his whole being to praise, the psalmist pictures the Lord within the wonderful Majesty of His creation. The heavens are spread forth as a canopy; His abode is supported by pillars and is surrounded by the Angels. God is distinct from His universe, but He is anything but remote from it. His taking of its parts and powers as His robe, palace and chariot indicates He delights in His world. The psalm shows God as both the creator and the sustainer of all life. He has not only created the inhabitants of earth, but has given each creature its own ability to gather food, protect themselves and to procreate. Nothing could exist or continue to exist without the breath of God.

This psalm, from first to last, beginning to end, hallows the name of God. Love, rather than fear, motivated this psalm. So the final words, "Bless the

Lord, all my soul" have come full circle, having not only responded to the glory that is, but also *hinting* to the prospect of its final consummation.

PSALM 105

¹O give thanks unto the LORD; call upon his name:
make known his deeds among the people.
²Sing unto him, sing psalms unto him:
talk ye of all his wondrous works.
³Glory ye in his holy name:
let the heart of them rejoice that seek the LORD.
⁴Seek the LORD, and his strength:
seek his face evermore.
⁵Remember his marvelous works that he hath done;
his wonders, and the judgments of his mouth;
⁶O ye seed of Abraham his servant,
ye children of Jacob his chosen.
⁷He [is] the LORD our God: his judgments
[are] in all the earth.
⁸He hath remember his covenant for ever, the word
[which] he commanded to a thousand generations.
⁹Which [covenant] he made with Abraham,
and his oath unto Isaac;
¹⁰And confirmed the same unto Jacob, for a law,
[and] to Israel [for] and everlasting covenant:
¹¹Saying, Unto thee will I give the land of Canaan,
the lot of your inheritance:
¹²When they were [but] a few men in number; yea,
very few, and strangers in it.

¹³When they went from one nation to another, from
[one] kingdom to another people;
¹⁴He suffered no man to do them wrong: yea, he
reproved kings for their sakes;
¹⁵[Saying], Touch not mine anointed, and do my
prophets no harm.
¹⁶Moreover he called for a famine upon the land: he
brake the whole staff of bread.
¹⁷He sent a man before for them, [even] Joseph,
[who] was sold for a servant:
¹⁸Whose feet they hurt with fetters:
he was laid in iron.
¹⁹Until the time that his word came:
the word of the LORD tried him.
²⁰The King sent and loosed him;
[even] the ruler of the people, and let him go free.
²¹He made him lord of his house,
and ruler of all his substance:
²²To bind his princes at his pleasure;
and teach his senators wisdom.
²³Israel also came into Egypt;
and Jacob sojourned in the land of Ham.
²⁴And he increased his people greatly;
and made them stronger than their enemies.
²⁵He turned their heart to hate his people, to deal
subtly with his servants.
²⁶He sent Moses his servant; [and]
Aaron whom he had chosen.
²⁷They showed his signs among them, and wonders
in the land of Ham.

²⁸He sent darkness, and made it dark;
and they rebelled not against his word.
²⁹He turned their waters into blood,
and slew their fish.
³⁰Their land brought forth frogs in abundance,
in the chambers of their kings.
³¹He spake, and there came divers sorts of flies,
[and] lice in all their coasts.
³²He gave them hail for rain,
[and] flaming fire in their land.
³³He smote their vines also and their fig trees; and
brake the trees of their coasts.
³⁴He spake, and the locusts came, and caterpillars,
and that without number,
³⁵And did eat up all the herbs in their land, and
devoured the fruit of their ground.
³⁶He smote also all the firstborn in their land, the
chief of all their strength.
³⁷He brought them forth also with silver and gold:
and [there was] not one feeble
[person] among their tribes.
³⁸Egypt was glad when they departed:
for the fear of them fell upon them.
³⁹He spread a cloud for a covering; and fire to give its
light in the night.
⁴⁰[The people] asked, and he brought quails, and
satisfied them with the bread of heaven.
⁴¹He opened the rock, and the waters gushed out;
they ran in the dry places [like] a river.
⁴²For he remembered his holy promise, [and]
Abraham his servant.

⁴³And he brought forth his people with joy,
[and] his chosen with gladness:
⁴⁴And gave them the lands of the heathen:
and they inherited the labor of the people;
⁴⁵That they might observe his statutes, and keep his laws. Praise ye the LORD.

PSALM 105
Title: Thirteenth Psalm of Praise
Author: anonymous
Superscription: none
Theme: The Everlasting Faithfulness of God

Israel's sacred history is the subject of both Psalms 104 and 105. These psalms, written near the same time, were used for corporate worship at one of the annual feasts: the Feast of Weeks, Pentecost or at the Feast of Tabernacles. Here the worshipers are reminded of God's work on their behalf and encouraged to show gratitude for past forgiveness and mercy. The history of Israel, as told here, belongs to every Christian. In Galatians 3:6 and 4:28, every Christian belongs to the family of God; this is the history believers in Christ have inherited.

The song centers upon the covenant, which God made with Abraham to give the land of Canaan to his descendants. The unusual use of "mine anointed ones and my prophets" refers to the patriarchs of old. Yet, while centered in days past, the relativity of such a pledge must be noted: first, that the earth itself might perish (102:25) and second that even God's "forever" can be forfeited by man's apostasy as seen in 1 Samuel 2:30 and Matthew 21:43.

Told here is the story of all that occurred on the sojourn from Egypt to Canaan. He sent His servant Joseph, tested him, tried him and allowed him to be raised to power. This greatly increased the number of His people. As the number of Israelites increased, the Egyptians sought to enslave and overpower them as a people. God intervened and when it was time for their deliverance, He sent Moses and Aaron as His representatives. Everything done for the Israelites happened because God remembered His holy promise to them.

The psalm ends on the positive note, which it has sustained from the beginning. Dwelling completely in the grace of God, it has ignored the sins of the redeemed, which occurred at almost every turn. Verse 45 explains why God has given His grace and mercy to such a people as the Israelites that they may observe His statutes and keep His laws. As in Romans 8:4 they were saved, not that sin may abound, but that the righteousness of the Law may fulfilled in those who walk after the spirit and not the flesh.

Note: The psalmist places special emphasis upon the plagues as signs of God's power. He moved the ninth plague to the head of the list, reverses the order of the third and fourth and updates the fifth and sixth completely, but the story remains the same.

PSALM 106

¹Praise ye the LORD. O give thanks unto the LORD;
for [he is] good: for his mercy [endureth] for ever.
²Who can utter the mighty acts of the LORD?
[who] can show forth all his praise?
³Blessed [are] they that keep judgment, [and] he
that doeth righteousness at all times.
⁴Remember me, O LORD, with the favor
[that thou bearest unto] thy people:
O visit me with thy salvation;
⁵That I may see the good of thy chosen,
that I may rejoice in the gladness of thy nation,
that I may glory with thine inheritance.
⁶ We have sinned with our fathers, we have committed iniquity, we have done wickedly.
⁷Our fathers understood not thy wonders in Egypt;
they remembered not the multitude of thy mercies,
but provoked [him] at the sea, [even] at the Red sea.
⁸Nevertheless he saved them for his name's sake,
that he might make his mighty power to be known.
⁹He rebuked the Red Sea also, and it was dried up:
so he led them through the depths,
as through the wilderness.
¹⁰And he saved them from the hand of him that
hated [them], and redeemed them from
the hand of the enemy.
¹¹And the waters covered their enemies:
there was not one of them left.
¹²Then believed they his words; they sang his praise.

¹³They soon forgat his works;
they waited not for his counsel:
¹⁴But lusted exceedingly in the wilderness,
and tempted God in the desert.
¹⁵And he gave them their request;
but sent leanness into their soul.
¹⁶They envied Moses also in the camp,
[and] Aaron the saint of the LORD.
¹⁷The earth opened and swallowed up Dathan,
and covered the company of Abiram.
¹⁸And a fire was kindled in their company;
the flame burned up the wicked.
¹⁹They made a calf in Horeb,
and worshipped the molten image.
²⁰Thus they exchanged their glory
into the similitude of an ox that eateth grass.
²¹They forgat God their Savior,
which had done great things in Egypt;
²²Wondrous works in the land of Ham,
[and] terrible things by the Red Sea.
²³Therefore he said that he would destroy them,
had not Moses his chosen stood before him in the
breach, to turn away his wrath,
lest he should destroy [them].
²⁴Yea, they despised the pleasant land,
they believed not his word.
²⁵But murmured in their tents, [and] hearkened not
unto the voice of the LORD.
²⁶Therefore he lifted up his hand against them,
to overthrow them in the wilderness:

²⁷To overthrow their seed also among the nations,
and to scatter them in the lands.
²⁸They joined themselves also unto Baalpeor,
and ate the sacrifices of the dead.
²⁹Thus they provoked [him] to anger with their
inventions: and the plague brake in upon them.
³⁰Then stood up Phinehas, and executed judgment:
and [so] the plague was stayed.
³¹And that was counted unto him for righteousness
unto all generations for evermore.
³²They angered [him] also at the waters of strife, so
that it went ill with Moses for their sakes:
³³Because they provoked his spirit, so that he spake
unadvisedly with his lips.
³⁴They did not destroy the nations,
concerning whom the LORD commanded them:
³⁵But were mingled among the heathen,
and learned their works.
³⁶And they served their idols:
which were a snare unto them.
³⁷Yea, they sacrificed their sons and
their daughters unto devils,
³⁸And shed innocent blood, [even] the blood of their
sons and of their daughters,
whom they sacrificed unto the idols of Canaan:
and the land was polluted with blood.
³⁹Thus where they defiled with their own works, and
went a whoring with their own inventions.
⁴⁰Therefore was the wrath of the LORD kindled
against his people, insomuch that
he abhorred his own inheritance.

⁴¹And he gave them into the hand of the heathen; and they that hated them ruled over them.
⁴²Their enemies also oppressed them, and they were brought into subjection under their hand.
⁴³Many times did he deliver them; but they provoked [him] with their counsel,
and were brought low for their iniquity.
⁴⁴Nevertheless he regarded their affliction, when he heard their cry:
⁴⁵And he remembered for them his covenant, and repented according to the multitude of his mercies.
⁴⁶He made them also to be pitied of all those that carried them captives.
⁴⁷Save us, O LORD our God, and gather us from among the heathen, to give thanks unto thy holy name, [and] to triumph in thy praise.
⁴⁸Blessed [be] the LORD God of Israel from everlasting to everlasting: and let all the people say, Amen. Praise ye the LORD.

PSALM 106
Title: Ninth Praise/Prayer Psalm
Author: anonymous
Superscription: none
Theme: Rejoice in God's Forgiveness

Beginning as a hymn (1-5), this sequel to Psalm 105 is both a national lament and a confession of sin. The song starts at the time of the Exodus and continues through the Babylonian exile, showing the shadow of sin that continually hangs over the

PSALMS 90-106 Referred to as the Numbers Psalms

Israelites. They did not trust God at the Red Sea or in the wilderness, but instead, constantly struggled with human self-will as they strained to reach the light.

The last two verses, however, are quoted in the account of a much earlier event: David's procession with the ark to Jerusalem as seen in 1 Chronicles 16:35. Whether this means that the psalm refers to the captivity of earlier days is unclear, yet it illustrates the extreme rejoicing and praying that God deserves from a *frequently* disobedient people. In spite of the clarity of man's failures, this is psalm does not praise man's weakness, but God's extraordinary patience and long-suffering.

In the fashion of a poem, the author issues a call to praise, followed by an expression of the attitude, personal prayer and a confession of the nation. The psalm catalogs many of the failures of the Israelite nation, but at the same time shows how God's tolerance and righteousness have been uninterrupted. The Israelites created many of their own problems by murmuring and rebelling for 40 years. Moses struck the rock twice in anger. He acted as he wanted, not doing what God had told him to do, but what his anger told him to do. Aaron made the golden calf fully knowing this was wrong, but he gave in to the wishes of others and gave way to idol worship. Backslidden and faithless, they became defiled by their own sins.

Many generations have passed, yet history combines them and still none may be called sinless. It is one thing to condemn an earlier generation; quite another to see one's self mirrored in their behavior.

In this admission of sin, past and present become one and the indictment of the past is the confession of the present. YET GOD, being faithful to His word (and His covenant with Abraham) allowed them to enter the Promised Land. Only God proved faithful in this alliance, however, for upon entering the land God had promised Abraham, the people repeatedly proved unfaithful. They became totally apostate at times, taking part in idol worship and human sacrifice. In the New Testament, 1 Corinthians 8 shows that the sin of paganism continued. The cycle of sin, confession, apostasy, the cry for help and God's forgiveness continues today and will until time ends.

In verses 47 and 48 are the doxology. The lengthy confession pleads for mercy and restoration. The theme has been that God's steadfastness is greater than man's perversity and failures. This stands as a fitting close to both this psalm and the Fourth Book of the Psalter.

Note: The phrase "righteous at all times" is comparable to Paul's urgent words, "in season and out of season", as seen in 2 Timothy 4:2.

If the natural mind gives no concern or thought to the character of God, this absence will become the instigator of sin.

NOTES ON BOOK FOUR
Major Themes:

- God granted Israel's requests
- Sin carries consequences

- Sin is not historical-but continues (prodigal son, story of Lot, etc.)
- Man, like Jesus, needs God's counsel for empowerment
- The church needs confession and intercession
- Humble postures reflect a humble heart
- A wise person welcomes God's discipline
- God hates procrastination and time-wasters
- Faith is a forward focus on God
- Faith looks back at the blessings of God
- Faith allows confidence when in distress
- Not to stare or meditate on inappropriate things

BOOK FIVE

PSALMS 107-150
Deuteronomy Psalms

The Fifth Book of Psalms is a cluster of several smaller groups of psalms combined to form the final portion of the Psalter. Each grouping has a subtitle, yet all of the teachings in these psalms are focused around the word of God, showing His great love and His great power.

This section opens with Psalm 107, which gives the key, "he sent His word and healed them." Included within this group is Psalm 119, which is the longest and possibly the greatest psalm in the Psalter. It rejoices in the word of God and leads man into the heart and the mind of The Lord.

Psalms 120 through 134 are known as the *Psalms of Ascents or Degrees.* Pilgrims sang these psalms as they made their way into the Temple courts. Psalms 111-113, 115-117 and Psalms 146-150 are the *Hallelujah Psalms.* Psalms 113-118 are the *Egyptian Hallel* (corporate, liturgical songs used at great festivals such as Passover, the Festival of Weeks or the Feast of Tabernacles). At Passover, Psalm 113 and 114 were sung before the second cup was passed and Psalm 115-118 after the meal when the fourth cup had been filled. These *Hallel Psalms* are the hymns that Jesus and His disciples sang at the Last Supper in Matthew 26:30.

Each of Psalms 146-150 begins and ends with the word *hallelujah*, meaning *praise the Lord*. An overall liturgical purpose is evident throughout, resulting in a deep sense of public worship, which culminates in the closing words of Psalm 150.

Many of the thoughts expressed here become the foundation for the coming Christ. Some of the themes which help *transition* the Old Testament to the New Testament are from the Psalms and will be seen both as history and prophecy. Continuing themes include how God will:

- Bless His little children-Matthew 19:24
- Strengthen young men-1 John 2:14
- Sanctify and cleanse all who read it-Ephesians 5:26
- Give protection to the widows-Exodus 22:22
- Honor the aged-Leviticus 19:32
- Offer eternal life to everyone-John 3:36

PSALM 107

¹O, give thanks unto the LORD, for [he is] good: for his mercy [endureth] for ever.
²Let the redeemed of the LORD say [so], whom he hath redeemed from the hand of the enemy;

³And gathered them out of the lands,
from the east, and from the west, from the north,
and from the south.
⁴They wandered in the wilderness in a solitary way;
they found no city to dwell in.
⁵Hungry and thirsty, their soul fainted in them.
⁶Then they cried unto the LORD in their trouble,
[and] he delivered them out of their distresses.
⁷And he led them forth by the right way, that they
might go to a city of habitation.
⁸Oh that [men] would praise the LORD [for] his
goodness, and [for] his wonderful works
to the children of men!
⁹For he satisfieth the longing soul, and filleth the
hungry soul with goodness.
¹⁰Such as sit in darkness and in the shadow of death,
[being] bound in affliction and iron;
¹¹Because they rebelled against the words of God,
and contemned the counsel of the most High:
¹²Therefore he brought down their heart with labor;
they fell down, and [there was] none to help.
¹³Then they cried unto the LORD in their trouble,
[and] he saved them out of their distresses.
¹⁴He brought them out of darkness and the shadow
of death, and brake their bands in sunder.
¹⁵O that [men] would praise the LORD [for] his goodness, and [for] his wonderful works
to the children of men!
¹⁶For he hath broken the gates of brass,
and cut the bars of iron in sunder.

¹⁷Fools because of their transgression,
and because of their iniquities, are afflicted.
¹⁸Their soul abhorteth all manner of meat; and they
draw near unto the gates of death.
¹⁹Then they cry unto the LORD in their trouble, [and]
he saveth them out of their distresses.
²⁰He sent his word, and healed them, and delivered
[them] from their destructions.
²¹Oh that [men] would praise the LORD [for] his
goodness, and [for] his wonderful
works to the children of men!
²²And let them sacrifice the sacrifices of thanksgiving, and declare his works with rejoicing.
²³They that go down to the sea in ships, they that do
business in great waters;
²⁴These see the works of the LORD
and his wonders in the deep.
²⁵For he commandeth, and raiseth the stormy wind,
which lifteth up the waves thereof.
²⁶They mount up to the heaven,
they go down again to the depths: there soul
is melted because of trouble.
²⁷They reel to and fro, and stagger like a drunken
man, and are at their wit's end.
²⁸Then they cried unto the LORD in their trouble,
and he bringeth them out of their distresses.
²⁹He maketh the storm a calm,
so that the waves of thereof are still.
³⁰Then are they glad because they be quiet; so he
bringeth them unto their desired haven.

³¹O that [men] would praise the LORD [for] his goodness, and [for] his wonderful works to the children of men!
³²Let them exalt him also in the congregation of the people, and praise him in the assembly of the elders.
³³He turneth rivers into a wilderness, and the watersprings into dry ground;
³⁴A fruitful land into barrenness, for the wickedness of them that dwell therein.
³⁵He turneth the wilderness into a standing water, and dry ground into watersprings.
³⁶And there he maketh the hungry to dwell, that they may prepare a city for habitation;
³⁷And sow the fields, and plant vineyards, which may yield fruits of increase.
³⁸He blesseth them also, so that they are multiplied greatly; and suffereth not their cattle to decrease.
³⁹Again, they are minished and brought low through oppression, affliction, and sorrow.
⁴⁰He poureth contempt upon princes, and causeth them to wander in the wilderness, [where there is] no way.
⁴¹Yet setteth he the poor on high from affliction, and maketh [him] families like a flock.
⁴²The righteous shall see [it], and rejoice: and all iniquity shall stop her mouth.
⁴³Whoso [is] wise, and will observe these [things], even they shall understand the loving kindness of the LORD.

PSALM 107
Title: Fourteenth Psalm of Praise
Author: anonymous
Date: After the Babylonian Exile
Superscription: none
Theme: Thanksgiving to God for His Deliverance

Psalms 105, 106 and 107 are definitely linked together. At editing, a division between 106 and 107 may have been arbitrarily added as way of making the five books of psalms, thus matching the Five Books of Moses. As occurs so often in the Book of Psalms, this division is neither damaging nor mandatory to the praise it holds. This song was composed primarily for liturgical use at one of the annual religious festivals. The most likely use of this psalm was in thanksgiving for their return from Babylon and sung to honor God's unfailing faithfulness to those who cry out to Him in the midst of crises.

At the heart of this beautiful psalm is a striking set of word pictures that show the human dilemma. These situations are not specifically for this time and place, but rather show the many ways of depicting the how God delivers His people. In each instance, the author describes the helpless condition of those in trouble, their cry to God and the deliverance which He gives.

The *rescued man* includes one who is lost in the world or one who has been imprisoned. The sickness in 17-22 could refer to a literal sickness or a sickness of the heart brought about through sin. Many troubles are self-inflicted. The wages of sin or at least an interim payment, emphasizes man's fundamental guilt of spurning God's counsel. This may serve as the general conclusion drawn from the moral situations described in verses 4 through 32. It is, however, a reminder that life is through God's permission, not by any man's method of *sin management.*

The epilogue in verses 35-38 make it doubly clear that God is a man's only true resource. There is a sober reminder that eloquence, shallow responses or leaning on man's understanding is not the answer to life's problems. It is in God Himself that man has life and to glorify Him is the only correct response. Each man is to recognize the pictures of life and salvation presented here and to find his own life in the midst of them.

Note: Loss, hunger, thirst and exhaustion are all trials that Jesus was to experience. Against this background the Lord's proclamations found in Luke 4:18 is read with a livelier and more personal understanding.

PSALM 108

¹A Song [or] Psalm of David. O God, my heart is fixed; I will sing and give praise, even with my glory.
²Awake, psaltery and harp:
I [myself] will awake early.
³I will praise thee, O LORD, among the people: and I will sing praises unto thee among the nations.
⁴For thy mercy [is] great above the heavens:
and thy truth [reacheth] unto the clouds.

⁵Be thou exalted, O God, above the heavens:
and thy glory above all the earth;
⁶That thy beloved may be delivered: save [with] thy
right hand, and answer me.
⁷God has spoken in his holiness; I will rejoice, I will
divide Shechem, and mete out the valley of Succoth.
⁸Gilead [is] mine; Manasseh [is] mine;
Ephriam also [is] the strength of mine head;
Judah [is] my lawgiver;
⁹Moab, [is] my washpot; over Edom will I cast out
my shoe; over Philistia will I triumph.
¹⁰Who will bring me into the strong city?
who will lead me into Edom?
¹¹[Wilt] not [thou], O God, [who] hast cast us off?
and wilt not thou, O God, go forth with our hosts?
¹²Give us help from trouble: for vain
[is] the help of man.
¹³Through God, we shall do valiantly: for he [it is
that] shalt tread down our enemies.

PSALM 108
Title: Nineteenth Psalm of Instruction
Author: a Psalm of David
Superscription: none
Theme: Guarantee of God's Victory over Enemies

Psalm 108 combined extracts from Psalm 57:7-11 and Psalm 60:5-12. This psalm is both a hymn and a lament. The divine name Yahweh used in verse 3, rather than the Adonai of Psalm 57, indicates that the present psalmist undoubtedly drew his material from the two earlier works. Perhaps this combination met the needs of a new situation. The celebration of the greatness of God's love links this psalm thematically with Psalm 103.

Psalms 57 and 60 show great stress in the life of David. In Psalm 57, he was *hunted down* only to be *defeated* in Psalm 60. Starting on a positive point, this song exhibits discipline (11), yet outlines that of an *inheritance* not yet received. The earlier psalms provided insight into times of personal or corporate trials, but the present time calls for new ideas and stronger faith.

Praise is the total focus of verses 7-10, where each of the cities are described as belonging to God, using terms that are parallel to everyday things in life. Just as a man is over his household and uses his own things at his will, so it is with God. All of the kingdoms of man are at His disposal and for His personal use. No man can rely upon anything except the most excellent and divine power of God.

The final lines are the entire psalm in short: "The help of man is useless" and "through God, we will do valiantly."

PSALM 109

[1]To the chief Musician, A Psalm of David. Hold not thy peace, O God of my praise;
[2]For the mouth of the wicked and the mouth of the deceitful are opened against me: they have spoken against me with a lying tongue.

³They compassed me about also with words of
hatred, and fought against me without a cause.
⁴For my love they are my adversaries:
but I [give myself unto] prayer.
⁵And they have rewarded me evil for good,
and hatred for my love.
⁶Set thou a wicked man over him:
and let Satan stand at his right hand.
⁷When he shall be judged, let him be condemned:
and let his prayer become sin.
⁸Let his days be few; [and] let another take his office.
⁹Let his children be fatherless, and his wife a widow.
¹⁰Let his children be continually vagabonds,
and beg: let them seek [their bread]
also out of their desolate places.
¹¹Let the extortioner catch all that he hath;
and let the strangers spoil his labor.
¹² Let there being none to extend mercy unto him:
neither let there be any to favor
his fatherless children.
¹³Let his posterity be cut off; [and] in the generation
following let their name be blotted out.
¹⁴Let the iniquity of his fathers be remembered
with the LORD; and let not the sin
of his mother be blotted out.
¹⁵Let them be before they LORD continually, that he
may cut off the memory of them from the earth.
¹⁶Because that he remembered not to show mercy,
but persecuted the poor and needy man, that he
might even slay the broken in heart.

¹⁷As he loved cursing, so let it come unto him: as he delighted not in blessing, so let it be far from him. ¹⁸As he clothed himself with cursing like as with his garment, so let it come into his bowels like water, and like oil into his bones. ¹⁹Let it be unto him as the garment [which] covereth him, and for a girdle wherewith he is girded continually. ²⁰[Let] this [be] the reward of mine adversaries from the LORD, and of them that speak evil against my soul. ²¹But do thou for me, O GOD the Lord, for thy name's sake: because thy mercy [is] good, deliver thou me. ²²For I [am] poor and needy, and my heart is wounded within me. ²³I am gone like the shadow when it declineth: I am tossed up and down as the locust. ²⁴My knees are weak through fasting; and my flesh faileth of fatness. ²⁵I became also a reproach unto them: [when] they looked upon me they shaked their heads. ²⁶Help me, O LORD my God: O save me according to thy mercy: ²⁷That they may know that this [is] thy hand; [that] thou, LORD, hast done, it. ²⁸Let them curse, but bless thou: when they arise, let them be ashamed; but let thy servant rejoice. ²⁹Let mine adversaries be clothed with shame, and let them cover themselves with their own confusion, as with a mantle.

³⁰I will greatly praise the LORD with my mouth; and yea, I will praise him among the multitude.
³¹For he shall stand at the right hand of the poor, to save [him] from those that condemn his soul.

PSALM 109
Title: Sixteenth Psalm of Distress
Author: a Psalm of David
Superscription: to the chief Musician
Theme: Prayer for God to Judge False Witnesses

David is clearly angry as he discovers that those he has treated well have returned his goodness with evil. The continual attacks have reduced him to a mere shadow (1-4; 22-25) of his former self. One can understand and even visualize his hostility, yet the tirade of verses 6-20 seem to be a bit excessive. His feeling of betrayal shows itself in in the repeated phrase *"in return for my love"*. It was a betrayal almost worthy of Judas. Though occasionally counted among the corporate psalms, this psalm carries too much personal character and expression to be anything other than a personal lament.

There is a righteous indignation against evil as seen in Matthew 23:13 and it is with that same feeling that his enemies are also the enemies of God. As the psalm begins, the complaints of the psalmist also begin. He launches into the penalties that he wants God to impose upon those who have assaulted him. The judgment is clear and now the psalmist sets forth the sentence of the guilty evil ones. He states that at the death of the accused, someone else will take his office; his children and wife will face hardship and trouble and in a very short time, all memory of him is forgotten.

It is reminiscent of David's horrific curse on the house of Joab in 2 Samuel 3:29. At the same time, it is not a fantasy; judgments are shown elsewhere to be the dark side of human solidarity and David's curse, however ugly in its motivation, could still have been the vehicle of God's judgment. The Law, the prophets and the Gospels all give warnings, though not with relish, of what the father's sin can bring upon the children. Exodus 20:5, 1 Samuel 31, Luke 19:41 also show this concept.

Worn out from pleading, thoughts turn into prayers of deliverance. Up to this point, it seems that God has been silent, yet the psalmist knows that it will not always be so. In spite of what David has placed upon the heads of his enemies, the whole mood changes with the pivotal phrase "but thou delivereth me". His appeal is on the surest basis of all: for thy name's sake. The psalmist prays that God will have mercy upon him in his sick and needy condition and vindicate him, so that his enemies may realize that God's hand is upon him. He closes with the knowledge that very soon he will have an opportunity to praise God for answered prayer.

The figure of the accuser represents (Satan) standing at the right hand of his victim, who is now replaced by God standing at the right side of the needy. In this awareness, God is no longer silent; His answer is complete.

Note: we can see the hint of prophecy which the Holy Spirit spoken by the mouth of David concerning Judas (Acts 1:16). Therefore, we can thoroughly understand righteous anger (compare to Job and Jeremiah). These outbursts of anger are recorded for learning, not for imitation. Yet they voice to cry of innocent blood, which God has pledged to hear (Matthew 23:35; Luke 18:8). It is presented here only as David's cry-the men of Christ are to bless and not to curse others.

PSALM 110

¹A Psalm of David. The LORD said unto my Lord,
Sit thou at my right hand,
until I make thine enemies thy footstool.
²The LORD shall send the rod of thy strength out of Zion: rule thou in the midst of thine enemies.
³Thy people [shall be] willing in the day of thy power, in the beauties of holiness from the womb of the morning: thou hast the dew of thy youth.
⁴The LORD hath sworn, and will not repent, Thou [art] a priest for ever after the order of Melchizedek.
⁵The Lord at thy right hand shall strike through kings in the day of his wrath.
⁶He shall judge among the heathen, he shall field [the places] with the dead bodies; he shall wound the heads over many countries.
⁷He shall drink of the brook in the way: therefore shall he lift up the head.

PSALM 110
Title: Eighteenth Messianic Psalm
Author: a Psalm of David
Superscription: none
Theme: Proclaiming the Messiah's Reign

Men from Abraham to Simon of the Maccabean times have suggested David as the recipient of this oracle. The term "Oracle of the Lord" is nowhere else in the Psalter, but was a term frequently used by the prophets. While some commentators limit the stand of the Oracle to verse 1, it seems better to extend it through verse 4. The Messianic King is commanded to occupy the position of the highest honor and share the divine rule until His enemies are completely vanquished (Joshua 10:24; 1 Kings 5:3). The King is to rule from the authority He has through His relationship with God. His rule is to be universal and his subjects are to be willing volunteers.

This psalm, which is similar to Psalm 2, is a basis for many thoughts in the New Testament. It bears the earmark of a coronation psalm used to crown a new king. In this prophetic psalm, the new King would be Jesus. Before the Christian era, Jews already viewed it as messianic. Its powerful usage in the New Testament by Jesus, Peter and the writer of Hebrews indicates that this is the most prophetic of all the psalms. The king which is spoken of may have been the present ruler and if so has been greatly idealized, or this may refer to one greater—*the coming king*. The apostles later spell out the startling fact that David spoke of the King as "My King" leaving his peers to think out the implications.

The King, as described by this psalm, will be:

- Greater than David (Acts 2:34)
- Seated at God's right hand (Acts 2:34)
- Greater than the angels (Hebrews 1:13)
- Savior and intercessor (Acts 5:31)
- Exalted by God (Acts 5:31)
- A completed offering (Hebrews 10:10)
- Taken to Heaven to sit with God (Hebrews 10:12)
- Wait for the surrender of His enemies
- Rejected by man (Mark 8:31)
- Have His enemies as a footstool (1 Corinthians 15:25)

This is the divine person of Christ. The description herein is beyond any of the Abrahamic people and above the priesthood. While it is clearly the human king in the foreground, verse 7 shows how the earthly king is bound to the coming King. The psalm leaves readers with a vision of the warrior who, following a victory, pauses briefly, renews his strength, then rises to complete the battle. David was King, Christ is King; God never separates Himself from His people.

PSALM 111

¹Praise ye the LORD. I will praise the LORD with [my] whole heart, in the assembly of the upright, and [in] the congregation.
²The works of the LORD [are] great, sought out of all them that have pleasure therein.
³His work [is] honorable and glorious: and his righteousness endureth for ever.
⁴He has made his wonderful works to be remembered: the LORD [is] gracious and full of compassion.
⁵He hath given meat unto them that fear him: he will ever be mindful of his covenant.
⁶He hath showed his people the power of his works, that he may give them the heritage of the heathen.
⁷The works of his hands [are] verity and judgment; all his commandments [are] sure.
⁸They stand fast for ever and ever, [and are] done in truth and uprightness.
⁹He sent redemption unto his people: he hath commanded his covenant for ever: holy and reverend [is] his name.
¹⁰The fear of the LORD [is] the beginning of wisdom: a good understanding have all they that do [his commandments]: his praise endureth for ever.

PSALM 111
Title: Third Psalm of God
Author: anonymous
Superscription: none
Theme: Praise for God's Justice

Psalms 111-113 each begin with the praise of *hallelujah*. Psalm 111 and Psalm 112 are very similar: both are acrostics (each having 22 lines beginning with successive letters of the Hebrew alphabet) and more importantly, they match in their subject matter, which describes the God of man and the man of God and gives illustrations of both. The word *"forever"* dominates the psalm and reflects two aspects of His work, rarely noticed: that everything He makes will endure (8, 9) and as they are His, they are in His care (5).

A central theme is the steady goodness of God as displayed in His works. In the psalms, the Lord's *works* often refer to His deeds, but more often focuses upon heaven, earth and all of nature. This hymn honors not only God's creative works, but also the redemption and deliverance of His people. It shows the personality of God as righteous, merciful, just, faithful, true, holy and eternal. This respect and understanding of God, albeit limited to human capacity, is the true starting point of all human wisdom.

The psalm begins with an annunciation of praise, "I will praise the Lord." This signifies that the message in the Temple was spoken by a solo voice. In verses 2 through 4, the author attempts to describe God's work in general. He speaks of the Lord's work as great, honorable and glorious. He then speaks of the Lord's eternal righteousness, graciousness and His compassion-all attributes revealed in His mighty acts. The wisdom of God and His creations have leant themselves to centuries of research and study. The result of this arduous labor has shown that the mere thoughts of the faithful are now accepted by the scientific world as fact.

The psalm concludes with a note on godly wisdom. The fear of the Lord of the beginning of wisdom. This is the classical Old Testament statement concerning the religious basis of what it means to be wise. People who follow His precepts literally are those who do them. This type of fear is a reverence and awe of God that pervades every area of life. It is the beginning of true faith; insight and understanding will follow.

PSALM 112

¹Praise ye the LORD. Blessed [is] the man [that]
feareth the LORD, [that] delighteth greatly
in his commandments.
²His seed shall be mighty upon the earth:
the generation of the upright shall be blessed.
³Wealth and riches [shall be] in his house: and his
righteousness endureth for ever.
⁴Unto the upright there ariseth light in the darkness:
[he is] gracious, and full of
compassion, and righteous.
⁵A good man showeth favor, and lendeth:
he will guide his affairs with discretion.

⁶Surely he shall not be moved for ever: the righteous shall be in everlasting remembrance.
⁷He shall not be afraid of evil tidings: his heart is fixed, trusting in the LORD.
⁸His heart [is] established, he shall not be afraid, until he see [his desire] upon his enemies.
⁹He hath dispersed, he hath given to the poor; his righteousness endureth for ever; his horn shall be exalted with honor.
¹⁰The wicked shall see [it], and be grieved; he shall gnash with his teeth, and melt away: the desire of the wicked shall perish.

PSALM 112
Title: Seventh Psalm of the Righteous
Author: anonymous
Superscription: none
Theme: Blessed are the Righteous

Psalm 112 is a companion to Psalm 111 in both its acrostic construction and subject matter. Psalm 111 expounds upon the wisdom that begins with the fear of God. Psalm 112 takes wisdom, places it into the life of man and shows the blessings that await those who fear and obey God. Similar to Psalm 1:1, the opening lines bring to mind the character of Job tested at the hand of Satan, yet still proved faithful to God.

A man who fears the Lord naturally finds delight in keeping the divine commandments. Serving God has become a joy rather than a burden and he sees God's work as fascinating as His word. The outlook for the wise man is as wonderful as the evil man's is bleak. His children will inherit his spiritual and material blessings. Family continuity is future prosperity linked to the present. While the verses may largely seem material, a closer look reveals the moral and spiritual terms, which make it an instrument of good. This is an application of the eternal truth that man will becomes more and more like the object of his worship.

This psalm deals realistically with the temptations that go with the prosperity. The greatest temptation is the impulse to abuse the *power* of wealth. Other pitfalls seen in verses 7 and 8 are the fear that what one possesses will be lost or stolen and the overwhelming temptation to become miserly. This psalm commands both graciousness and fairness by the lender, who has a powerful advantage over the borrower. Verses 5, 6 and 9 all indicate what potential problems could arise if a man of prosperity is unwise in his dealings.

In 2 Corinthians, there is an echo of verse 9 as it speaks of what a wise man does with the profit he earns from his harvest. There, as here, the accent is on the fact that Godly things will never lose their value. The previous psalm had as its subject the goodness of the Lord. It finished with a verse that invited man's response. The present psalm, having expanded upon that response, closes the matter neatly by showing how bitter and futile is the life of any man who does not follow God. An evil and wicked man cannot know God and here one can easily see his fate compared to the fate of the righteous.

PSALM 113

¹Praise ye the LORD. Praise O ye servants of the LORD, praise the name of the LORD.
²Blessed be the name of the LORD from this time forth and for evermore.
³From the rising of the sun until the going down of the same the LORD's name [is] to be praised.
⁴The LORD [is] high above all nations, [and] his glory above the heavens.
⁵Who [is] like unto the LORD our God, who dwelleth on high,
⁶Who humbleth [himself] to behold [the things that are] in heaven, and in the earth!
⁷He raiseth up the poor out of the dust, [and] lifteth the needy out of the dunghill;
⁸That he may set [him] with princes, [even] with the princes of his people.
⁹He maketh the barren woman to keep house, [and to be] a joyful mother of children.
Praise ye the LORD.

PSALM 113
Title: Fourth Psalm of God
Author: anonymous
Superscription: none
Theme: The Majesty of God

This is the first psalm in the collection known as the *Egyptian Hallel*. Each song of praise begins and ends with "hallelujah", meaning *"praise God forever"*.

The *Egyptian Hallel* was given this name from the repeated use of the word "halleluiah" and of the frequent references in Psalms 113 and 114 to the events of great Exodus from Egypt. As the psalms continue, the purpose of this *group* is made clear. The purpose of these psalms is to raise the downtrodden man.

This story marks the salvation which began in Egypt and will be spread throughout the nations. When one comes to pray and worship God, it must be more than flattery or rote recitation. A loving humility flows from worshipers as they call upon His name. Each worshiper is unique, but they are also part of a vast company, extending unimaginably in time (2) and space (3) as befits His sovereignty in heaven and in earth (4).

This psalm shows that God is incomparable. He is beyond creation and yet He is closely concerned for the humblest of His people. Thematically, this psalm has strong links with the song of Hannah (1 Samuel 2:1-15) and the song of Mary (Luke 1:46-55). Both of these songs make the same point: that the Most High cares for the most humiliated. Hannah's joy became the joy of Israel; Mary's child became the future of the world.

"Who is like our God?" is the same question which Isaiah asked in Isaiah 40:12 and has numerous occurrences through the Bible. In this psalm, the question ends with praise as the psalmist tells of the God who raises the man from the dust, picks up the poor and needy and seats them on the thrones of princes.

Note: Seven verbs are used to praise God: exalted, set on high, stooped down, raises, lifts, seeds and settles. Biblically, seven is the number of completeness.

PSALM 114

¹When Israel went out of Egypt, the house of Jacob
from a people of strange language;
²Judah was his sanctuary, [and] Israel his dominion.
³The sea saw [it], and fled: Jordan was driven back.
⁴The mountains skipped like rams,
[and] the little hills like lambs.
⁵What [ailed] thee, O thou sea, that thou fleddest?
thou Jordan, [that] thou wast driven back?
⁶Ye mountains, [that] ye skipped like rams;
[and] ye little hills, like lambs?
⁷Tremble, thou earth, at the presence of the Lord,
at the presence of the God of Jacob;
⁸ Which turned the rock [into] a standing water,
the flint into a fountain of waters.

PSALM 114
Title: Fifth Psalm of God
Author: anonymous
Superscription: none
Theme: God's Power to Deliver Israel

The terror of pursuit, the wild elation on the far shore, the trembling at Mount Sinai and the crossing of the Jordan are all found in this psalm. Verses 1-4 recall the great events of the Exodus; verses 5 and 6 are hypothetical statements placed in question form. The answer comes swiftly in the statement that God will provide for His people just as He took care of the wanderers in the wilderness.

Verses 7 and 8 are an admonishment to all of nature to tremble at the presence of God. There is within Him the power to turn rock into springs and flint into a fountain. In this quiet story of Exodus and Joshua the psalmist recaptures the magnitude of what Israel had experienced. This psalm shows God's power directed to its point of need, transforming their promise into a place of plenty and a source of joy.

PSALM 115

¹Not unto us, O LORD, not unto us,
but unto thy name give glory, for thy mercy,
[and] for thy truth's sake.
²Wherefore should the heathen say,
Where [is] now there God?
³But our God [is] in the heavens:
he hath done whatsoever he hath pleased.
⁴Their idols [are] silver and gold,
the work of men's hands.
⁵They have mouths, but they speak not:
eyes have they, but they see not:
⁶They have ears, but they hear not:
noses have they, but they smell not:

⁷They have hands, but they handle not:
feet have they, but they walk not;
neither speak they through their throat.
⁸They that make them are like unto them;
[so is] everyone that trusteth in them.
⁹O Israel, trust thou in the LORD:
he [is] their help and their shield.
¹⁰O house of Aaron, trust in the LORD:
he [is] their help and their shield.
¹¹Ye that fear the LORD, trust in the LORD:
he [is] their help and their shield.
¹²The LORD hath been mindful of us:
he will bless [us]; he will bless the house of Israel;
he will bless the house of Aaron.
¹³He will bless them that fear the LORD,
[both] small and great.
¹⁴The LORD shall increase you more and more,
you and your children.
¹⁵Ye [are] blessed of the LORD
which made heaven and earth.
¹⁶The heaven, [even] the heavens, [are] the LORD's:
but the earth hath he given to the children of men.
¹⁷The dead praise not the LORD,
neither any that go down into silence.
¹⁸But we will bless the LORD from this time forth and
for evermore. Praise the LORD.

PSALM 115
Title: Sixth Psalm of God
Author: anonymous
Date: The Dedication of the Second Temple
Superscription: none
Theme: Uselessness of Idols, Faithfulness of God

To God be the glory! This psalm is a story of God's unchangeable nature and the goodness He continues to give to His righteous people. The energetic poetry here suggests a time shortly after the Babylonian Exile when Israel had suffered the taunts of their captors. The people praise the Lord, who is their only God.

The psalm begins with a contrast of the God of heaven and earth as compared to the value of fabricated idols. There is a strong, almost sarcastic contrast between the spiritual God reigning over everything and the idols of man. No matter how carefully made, an idol cannot speak, does not know, cannot hear and cannot walk. The traits of the idol are like those of the man who made them, unable to compete with a living God. This contrast makes idolatry appear completely absurd.

This psalm was designed for use in temple worship, led by a single singer with the response coming from the congregation. The *complaints* in verses 1 and 2 do not change the focus of the hymn, but give the historical basis for the psalm. This psalm was for celebration at various festivals, with Psalms 115-118 sung at the conclusion of the Passover meal.

Sadly, the heathen man can only enjoy things that he can see and he holds only contempt for what he cannot. God, however, is unlimited. He is not a creation-He is the Creator. He has no need to bow down to circumstances-He creates and guides them instead. He is to be trusted, not in the useless sense of idols, but in His personal bond and steadfast love. In trusting anything but God renders both the idol and its worshiper as useless (Jeremiah 2:5, 2 Kings 17:15).

The phrase "the Lord has been mindful of us" marks the praise, enhanced by their previous enslavement, which exhibits the love they have for the great God of Israel. The God who made heaven and earth has now made us His heirs and trustees. Within His generosity, however, there is responsibility; He has given us the earth and we must care for it. We are not its maker, nor is it something we are to exploit. Behind the gift is the giver and the response must be altogether positive. This psalm may appear to be no more than an undying Israel offering praise, however, it may be saying that those who serve the living God will live on, unlike the worshipers of lifeless objects.

PSALM 116

¹I love the LORD, because he hath heard my voice,
[and] my supplications.
²Because he hath inclined his ear unto me,
therefore will I call upon [him] as long as I live.

³The sorrows of death compassed me,
and the pains of hell gat hold upon me:
I found trouble, and sorrow.
⁴Then I called upon the name of the LORD;
O LORD, I beseech thee, deliver my soul.
⁵Gracious [is] the LORD, and righteous;
yea, our God [is] merciful.
⁶The LORD preserveth the simple:
I was brought low, and he helped me.
⁷Return unto thy rest, O my soul;
for the LORD hath dealt bountifully with thee.
⁸For thou hast delivered my soul from death, mine
eyes from tears, [and] my feet from falling.
⁹I will walk before the LORD in the land of the living.
¹⁰I believed, therefore, have I spoken:
I was greatly afflicted:
¹¹I said in my haste, All men [are] liars.
¹²What shall I render unto the LORD
[for] all his benefits toward me?
¹³I will take the cup of salvation,
and call upon the name of the LORD.
¹⁴I will pay my vows unto the LORD now
in the presence of all his people.
¹⁵Precious in the sight of the LORD [is]
the death of his saints.
¹⁶O LORD, truly I [am] thy servant; I [am] thy servant,
[and] the son of thine handmaid:
thou hast loosed my bonds.
¹⁷I will offer to thee the sacrifice of thanksgiving, and
I will call upon the name of the LORD.

¹⁸I will pay my vows unto the LORD now in the presence of all his people,
¹⁹In the courts of the LORD's house, in the midst of thee, O Jerusalem. Praise ye the LORD

PSALM 116
Title: Third Prayer/Testimony Psalm
Author: a Psalm of David
Superscription: none
Theme: Deliverance from the Grave

Sometimes it is difficult to find the words to express the emotions that one feels. This psalm is one that, as it passed through the church, would lend itself to that situation. The words are very spontaneous and reach into the depths of the psalmist's soul. In verses 1-4, the psalmist is making a lifelong resolve to trust God exclusively and to worship Him as the one and only true God. It is obvious that the psalmist knows firsthand the love and the protection of God.

This psalm appears as a part of the Egyptian Hallel and suggests that God has brought this man through many trials. God has heard the prayer of His child and brought him through the darkness into the sunlight. He pours out his heart in gratitude. From this experience of answered prayer, he has come to know God is gracious, righteous and merciful. He knows that God preserves, helps, deals bountifully and delivers His people.

In the midst of his exultation, he recalls that at times he had not clung to his faith, saying that all men are liars and that when he needed help, no one was there to assist him. This quoting of Psalm 31:22 shows that he now realizes that in the worst times of life, God is his only source of refuge. The author makes the point that to feel crushed or disillusioned and to say so, even to the point of anguish, is still no proof that faith is dead; in many cases it is simply a reminder of the complete necessity of living under the hand of God.

To walk in the presence of the Lord is both demanding and reassuring, since in the presence of the Lord one is wholly exposed, but also wholly befriended.

PSALM 117

¹O Praise the LORD, all ye nations:
praise him, all ye people.
²For his merciful kindness is great toward us:
and the truth of the LORD [endureth] for ever.
Praise ye the LORD.

PSALM 117
Title: Fifteenth Psalm of Praise
Author: anonymous
Superscription: none
Theme: In Praise of the Lord

This psalm, although short in its words, is very great in faith. In some manuscripts, this psalm is a part of the preceding poem. However, both the Hebrew text and the Septuagint have treated them as separate psalms. These two verses contain the complete act of praise. The first verse employs strict parallelism of form and sends forth a call to worship to the world. The second verse, which is in similar form, completes the call by expressing the reasons for giving praise. Truly universal, the call includes all nations of all peoples and times.

This may be the first time that the Israelites and the Gentiles are praising side-by-side as one people under God. The very diversity of this song is a challenge not to ignore God's kingship or to assume that one's birthplace entitles them to expect different fates in life or different affection from God. His steadfast love belongs to everyone—forever. His promises plans and plans are as fresh now as on the day that He made them.

PSALM 118

¹O give thanks unto the LORD; for [he is] good:
because his mercy [endureth] for ever.
²Let Israel now say, that his mercy
[endureth] for ever.
³Let the house of Aaron now say,
that his mercy [endureth] for ever.
⁴Let them now that fear the LORD say,
that his mercy [endureth] for ever.
⁵I called upon the LORD in distress: the LORD answered me, [and set me] in a large place.
⁶The LORD [is] on my side; I will not fear:
what can man do unto me?

⁷The LORD taketh my part with them that help me:
therefore shall I see [my desire]
upon them that hate me.
⁸[It is] better to trust in the LORD that
to put confidence in man.
⁹[It is] better to trust the LORD then
to put confidence in princes.
¹⁰All nations compassed me about:
but in the name of the LORD will I destroy them.
¹¹They compassed me about; yea, they compassed
me about: but in the name of the LORD,
I will destroy them.
¹²They compassed me about like bees;
they are quenched as the fire of thorns: for in the
name of the LORD I will destroy them.
¹³Thou has thrust sore at me that I might fall:
but the LORD helped me.
¹⁴The LORD [is] my strength and song,
and is become my salvation.
¹⁵The voice of rejoicing and salvation [is] in the
tabernacles of the righteous:
the right hand of the LORD doeth valiantly.
¹⁶The right hand of the LORD is exalted: the right
hand of the Lord, doeth valiantly.
¹⁷I shall not die, but live,
and declare the works of the LORD.
¹⁸The LORD hath chastened me sore:
but he hath not given me over unto death.
¹⁹Open to me the gates of righteousness: I will go
into them, [and] I will praise the LORD:

²⁰This gate of the LORD,
into which the righteous shall enter.
²¹I will praise thee: for thou hast heard me,
and art become my salvation.
²²The stone [which] the builders refused is become
the head [stone] of the corner.
²³This is the LORD's doing;
it [is] marvelous in our eyes.
²⁴This [is] the day [which] the LORD hath made;
we will rejoice and be glad in it.
²⁵Save now, I beseech thee, O LORD: O LORD,
I beseech thee, send now prosperity.
²⁶Blessed [be] he that cometh in the name of the
LORD: we have blessed you out of
the house of the LORD.
²⁷God [is] the LORD, which hath showed us light:
bind the sacrifice with cords,
[even] unto the horns of the altar.
²⁸Thou [art] my God, and I will praise thee:
[thou art] my God, I will exalt thee.
²⁹O give thanks unto the LORD; for [he is] good:
for his mercy [endureth] for ever.

PSALM 118
Title: Nineteenth Messianic Psalm
Author: anonymous
Superscription: none
Theme: Thanksgiving for God's Mercies

Standing at the end of the Hallel collection is Psalm 118. While known to be a processional psalm, the exact reasons for its writing remain obscured. There are four viable reasons for the creation of this psalm. This psalm may indicate a Davidic king giving thanks for victory in battle; it may show the celebration of the Israelites leaving Egypt and subsequent victory over Canaan; the joy of either the rebuilding the walls of Jerusalem; perhaps a song in dedication of the Second Temple. Following the first possibility makes the speaker the King while the balance would have the Levitical Choir speaking on behalf of the people.

The notes that follow will assume the first interpretation. Verses 5-21 and verse 22 appear to speak in a singular voice, which gives an indication that the first four verses may have later been added to adapt it to usage in public worship.

Verses 10-14 give a continual reminder of the contempt that other nations have directed toward Jerusalem since its first inhabitation by the Israelites. History shows that the world's conspiracy against the city may have been a direct desire to destroy the *City of God* from other nations and sadly from within Israel itself, as is seen in Acts 4:27. This rejection was much more personal in that it was also rejection of the Lord and His anointed ones, a matter expressed much earlier in Psalm 2:2.

As the New Testament unfolded in Luke 11:53, the *Great King* was disdained by the builders of their own *worldly* empires. The battle between men of righteousness and men of evil started in the Garden of Eden and will continue until the Lord makes His triumphant return. Though the *warriors* on both sides of this battle fight with vigor and vengeance, only one will emerge victorious. Surely as He had delivered them at the Red Sea, He would later be victorious, not only in battle, but later in the provision of eternal salvation as well.

Jesus would experience the same opposition as the Israelites faced (Luke 11:52-54). The last song of this liturgy may have been the one sung by Jesus and His disciples at the conclusion of the Last Supper. Following the liturgical call to praise the King offers a song for deliverance and victory in battle. The call to thanksgiving is the signal for the procession toward the Temple to begin. The King speaks his final word of praise and the liturgical conclusion repeats the opening call, thus framing the whole psalm.

Note: "The stone the builders rejected." These words in verse 22 are repeated five times in the New Testament. Taken literally, it means the head of the corner—a large stone used to anchor and align the corner of a wall. The stone hated by worldly powers has now become the most important stone in the structure of God's new Kingdom for humanity. This rejection of the stone (Jesus) would one day act itself out on the road to Jerusalem, unrehearsed and with explosive force. When God's realities broke through His symbols and shadows (Hebrews 10:1), the horns of the altar became the arms of the cross and the festival itself found fulfillment in Christ, the Passover Lamb.

PSALM 119

¹Blessed [are] the undefiled in the way,
who walk in the law of the LORD.
²Blessed [are] they that keep his testimonies, [and that] seek him with the whole heart.
³They also do no iniquity: they walk in his ways.
⁴Thou hast commanded [us]
to keep thy precepts diligently.
⁵O that my ways were directed to keep thy statutes!
⁶Then shall I not be ashamed, when I have respect unto all thy commandments.
⁷I will praise thee with uprightness of heart, when I shall have learned thy righteous judgments
⁸I will keep thy statutes: O forsake me not utterly.
⁹Wherewith all shall a young man cleanse his way?
by taking heed [thereto] according to thy word.
¹⁰With my whole heart, I have sought thee:
O let me not wander from thy commandments.
¹¹Thy word have I hid in mine heart,
that I might not sin against thee.
¹²Blessed [art] thou, O LORD: teach me thy statutes.
¹³With my lips have I declared all
the judgments of thy mouth.
¹⁴I have rejoiced in the way of thy testimonies,
as [much as] in all riches.
¹⁵I will meditate in thy precepts,
and have respect unto thy ways.
¹⁶I will delight myself in thy statutes:
I will not forget thy word.

¹⁷Deal bountifully with thy servant,
[that] I may live, and keep thy word.
¹⁸Open thou mine eyes, that I may behold
wondrous things out of thy law.
¹⁹I [am] a stranger in the earth:
hide not thy commandments from me.
²⁰My soul breaketh for the longing [that it hath]
unto thy judgments at all times.
²¹Thou hast rebuked the proud [that are] cursed,
which do err from thy commandments.
²² Remove from me reproach and contempt;
for I have thy testimonies.
²³Princes also did sit [and] speak against me:
[but] thy servant did meditate in thy statutes.
²⁴Thy testimonies also [are] my delight
[and] my counselors.
²⁵My soul cleaveth unto the dust:
quicken thou me according to thy word.
²⁶I have declared my ways, and thou heardest me:
teach me thy statutes.
²⁷Make me to understand the way of thy precepts:
so shall I talk of thy wondrous works.
²⁸My soul melteth for heaviness: strengthen thou
me according unto thy word.
²⁹Remove from me the way of lying:
and grant me thy law graciously.
³⁰I have chosen the way of truth:
thy judgments have I laid [before me].
³¹I have stuck unto thy testimonies:
O LORD, put me not to shame.

³²I will run the way of thy commandments,
when thou shalt enlarge my heart.
³³Teach me, O LORD, the way of thy statutes;
and I shall keep it [unto] the end.
³⁴Give to me understanding, and I shall keep thy law;
yea, I shall observe it with [my] whole heart.
³⁵Make me to go in the path of thy commandments;
for therein do I delight.
³⁶Incline my heart unto thy testimonies,
and not to covetousness.
³⁷Turn away mine eyes from beholding vanity;
[and] quicken thou me in thy way.
³⁸Stablish thy word unto thy servant,
who [is devoted] to thy fear.
³⁹Turn away my reproach which I fear:
for thy judgments [are] good.
⁴⁰Behold, I have longed after thy precepts:
quicken me in thy righteousness.
⁴¹Let thy mercies come also unto me, O LORD,
[even] thy salvation, according to thy word.
⁴²So shall I have wherewith to answer him that
reproacheth me: for I trust in thy word.
⁴³And take not the word of truth utterly out of my
mouth; for I have hoped in thy judgments.
⁴⁴So shall I keep thy law
continually for ever and ever.
⁴⁵And I will walk at liberty: for I seek thy precepts.
⁴⁶I will speak of thy testimonies also before kings,
and will not be ashamed.
⁴⁷And I will delight myself in thy
commandments, which I have loved.

⁴⁸My hands also will I lift up unto thy
commandments, which I have loved;
and I will meditate in thy statutes.
⁴⁹Remember the word unto thy servant,
upon which thou hast caused me to hope.
⁵⁰This [is] my comfort in my affliction:
for thy word hath quickened me.
⁵¹The proud have had me greatly in derision:
[yet] have I not declined from thy law.
⁵²I remembered thy judgments of old, LORD;
and have comforted myself.
⁵³ Horror hath taken hold upon me because
of the wicked that forsake thy law.
⁵⁴Thy statutes have been my songs in the house
of my pilgrimage.
⁵⁵I have remembered thy name,
O LORD, in the night, and had kept thy law.
⁵⁶This I had, because I Thy precepts.
⁵⁷[Thou art] my portion, O LORD: I have said that
I would keep thy words.
⁵⁸I entreated thy favor with [my] whole heart:
be merciful unto me according to thy word.
⁵⁹I thought on my ways,
and turned my feet unto thy testimonies.
⁶⁰I made haste, and delayed not
to keep thy commandments.
⁶¹The bands of the wicked have robbed me:
[but] I have not forgotten thy law.
⁶²At midnight I will rise to give thanks unto thee
because of thy righteous judgments.

⁶³I [am] a companion of all [them] that fear thee,
and of them that keep thy precepts.
⁶⁴The earth, O LORD, is full of thy mercy:
teach me thy statutes.
⁶⁵Thou hast dealt well with thy servant,
O LORD, according unto thy word.
⁶⁶Teach me good judgment and knowledge: for I
have believed thy commandments.
⁶⁷Before I was afflicted I went astray:
but now I have kept thy word.
⁶⁸Thou [art] good, and doest good;
teach me thy statutes.
⁶⁹The proud have forged a lie against me: [but] I will
keep thy precepts with [my] whole heart.
⁷⁰Their heart is as fat as grease;
[but] I delight in thy law.
⁷¹[It is] good for me that I have been afflicted;
that I might learn thy statutes.
⁷²The law of thy mouth [is] better unto me,
than thousands of gold and silver.
⁷³Thy hands have made me,
and fashioned me: give me understanding,
that I may learn thy commandments.
⁷⁴They that fear thee will be glad when they see me;
because I have hoped in thy word.
⁷⁵I know, O LORD, that thy judgments [are] right, and
[that] thou in faithfulness hast afflicted me.
⁷⁶Let, I pray thee, thy merciful kindness be for my
comfort, according to thy word unto thy servant.
⁷⁷Let thy tender mercies come unto me, that I may
live: for thy law [is] my delight.

⁷⁸Let the proud be ashamed; for they dealt perversely with me without a cause:
[but] I will meditate in thy precepts.
⁷⁹Let those that fear thee turn unto me,
and those that have known thy testimonies.
⁸⁰Let my heart be sound in thy statutes;
that I be not ashamed.
⁸¹My soul fainteth for thy salvation:
[but] I hope in thy word.
⁸²Mine eyes fail for thy word, saying,
When wilt thou comfort me?
⁸³For I am become like a bottle in the smoke; [yet]
do I not forget thy statutes.
⁸⁴How many [are] the days of thy servant? when wilt thou execute judgment on them that persecute me?
⁸⁵The proud have digged pits for me,
which [are] not after thy law.
⁸⁶All thy commandments [are] faithful:
they persecute me wrongly; help thou me.
⁸⁷They had almost consumed me upon earth;
but I forsook not thy precepts.
⁸⁸Quicken me after thy lovingkindness; so shall I
keep the testimony of thy mouth.
⁸⁹For ever, O LORD, thy word is settled in heaven.
⁹⁰Thy faithfulness [is] unto all generations: thou hast
established the earth, and it abideth.
⁹¹They continue this day according to thine ordinances: for all [are] thy servants.
⁹²Unless by law [had been] my delights, I should
then have perished in mine affliction.

⁹³I will never forget thy precepts:
for with them thou hast quickened me.
⁹⁴I [am] thine, save me;
for I have sought thy precepts.
⁹⁵The wicked have waited for me to destroy me:
[but] I will consider thy testimonies.
⁹⁶I have seen an end of all perfection:
[but] thy commandment [is] exceeding broad.
⁹⁷O how I love thy law!
it [is] my meditation all the day.
⁹⁸Thou through thy commandments hast made me
wiser than mine enemies:
for they [are] ever with me.
⁹⁹I have more understanding than all my teachers:
for thy testimonies [are] my meditation.
¹⁰⁰I understand more than the ancients,
because I keep thy precepts.
¹⁰¹I have refrained my feet from every evil way,
that I might keep thy word.
¹⁰²I have not departed from thy judgments:
for thou hast taught me.
¹⁰³How sweet are thy words unto my taste!
[yea, sweeter] than honey to my mouth!
¹⁰⁴Through thy precepts I get understanding:
therefore I hate every false way.
¹⁰⁵Thy word [is] a lamp unto my feet,
and a light unto my path.
¹⁰⁶I have sworn, and I will perform [it],
that I will keep thy righteous judgments.
¹⁰⁷I am afflicted very much: quicken me,
O LORD, according to thy word.

¹⁰⁸Accept, I beseech thee, the freewill offerings of my mouth, O LORD, and teach me thy judgments.
¹⁰⁹My soul [is] continually in my hand:
yet do I not forget thy law.
¹¹⁰The wicked have laid a snare for me:
yet I erred not from thy precepts.
¹¹¹Thy testimonies have I taken as and heritage for ever: for they [are] the rejoicing of my heart.
¹¹²I have inclined mine heart to perform thy statutes alway, [even unto] the end.
¹¹³I have [vain] thoughts: but thy law do I love.
¹¹⁴Thou [art] my hiding place and my shield:
I hope in thy word.
¹¹⁵Depart from me, ye evildoers:
for I will keep the commandments of my God.
¹¹⁶Uphold me according unto thy word, that I may live: and let me not be ashamed of my hope.
¹¹⁷Hold thou me up, and I shall be safe: and I will have respect unto thy statutes continually.
¹¹⁸Thou hast trodden down all them that err from thy statutes: for their deceit [is] falsehood.
¹¹⁹Thou puttest away all the wicked of the earth [like] dross: therefore I love thy testimonies.
¹²⁰My flesh trembleth for fear of thee;
and I am afraid of thy judgments.
¹²¹I have done judgment and justice:
leave me not to mine oppressors.
¹²²Be surety for thy servant for good:
let not the proud oppress me.
¹²³Mine eyes fail for thy salvation,
and for the word of thy righteousness.

¹²⁴Deal with thy servant according unto thy mercy,
and teach me thy statutes.
¹²⁵I [am] thy servant; give me understanding,
that I might know thy testimonies.
¹²⁶[It is] time for [thee], LORD, to work:
[for] they have made void thy law.
¹²⁷Therefore, I love thy commandments
above gold; yea, above fine gold.
¹²⁸Therefore I esteem all [thy] precepts [concerning]
all [things to be] right; [and] I hate every false way.
¹²⁹Thy testimonies [are] wonderful:
therefore doth my soul keep them.
¹³⁰The entrance of thy words giveth light; it giveth
understanding unto the simple.
¹³¹I opened my mouth and panted:
for I longed for thy commandments.
¹³²Look thou upon me, and be merciful unto me,
as thou usest to do unto those that love thy name.
¹³³Order my steps in thy word: and let not any
iniquity have dominion over me.
¹³⁴Deliver me from the oppression of man:
so will I keep thy precepts.
¹³⁵Make thy face to shine upon thy servant;
and teach me thy statutes.
¹³⁶Rivers of waters run down mine eyes,
because they keep not thy law.
¹³⁷Righteous [art] thou, O LORD,
and upright [are] thy judgments.
¹³⁸Thy testimonies [that] thou hast commanded [are]
righteous and very faithful.

¹³⁹My zeal hath consumed me, because mine enemies have forgotten thy words.
¹⁴⁰Thy word [is] very pure:
therefore thy servant loveth it.
¹⁴¹I [am] small and despised:
[yet] do not I forget thy precepts.
¹⁴²Thy righteousness [is] an everlasting righteousness, and thy law [is] the truth.
¹⁴³Trouble and anguish have taken hold on me: [yet] thy commandments [are] my delights.
¹⁴⁴The righteousness of thy testimonies [is] everlasting: give me understanding, and I shall live.
¹⁴⁵I cried with [my] whole heart; hear me, O LORD:
I will keep thy statutes.
¹⁴⁶I cried unto thee; save me,
and I shall keep thy testimonies.
¹⁴⁷I prevented the dawning of the morning,
and cried: I hoped in thy word.
¹⁴⁸Mine eyes prevent the [night] watches, that I might meditate in thy word.
¹⁴⁹Hear my voice according unto thy lovingkindness:
O LORD, quicken me according to thy judgment.
¹⁵⁰They draw nigh that follow after mischief:
they are far from thy law.
¹⁵¹Thou [art] near, O LORD;
and all thy commandments [are] truth.
¹⁵²Concerning thy testimonies, I have known of old that thou hast founded them for ever.
¹⁵³Consider mine affliction, and deliver me:
for I do not forget thy law.

¹⁵⁴Plead my cause, and deliver me:
quicken me according to thy word.
¹⁵⁵Salvation [is] far from the wicked:
for they seek not thy statutes.
¹⁵⁶Great [are] thy tender mercies, O LORD: quicken
me according to thy judgments.
¹⁵⁷Many [are] my persecutors and mine enemies;
[yet] do I not decline from the thy testimonies.
¹⁵⁸I be held the transgressors, and was grieved;
because they kept not thy word.
¹⁵⁹Consider how I love thy precepts: quicken me,
O LORD, according to thy lovingkindness.
¹⁶⁰Thy word [is] true [from] the beginning: and every
one of thy righteous judgments [endureth] for ever.
¹⁶¹Princes have persecuted me without a cause: but
my heart standeth in awe of thy word.
¹⁶²I rejoice at thy word,
as one that findeth great spoil.
¹⁶³I hate and abhor lying: [but] thy law do I love.
¹⁶⁴Seven times a day, do I praise thee
because of thy righteous judgments.
¹⁶⁵Great peace have they which love thy law: and
nothing shall offend them.
¹⁶⁶LORD, I have hoped for thy salvation,
and done thy commandments.
¹⁶⁷My soul hath kept thy testimonies;
and I love them exceedingly.
¹⁶⁸I have thy precepts and thy testimonies:
for all my ways [are] before thee.
¹⁶⁹Let my cry come near before thee, O LORD: give
me understanding according to thy word.

¹⁷⁰Let my supplication come before thee:
deliver me according to thy word.
¹⁷¹My lips shall utter praise,
when thou hast taught me thy statutes.
¹⁷²My tongue shall speak of thy word: for all thy
commandments [are] righteousness.
¹⁷³Let thine hand help me;
for I have chosen thy precepts.
¹⁷⁴I have longed for thy salvation, O LORD;
and thy law [is] my delight.
¹⁷⁵Let my soul live, and it shall praise thee; and let
thy judgments help me.
¹⁷⁶I have gone astray like a lost sheep; seek thy
servant; for I do not forget thy commandments.

PSALM 119
Title: Psalm of the Word of God
Author: anonymous
Date: Post-exilic
Superscription: none
Theme: The Excellence of God's Word

This is the longest chapter in the Bible with a length of 176 verses. It is also the most intricate and ceremonious of the 150 psalms in the Psalter. Within the exception of four verses, each contains one or more of these words: law, statutes, ordinances, commandments, word, precepts, testimony, judgment or way. The psalm itself is a series of acrostics, with each of the 22 stanzas divided into eight couplets. Each couplet begins with a corresponding letter of the Hebrew alphabet. In these verses, the psalmist takes delight in God's word, using it as a guide for life. His confidence in the Law is unbounded and seeing it broken brings him pain. He is humble in his countenance and willing to accept the discipline that he has *earned*. With the coming of Christ and the New Testament, there are volumes that speak to God's glory and yet this devotion to God puts many to shame.

No chronology is in this psalm, neither is there a cohesive focus on any topic such as victory, forgiveness or thanksgiving. As such, readers here must search for themes found among its verses. The thoughts are the reflections of a man reliving his prayers, his joys and his failures. For ease of understanding, the psalm is divided into smaller portions, leaving the thematic groupings the assignment of each individual.

Verse 1-8: The first part of the psalm devotes itself to obedience to the Law of God. All eight verses devote themselves to the joy, happiness and necessity of being obedient to God's word. Blessed are those who walk in the way of the Lord. Scripture is God's word for living life, not something to bring shame when one experiences failure or distress. The psalmist vows to keep the Law of the Lord as his guide forever.

Verses 9-16 address the way in which a man can operate within the Law of God. He asks, "Wherewithal shall a man cleanse his way?" The answer is timeless. Keeping God's word requires *knowing* God's Word

(9); keeping actions within the commandments (10); keeping the Laws in memory (11); being willing to learn (12); declaring His judgments and meditating on His words (13-14); placing their value above all else (14); reflecting on them (15) and being delighted that God cares enough for humanity to give them a guide to follow (16).

Verses 17-24: The psalmist has depended upon God in numerous times of persecution, a hint of sorrow is seen, but this section ends in joy and delight. Verse 17 "that I may live" becomes the first of many joyous expressions. He asks God to keep him aware of the Law in order that he may rejoice in its beauty. Even though the writer knows that in desiring to keep God's Law he will fail, he welcomes the discipline as the caring hand of God. His joy is not in the kingdom of princes, but in the guiding counsel of God.

Verses 25-32 revolve around strength and understanding. The psalmist calls for strength and comfort, quickly realizing that these things can only come from God. The words *"graciously teach"* are an invitation to God to share with man the knowledge of His love and to give him the courage to use that knowledge to strengthen him regardless of circumstances.

Verses 33-40: These verses seem to given the indication that if the psalmist knew and understood the words of God, that he would more than gladly walk in their ways. Vaguely he seems to reference that it is

God's *duty* to make him to understand and to follow the Laws, to keep him from evil deeds and to *quicken* him in righteousness. In reality, the psalmist is making confession that he knows he needs these things and that they can only come from God.

Verses 41-48 appeal for God to assist man to have the courage to respond to those who treat him with reproach, taunting both David and his God. It takes courage to stand on God's word in the face of the kings of the world without feeling fearful or ashamed. Still, the psalmist commits himself to walking in God's word and asks that God does not take his words of faith from his mouth. "I lift my hands" is used mainly in the context of prayer, but here it is bold expression of the psalmist indicating that the word of God is worthy to be praised.

Verses 49-56: The psalmist asks God to keep His word in his memory for comfort in times of persecution or affliction. He has discovered through his lifetime that God's words have always been able to rescue him in times of trouble and turn his grief into joy.

Verses 57-64 find the psalmist recalling his life and God's testimonies. He submits that he has always been faithful to the Law once he learned of their wonder. His thankfulness to God prompts him to rise both early in the morning and late in the night simply to glorify God. Yet, as before, he acknowledges that he does not know everything and asks again for God to "teach me thy statutes".

Verses 65-72: the psalmist remembers how he had been *away from God* prior to his afflictions and now begins to understand a benefit in God's wrath upon men. Before his own understanding of God's words, he went *astray* and it was through God's discipline that He reached understanding. In verse 66, the word *"judgment"* literally means "taste". The text refers to spiritual taste rather than physical taste and describes spiritual discrimination. The heart is to test words and actions much as the body *tastes* and tests foods. A companion piece to this occurs in Job 34:3.

Verses 73-80: The psalmist asks for blessings upon himself and humiliation for his enemies. He wants the proud to become ashamed and receive justice. He thanks God for His loving mercy and kindness and pleads that no matter what happens in his life, he will never be ashamed of his faithfulness. It is his hope that as others see his righteousness, they will also begin to see God.

Verse 81-88: With several examples, the psalmist gives a long list of his endless sorrow and sobs to God for his rescue. He has suffered from other men, yet has taken the stance that his faith has always been steadfast, never forsaking God. Although he has been beaten, bruised and battered, he begs God to quicken his spirit. Though he questions why so many negative things have come against him, he knows that only in God can he find hope in the darkest places of his life.

Verses 89-95 hold the victory which the preceding verses begged. The psalmist is revived by God's word, promising that he will never forget the precepts of God. These verses show that the complete and inerrant word of God is timeless and unchangeable. Cultures, opinions and seasons may change, but God will not. The psalmist, saved by his dependence upon God's Word, will continue to seek His testimonies.

Verses 97-104 appear to be those of an arrogant man. He meditates on the Law; he is wiser than his enemies are and has more understanding than his teachers have. He understands that more than ancient wisdom keeps him from evil ways and he has not departed from the words of God. To take these verses only in this light would be a mistake. The depth of the psalm lies behind the words. God has given him wisdom and understanding; both of which he has used to outsmart his enemies. His knowledge of the Law has kept him from falling into the temptation of evil and he acknowledges and thanks God for loving him and for being the source of all *his knowledge.*

Note: The New Testament cites verses 98-105 as a demonstration that true wisdom emanates from God, a gift at first hidden from worldly eyes. This theme will continue throughout the ministry of Christ, especially at the crucifixion, (1 Corinthians 2:6-8) and weaves itself into the entire New Testament.

Verses 105-112 show that mankind is far too incapable of living life without a guide. The Scripture lights the path that humankind is to follow. The psalmist, in gratitude to God, vows that he will perform according to His will and will keep His righteous judgments. Even though he has people trying to trap him in one way or another, he will not waver. He will trust and follow God unto the end. The most cherished example of God's word compared to the light is in the New Testament's recounting of the Lord's temptation when Jesus used God's word to back down Satan.

Verse 113-120: the psalmist emphasizes the loyalty of the believer and follower when he says, "Thou art my hiding place and my shield." This loyalty gives him a sense of safety and inspiration for the future. The worldly and the wicked possess no such safety, for their words are lies. An element of the fear of the Lord is in these verses as the psalmist testifies to the fate of the wicked, admitting that he is fearful of receiving such a judgment.

Verses 121-128 find the psalmist confidently declaring that he has been true to God's ways. Immediately following is an appeal for God to start taking action against those who have persecuted him and in doing so denied God. He knows how much God hates evildoers. In verse 123, the psalmist *instructs* God to get to work on the wicked ones of the earth. For them, the only appropriate judgment is divine judgment. The author states that God's words are to be valued more than precious metals and again, he asks for more understanding of God's word.

Verses 129-136 are the psalmist's testimonies of God's understanding and love. He acknowledges that God is the light that guides him in his path. He asks for freedom from those who oppress him. This is overshadowed by the despondency that he feels for those who fail to recognize the guiding hand of God, leading them through life. Failing to trust in the words of God will only lead to false knowledge or delusions of power as is seen in Proverbs 6:23.

Verses 137-144 show the strength of God in every circumstance. Opening with the phrase, "righteous art thou, O Lord," he describes how God has delivered him out of the hands of his enemies. His own trouble is caused by fretting and worrying; going back to the Word will bring him delight. God's understanding goes beyond anything the human mind can comprehend. All that He does or says bears His mark of purity. Verse 144 follow many of the previous verses, asking that God will give him more understanding of His word and of His ways.

Verses 145-152 hear the psalmist asking once again for God's divine health and power. He cries out to God for physical and spiritual health, making a brief acknowledgment regarding those who desire his ill fate. He cries once again for God's quickening power, "I cried; hear me O LORD." In his closing statement, the psalmist indicates that he has known the teachings of God forever and knows that God will stand by His word.

Verses 153-160 return to the psalmist's depth of agony. His personal needs ring out in the word *"quicken"* used in verses 154, 156 and 159. He is pondering those who have taken great efforts to make his life miserable. Although he stops short of asking God to condemn or destroy his enemies, he does state that they will find no salvation until they come under the wing of the true God. The writer has always stood his ground in the face of his enemies, confident in the unchanging nature of God's righteous judgments.

Verse 161-168: Surrounded by enemies and the Princes of nations, the psalmist still greatly admires the power of God's words. Even as he is surrounded by antagonists and wicked men, he has a great inner peace which comes from his love of the Law. Again, the psalmist recites what appears to be his own goodness: he rejoices in the word, he loves the Law, he praises God seven times a day, he has hoped for salvation and he has kept and loved the testimonies of the Lord. As before, he is not speaking proudly or arrogantly, but rather expressing the great love that he has for the scripture and the joy that he receives from honoring the Law of God.

Verses 169-176 are a summation of the psalm. There is a plea for more understanding followed by a promise to give more praise as his new knowledge leads him. He asks God to keep him from going astray and to *find him* should he begin to wander away from the Word. As he closes, the psalmist acknowledges that the words and the commandments are righteous and that he has chosen God's precepts.

Note: as the psalm ends, the psalmist has spent himself in reflection, praise and a plea for understanding from God. Though many scribes have spent their entire lives copying scripture, this psalm seems to push for worldwide knowledge and understanding of the Word of God. Studying the Word of God should not turn into simple scholarly pride. Using the knowledge of the Word of God to impress others is to stand with the Pharisees.

Verses 120-134 are a song sung by the pilgrims on their way to celebrate a festival in Jerusalem. These Songs of Degrees are also called the Song of Assents, to signify the steps upward to the Temple. Verses 120, 124, 125, 130 and 131 do not appear related to a journey to Jerusalem, indicating again that these portions may have been later additions.

Contained within its 176 verses are 21 traits of a man who is blessed; 15 great things God has done for man; 70 requests; 30 reasons to make vows to God; 30 vows which are made; 18 secrets to victory; a six-fold testimony; 198 references to God's word; 62 facts found in the word; 22 reasons God is happy and an enormous 610 personal pronouns.

PSALM 120

¹A Song of degrees. In my distress
I cried unto the LORD, and he heard me.
²Deliver my soul, O LORD, from lying lips,
[and] from a deceitful tongue.
³What shall be given unto thee?
or what shall be done unto thee?
or what shall be done unto thee, thou false tongue?
⁴Sharp arrows of the mighty, with coals of juniper.
⁵Woe is me, that I sojourn in Mesech,
[that] I dwell in the tents of Kedar!
⁶My soul hath long dwelt with
him that hateth peace.
⁷I [am for] peace: but when I speak,
they [are] for war.

PSALM 120
Title: Seventh Prayer of Distress
Author: anonymous
Date: Return from Babylon
Superscription: a Song of Degrees (Ascents)
Theme: Relief from Angry Foes

The beginning of the *Psalms of Ascents* is sharply personal as the psalmist cries out to the Lord to give him relief from those who have held him captive. It voices the longing and homesickness of those living among strangers and enemies. Their words, threats, hatred and anger show the resentment that often appeared between the righteous life of the Israelites and the ways of the pagan nations.

His question in verse 3 asks God what would be a fitting punishment to these foreigners who speak lies and offer nothing but struggle to their captives. He complains that he must sojourn among the bloodthirsty and barbaric enemies, especially those in Asia Minor and the Arabian Desert north of Damascus. A similar situation appears in verse 6:4 in the Book of Nehemiah when Israel was rebuilding the walls of Jerusalem.

The cry for deliverance passes through retribution toward a lament for peace. Although he has lived in this situation for quite some time, he still seeks a peaceful existence with his captors, they do not want peace, only war. There is no way the two can share the same nation. At psalm's end, he decrees that although his life has been painful, the evil ones will meet their destruction. His hope (4) is that they will be buried in a hail of sharp arrows and hot coals.

Note: This little passage is a pre-play of the New Testament comments about being equally yoked, referring especially to the joining of light and darkness. Nothing good can result through this union. The New Testament warns the Christian against two offenses: compromising (2 Corinthians) and animosity (Romans 12:14-21).

PSALM 121

¹A Song of degrees.
I will lift up mine eyes unto the hills,
from whence cometh my help.
²My help [cometh] from the LORD,
which made heaven and earth.
³He will not suffer thy foot to be moved:
he that keepeth thee will not slumber.
⁴Behold, he that keepeth Israel
shall neither slumber nor sleep.
⁵The LORD [is] thy keeper:
the LORD [is] thy shade upon thy right hand.
⁶The sun shall not smite thee by day,
nor the moon by night.
⁷The LORD shall preserve thee from all evil:
he shall preserve thy soul.
⁸The LORD shall preserve thy going out and thy
coming in from this time forth,
and even for evermore.

PSALM 121
Title: Seventh Psalm of God
Author: anonymous
Superscription: a Song of Degrees
Theme: Seeking God's Help

"From whence comes my help?" cries the psalmist. Looking toward the hills around Zion, the traveler voices the question that sets the mood for the psalm. The question expresses no doubt, but rather introduces the affirmation that carries throughout the balance of the psalm, namely that his helper is Jehovah God. As he journeys toward Jerusalem, he sees the dwelling place of God, the creator and guardian of all the earth.

The entire psalm speaks of the wonderful things that God does daily for His people. He will hold them upright, watch over them continually, keep them in the shade of His hand and protect them as they move about. God will keep them from all evil, He will preserve their souls and it is for this, that they sing His praise as they journey toward the Temple.

PSALM 122

¹A Song of degrees of David. I was glad when they said unto me, Let us go into the house of the LORD.
²Our feet shall stand within thy gates, O Jerusalem.
³Jerusalem is builded as a city
that is compact together:
⁴Whither the tribes go up, the tribes of the LORD,
unto the testimony of Israel,
to give thanks unto the name of the LORD.
⁵For there are set thrones of judgment,
the thrones of the house of David.
⁶Pray for the peace of Jerusalem:
they shall prosper that love thee.
⁷Peace be within thy walls,
[and] prosperity with in thy palaces.
⁸For my brethren and companions' sakes,
I will now say, Peace [be] within thee.

⁹Because of the house of the LORD our God
I will seek thy good.

PSALM 122
Title: Second Psalm of Zion
Author: a Psalm of David
Superscription: a Psalm of Degrees
Theme: The Joy of Entering the Temple

Psalm 122 is a prayer for the peace of Jerusalem. As the Pilgrims near the Temple gate within the city walls, they pray for the peace of the city, the center of worship and the seat of government for the entire nation. With Jerusalem in sight, the trials and the hazards of their pilgrimage are eclipsed by their feelings of joy. With travel now completed, this psalm is a sequel to the preceding one. Some commentators believe that rather than in *real time*, the psalm is a memory of one who has recently made this journey. Either way, the exuberant joy of being in Jerusalem leaves the psalmist overwhelmed.

What joy the psalmist felt as he responded to the invitation to join the pilgrims going to Jerusalem. He again rejoices in the fact that the testimony of the revealed Mosaic Law maintains Jerusalem as an orderly society and that Israel is governed by the fair and just rulings of God through King David. The future of Israel and many other nations and individuals revolve around verse 6, which states the promise of prosperity for those that love Israel.

Romans 10:1 indicates that there will be a restoration of Israel. In further support of Israel, Romans 10:12 indicates that the church needs to recognize its Jewish roots; the Gentiles were grafted into the church, but the roots belong to Israel. This view allows for fulfillment of Old Testament promises of blessings. Since Old Testament congregational worship was full of excitement, how much more joyous is the worship in the New Testament church to be, now that the full gospel of Jesus has been revealed.

Note: What Jerusalem was to the Israelite, the church is now to the Christian. Here are his closest ties, his brothers and his companions join with him to focus on the worship and praise of God. However limited or sinful a people may be, this is where God who has chosen to build His house. To the authorities of the time, the words of Jesus were decisive and dangerous (John 11:48) and had eventually become unthinkable (Luke 19:47). For the Christian, God's love is now seen as unbounded by culture or nation and anywhere the Christians gather together becomes the Temple. For the inspiring implications of this, see Acts 11:26; Acts 14:27; Hebrews 12:22-24 and Hebrews 13:1-3.

PSALM 123

[1]A Song of degrees. Unto thee lift I up mine eyes,
O thou that dwellest in the heavens.
[2]Behold, as the eyes of servants [look] unto the
hands of their masters, [and] as the eyes of a

maiden unto the hand of her mistress; so our eyes
[wait] upon the LORD our God,
until that he have mercy upon us.
³Have mercy upon us, O LORD, have mercy upon us:
for we are exceedingly filled with contempt.
⁴Our soul is exceedingly filled with the scorning of
those that are at ease,
[and] with the contempt of the proud.

PSALM 123
Title: Eighteenth Prayer of Distress
Author: anonymous
Superscription: a Song of Degrees
Theme: Mercy and Contempt

Psalm 123 is an intense lament by an individual who speaks for his people. As they travel, the pilgrims lift their eyes towards God. The change from the singular to the plural pronoun at the end of verse 1 suggests that the group may have sung this song as they made their sojourn. The simple prayer of God's humble people asks that God will show mercy upon them and in doing so will spoil the contempt of the proud. Just as Jesus looked up to heaven in recognition of His source of supply (John 17:1) and Stephen looked steadfastly into heaven for comfort during His persecution, so the psalmist looks toward God for His mercy.

The psalmist refers to the *eyes* four different times, adding emphasis to the idea that the pilgrims are *looking* for God's favor. As a servant requires the *mercy* of his master, so the pilgrims require the mercy of God. The measure of their desire is expressed in their cry, "Have mercy upon us, O God." With trained watchfulness, the servant is ready for the opportunity to be of service. The comparison must not be taken too literally, however, as God's servants are watching for relief, not for orders. Yet servants they remain and as such, they should be loyal and submissive. Yet these same "believers" refused to ease the strain of David's suffering. They neglected him, abandoned him and supported the contempt that surrounded him. Now, they seek mercy.

It is quite illuminating that *contempt* is singled out for specific mention. Other things can bruise and cause injuries, but this wound goes far deeper and pierces the spirit more than any other type of rejection. In the Sermon on the Mount, contempt ranks as more murderous than anger (Matthew 5:22). In Daniel 12:2 *contempt* is noted as one of the pains of hell. In Acts 5:41 suffering for faith is deemed as honorable. For mankind, the greatest acceptance of contempt came when Christ Himself suffered the contempt of others and through His own glory turned it into the redemption of humanity. The psalm ends with the determined acceptance of God's word as seen in Lamentations 3:18-24.

PSALM 124

^{1}A Song of degrees of David. If [it had not been] the LORD who was on our side, now may Israel say;
^{2}If [it had not been] the LORD, who was on our side, when men rose up against us:

³Then they had swallowed us up quick,
when their wrath is kindled against us:
⁴Then the waters had overwhelmed us,
the stream had gone over our soul:
⁵Then the proud waters had gone over our soul.
⁶Blessed [be] the LORD, who hath not given us
[as] a prey to their teeth.
⁷Our soul is escaped as a bird out of the snare of the fowlers: the snare is broken and we are escaped.
⁸Our help [is] in the name of the LORD, who made heaven and earth.

PSALM 124
Title: Third Psalm of Deliverance
Author: a Song of David
Superscription: a Psalm of Degrees
Theme: God defends His People

While the original purpose was undoubtedly to praise God for a particular act of deliverance, the placement of this psalm indicates that it may have had a general usage beyond the song of the pilgrims. In the structure of the psalm, a Levite speaks in verses 1-5, while worshipers answer in verses 6-8. The theme focuses on deliverance from very powerful enemies. Both the language and the theme suggest a post-exilic date. The author is designated as David, because of the echoes of Psalm 18 and 69.

The psalmist describes his enemies with three metaphors: a beast that would devour him, a flood of water that causes destruction and a bird hunter who traps with the use of snares. As a Psalm of David, insight is given into the peril of his kingdom, particularly from the Philistines, who hoped to see the last of Israel when they shattered the Kingdom of Saul. Second Samuel 5:17 shows how serious the threat was and how little confidence David placed in his own power. The Philistines had not invaded merely to gain territory, but meant to put an end to David and all of Israel. The description of the raging torrent is appropriate, as it was God who had broken through the Philistine army like a flood.

Verse 7 makes this psalm all the more accessible to the Christian as a song of praise. As a bird is released from a snare, so has humanity been set free from self-reliance and pride. While David's example in looking towards the Maker rather than things made inspires other pilgrims, the mention of "thy name" may be an echo of his own feelings in Psalm 20:7, where God is invisible and is more real and more potent than the most advanced army of the day.

PSALM 125

¹A Song of degrees. They that trust in the LORD
[shall be] as mount Zion, [which] cannot be
removed, [but] abideth for ever.
²As the mountains [are] round about Jerusalem,
so the LORD [is] roundabout his people
from henceforth even for ever.

³For the rod of the wicked shall not rest upon the lot of the righteous; lest the righteous put forth their hands unto iniquity.
⁴Do good, O LORD, unto [those that be] good, and [to them that are] upright in their hearts.
⁵As for such as turn aside unto their crooked ways, the LORD shall lead them forth with the workers of iniquity: [but] peace [shall be] upon Israel.

PSALM 125
Title: Sixth Psalm of Trust
Author: anonymous
Superscription: a Song of Degrees
Theme: The Protection of the Lord

In rousing song, Israel's security is celebrated in testimony and praise. This psalm, written after the Babylonian exile is similar to Psalm 124 and was not designed only as pilgrim song, but was one that was familiar enough to be sung by a group. A Levite probably led this liturgy.

After a long and difficult journey, the mountains roundabout Jerusalem slowly come into view. The Israelites trust that as Mount Zion is steady and immovable, so is the Lord. Symbolizing God's presence are the hills around Jerusalem, but also those who trust in the Lord are immovable, like the rock of Zion. True religion starts at the center, the Lord, in whom all things-Mount Zion included-will hold together. The phrase "those who trust in the Lord" shows that trust is a vital aspect of a relationship with God.

God encourages men to look inside themselves as well as toward Him. However, as Psalm 121 shows, the human mind is tempted to fall far short of what God desires. There have been many times when wicked men appear to have the upper hand and the righteous are seen as wavering. Evil always rejoices upon finding something it can corrupt as is seen in verse 3 and is similar to Matthew 24:12. No matter how things *look,* God shortens wickedness and strengthens love.

In verses 4 and 5, the prayer "Do good, O Lord" is the psalmist's request for favor upon the faithful. He fears that if the Israelites had remained under the rule of foreigners that their identity and perhaps their faith would slowly fade. The final words of the psalm are words of peace. Confident of the righteousness of Israel, he is equally confident that God will cast out those who reject Israel.

PSALM 126

¹A Song of degrees. When the LORD turned again the captivity of Zion, we were like them that dream.
²Then was our mouth filled with laughter, and our tongue with singing: then said they among the heathen, The LORD hath done great things for them.
³The LORD hath done great things for us;
[whereof] we are glad.
⁴Turn again our captivity,
O LORD, as the streams in the south.
⁵They that sow in tears shall reap in joy.

⁶He that goeth forth and weepeth, bearing precious seed, shall doubtless come again with rejoicing, bringing his sheaves [with him].

PSALM 126
Title: Fourth Psalm of Deliverance
Author: anonymous
Superscription: a Song of Degrees
Theme: Return to Zion

This psalm has been described as a song of *thanksgiving, lament, deliverance and restoration.* Although there is an obvious reference to the return from the exile, the conditions are not those that actually existed in the early post-exilic society. The psalmist instead refers to ideal conditions, which the exiles expected and the disillusionment that was to follow. They had dreams of their homeland while in captivity and the hope of the glorious restoration was idealized to the point that it proved too good to believe. What they had idealized and visualized while in captivity was not indicative of what had really happened.

Verses 4 to 6 further this beautiful vision of Jerusalem. The *beauty* of Jerusalem was never far from those in captivity. However, it was not to be. Conditions were anything but glorious and ideal. In Haggai 2:1-8 Yahweh speaks to the people and tells them that instead of worrying about their own things, they need to be about rebuilding the Temple. God promises that the latter glory will be greater than the former. Even as the farmer sows in anxiety and reaps in joy, so may Israel will realize the fullness of restoration. The planting of seeds accompanied by a spirit of brokenness can only bring about a spiritual harvest of joy.

The images of renewal carry excitement, the joy of seeing their Temple in its full splendor, followed by the solemn awareness of the future and the part that each man is to play in it. As seen in the beginning of the psalm, each person must now wonder what kind of deliverance God had given to them and what He would yet place in their hands. The sight of the city had been long awaited and they were heartbroken. The return from Babylon had been hard won (2 Corinthians 9:6) and long awaited (Galatians 6:7-10). However, there is new resolve and whatever the uncertainties of literal farming, the psalmist is sure of his harvest-God's blessing will "grow" within the lives of His people.

Note: This psalm reminds man to treat situations as measure of the future: dry places as potential rivers, hard toil and good seed as the certain prelude to a harvest. Hence, in the New Testament comes the admonishment not to fret, not to worry and above all, to be patient and keep faith in God.

PSALM 127

¹A Song of Degrees for Solomon. Except the LORD build the house, they labor in vain that build it:
except the LORD keep the city,
the watchmen waketh [but] in vain.

²[It is] vain for you to rise up early,
to sit up late, to eat the bread of sorrows:
[for] he giveth his beloved sleep.
³Lo, children [are] an heritage of the LORD:
[and] the fruit of the womb [is his] reward.
⁴As arrows [are] in the hand of a mighty man;
so [are] children of the youth.
⁵Happy [is] the man that hath his quiver full of them:
they shall not be ashamed, but they shall speak with
the enemies in the gate.

PSALM 127
Title: Seventh Psalm of Trust
Author: a Psalm for Solomon
Superscription: a Psalm of Degrees
Theme: Uniting with the Lord in Labor

It is likely that this is a combination of two psalms, one revolving around building the Temple and the other the building of the family. Emphasis is on the folly of building a family without the help of God. This psalm has an unknown origin, but through time, it has become a *folk song* of the pilgrims.

Here, as the pilgrims travel, they are reminded that life's securities and blessings are gifts from God rather from their own achievements. The song singles out three of man's most universal preoccupations: building, security and raising a family. It begs the question not only of what has been built, but who is the builder?

Verses 1 and 2 express a distinct dependence upon the Lord. Man's total dependence on God is illustrated in the reference to basic human endeavors. Nothing built by man will ever be equal to God's design. If God is not included in man's plans and efforts, even the diligent man who works from morning until late evening cannot hope for success. The work of creating and building can only have two possible ends: it will be by the Lord's doing, or it will be pointless.

The same concept is in the building of a family, it must be founded upon the rock which God has provided (Luke 6:49). God's covenant with Adam and Eve contained two primary provisions: descendants and dominion. It would physically be impossible for two people to take care of the entire earth. This was a task that would require (many) descendants. For believers, having children is a response to the command to be fruitful and multiply, fill the earth and subdue it (Genesis 1:28). God gives children to men just as a loving father passes his inheritance to his descendants. The children belong to their parents only in a secondary sense. When a couple marries, they make themselves available to serve God by loving and teaching the next generation. Especially important are a man's sons, as they can provide protection and safety to his aging parents.

Note: Jesus shows how much God values children. "Not one of these little ones is to be despised." He holds their faces toward God as an example for adults to be constantly looking upward. Loving and caring for

God's children is one of the principal ways in which He is invited to become the primary builder of a family.

PSALM 128

¹A Song of degrees. Blessed [is] every one that
feareth the LORD; that walketh in his ways.
²For thou shalt eat the labor of thine hands: happy
[shalt] thou [be], and [it shall be] well with thee.
³Thy wife [shall be] as a fruitful vine by the sides of
thine house: thy children like olive
plants round about thy table.
⁴Behold, that thus shall the man
be blessed that feareth the LORD.
⁵The LORD shall bless thee out of Zion:
and thou shalt see the good of Jerusalem
all the days of thy life.
⁶Yea, thou shalt see thy children's children,
[and] peace upon Israel.

PSALM 128
Title: a Psalm of Righteousness
Author: anonymous
Superscription: a Song of Degrees
Theme: Blessings of those Who Fear the Lord

In the psalm, a man pictures and describes everything a man of his own day could ask from life. Like the preceding psalm, the tone and style of the wisdom literature is present and it is not a pilgrim song, but rather a folk song of the travelers. The most prominent of the *wisdom* teachings is that the fear of the Lord is the only way one can enter the pathway to wisdom.

The psalmist begins by stating that happiness is the lot of those who have learned to fear the Lord and to walk in His ways. It is well with him because he eats the products of his labor, rather than losing them to his oppressive overlords. The ingredients of true happiness are reverence and obedience. Hard work is taken for granted, but this psalm as Psalm 127 make it clear that *enjoyment* of the fruit is a gift from God.

A faithful and loving wife is the symbol of fruitfulness. She is not like the fatherless, which speak continually and never stay at home. "Within the heart of your house" refers to the wife directly, not to the actual vine and is put here in marked contrast to what is said of the promiscuous wife in Proverbs 9:13. The attractiveness of a wife is her complete devotion to the ways of God.

While righteousness is personal and a family is confined, but dangers disappear during the gatherings held in Zion. In the gathering of the faithful one finds their personal blessings entwined with the welfare of the greater family of God. No barriers should exist between believers and they are to show themselves to have a commonality with all of God's *citizens.* A vital part of the blessing enjoyed by one who fears God comes from beyond the limits of his own home, perhaps all the way from Zion.

Note: The vine and the olive tree are frequently paired in the Old Testament as both were very long lived and produce the wine and the oil that played such a central role in the lives of the people.

PSALM 129

¹A Song of degrees. Many a time have they afflicted
me from my youth, may Israel now say:
²Many a time have they afflicted me from my youth:
yet they have not prevailed against me.
³The plowers plowed upon my back:
they made long their furrows.
⁴The LORD [is] righteous:
he hath cut asunder the cords of the wicked.
⁵Let them all be confounded
and turned back that hate Zion.
⁶Let them be as the grass [upon] the housetops,
which withereth afore it groweth up:
⁷Wherewith the mower filleth not his hand;
nor that he bindeth sheaves his bosom.
⁸Neither do they go which go by say, The blessing of
the LORD [be] upon you:
we bless you in the name of the LORD.

PSALM 129
Title: Fourth Prayer/Testimony Psalm
Author: Anonymous
Superscription: a Psalm of Degrees
Theme: Victory over Enemies

This is the plea of a suffering Israel and the lament of an anguished community. The characteristic of trust is present but some negative emotions appear as well. Israel looks back upon the Hand that has saved them so frequently. While most nations look back on what they have achieved, Israel reflects on what she has survived. It could be a disheartening exercise, for Zion still has many enemies. The singers take courage from the past, facing God with gratitude and facing their enemies with defiance.

In his mind, the psalmist hears the words, "I loved him and out of Egypt I called my son" (Hosea 11:1). The great Exodus was the best starting point for the reflections of the suffering of Israel, just as the cross and the resurrection are for the Christians. Here, the psalmist compresses the long history of Israel's troubles into a short statement. From the time of the Exodus to the current time, his nation has suffered severe affliction from every direction. The marks on their backs are similar to the furrows made by a plow and the cords of the oppressors are as harnesses on oxen. This suffering was not simply discomfort, but severe anguish.

Verse 5 brings an indictment upon Zion's enemies. The enemies of Israel should be humiliated and sent back to their homeland. If Zion were no more than a capital city, this curse on its enemies would be mere bluster. However, in the Psalter, Zion is the city of God (48:1) and the place of His earthly throne. To the inhabitants of Jerusalem, it is appropriate that those who reject God's city deserve severe punishment. Leaving metaphors aside, the wicked ones are not only choosing the way of hatred, but more importantly, they are setting themselves against God, which is more than foolish—it is self-destructive.

Note: The survival of this people, so hated yet so resilient, is their silent witness to God. The New Testament shows its fulfillment in Christ and calls the church to follow, as did the Israelites-not walking in circumstance, but walking in His power.

PSALM 130

^A 1 Song of degrees. Out of the depths have
I cried unto thee, O LORD.
²Lord, hear my voice: let thine ears be
attentive to the voice of my supplications.
³If thou, LORD, shouldest mark iniquities,
O Lord, who shall stand?
⁴But [there is] forgiveness with thee,
that thou mayest be feared.
⁵I wait for the LORD, my soul doth wait,
and in his word do I hope.
⁶My soul, [waiteth] for the Lord more than they that
watch for the morning: [I say, more than] they that
watch for the morning.
⁷Let Israel hope in the LORD: for with the LORD
[there is] mercy, and with him
[is] plenteous redemption.
⁸And he shall redeem Israel from all his iniquities.

PSALM 130
Title: Nineteenth Prayer of Distress
Author: anonymous
Superscription: a Psalm of Degrees
Theme: Wait for Redemption

Psalm 130 is one of the most eloquent of the prayers of distress. There is a steady climb from the voice of a pained and remorseful sinner towards assurance and at the end, there is redemption. This psalm was once the sixth penitential psalm as it seems to carry more references to the removal of iniquity than danger from an enemy. The beginning cry comes from the soul of one who knows his own failures; the closing plea is for all of Israel to place their trust in the Lord. Since the psalmist's troubles affected the entire nation, the psalm becomes appropriate for bands of pilgrims in the post-exilic society.

Sin is universal. If God counted the iniquities of each man, rather than blotting them out, there would not be enough books-no person is sinless. The only hope comes in God's forgiveness. The confession of verse 3 echoes many found in the Psalter. Here however, there is an expectancy of God's intervention. The psalmist shows that he is aware of God's timing when he says, "I wait for the Lord, my soul doth wait, and in His word do I hope."

At the end of the psalm, the writer is doing just this-he is waiting. He waits upon God the way a guard watches over his charge, always ready, always vigilant. Yet for all his watchfulness, he could not have known the true redemption of which he spoke. This Messianic link indicates that the men of the Old Testament knew "something" about the unmerited pardon that was to come through Christ (Romans 4:7-8). The lack of clarity in this however did not dampen this singer's spirit in any way. God's forgiveness has never been in doubt, in spite of what the future would hold. There can be no argument as to the inclusiveness of his word:, "for with the Lord there is mercy and with Him is plenteous redemption." Where sin abounded, grace did much more abound.

Note: The word "iniquity" is used frequently in the Psalms and carries a meaning greater than sin. "Iniquity" comes from the Hebrew word avon *meaning: evil, fault, sin, guilt, blame, moral illness, perversion and crookedness. Coming from the root* avah, *it adds the action of bending or distorting. Hence, iniquity becomes an evil bent, a crooked direction or a warped thought or action. The word "iniquity" appears more than 220 times in the Old Testament.*

PSALM 131

¹A Song of degrees of David. LORD, my heart is not haughty, nor mine eyes lofty: neither do I exercise myself in great matters, or in things too high for me.
²Surely I have behaved and quieted myself, as a child that is weaned of his mother:
my soul [is] even as a weaned child.

> ³ Let Israel hope in the LORD,
> from henceforth and for ever.

PSALM 131
Title: Ninth Psalm of the Righteous
Author: a Psalm of David
Superscription: a Song of Degrees
Theme: Simple Trust

Although this is essentially a song of trust, this beautiful literary composition reads like a confession. The picture of humble resignation to God's leading exemplifies a deep sense of personal discipline. While some interpreters label this is a corporate expression, the final plea for Israel suggests that an individual voice is speaking throughout. Ascribed to David, it has its ironies in light of the pathway of his life, but awakens memories of much simpler times. Easy to remember in its brevity, it was only natural that a beautiful expression of humility like this should become a *folk* song of the pilgrims.

This small Psalm anticipates the lesson of Matthew 18:1-4, where Jesus called a little child to him. In answer to the question, "Who is the greatest in the kingdom of heaven?" Jesus held up a little child as an example. Only those as trusting and humble as a child may enter the kingdom of God, which is total righteousness, peace and joy. Without these qualities, one will come to undervalue other people, overestimate and overreach themselves and forget the words of Deuteronomy 29:29.

After a long struggle, the psalmist can now declare himself free of his previous ambitions and hardness of heart. His soul is now calm and he now thinks like a child on his mother's lap, no longer struggling to be fed. The psalm shows that whereas a child once depended upon its mother for what it could not live without, he has now learned that he no longer requires this sustenance and can move forward. Now he is able to receive all he needs from God. It is a freedom from the need to fulfill one's own desires as well as from the bondage of unknown threats and fears.

David commits himself to do the will of Him who sent him and to accomplish the tough trials ahead for which he has already been tested. Jesus says almost the same thing in (John 4:34).

PSALM 132

¹A Song of degrees. LORD, remember David,
[and] all his afflictions:
²How he sware unto the LORD,
[and] vowed unto the mighty [God] of Jacob;
³Surely I will not come into the tabernacle of my
house, nor go up into my bed;
⁴I will not give sleep to mine eyes,
[or] slumber to mine eyelids,
⁵Until I find out a place for the LORD,
an habitation for the mighty [God] of Jacob.
⁶Lo, we heard of it at Ephratah:
we found it in the fields of the wood.

⁷We will go into his tabernacles:
we will worship at his footstool.
⁸Arise, O LORD, into thy rest; thou,
and the ark of thy strength.
⁹Let thy priests be clothed with righteousness;
and let thy saints shout for joy.
¹⁰For thy servant David's sake turn not away
the face of thine anointed.
¹¹The LORD hath sworn [in] truth unto David; he will
not turn from it; Of the fruit of thy
body will I set upon thy throne.
¹²If thy children will keep my covenant and
my testimony that I shall teach them, their children
shall also sit upon thy throne for evermore.
¹³For the LORD hath chosen Zion;
he hath desired [it] for his habitation.
¹⁴This [is] my rest for ever: here will I dwell;
for I have desired it.
¹⁵I will abundantly bless her provision:
I will satisfy her poor with bread.
¹⁶I will also clothe her priests with salvation: and her
saints shall shout aloud for joy.
¹⁷There will I make the horn of David to bud: I have
ordained a lamp for mine anointed.
¹⁸His enemies will I clothe with shame: but upon
himself shall his crown flourish.

PSALM 132
Title: Third Psalm of Zion
Author: a Psalm of David
Superscription: a Psalm of Degrees
Theme: Trust in the God of David

Unique among the songs in the Pilgrim collection, this appears to have been included because of its nature and historical importance. This psalm was composed early in David's monarchy. The reason for this writing may have been the dedication of the Temple or perhaps for a king's coronation. The more likely instance is that this psalm is connected with David's bringing the Ark of the Covenant back to the Temple-the short distance from Kiriath-jearim as told in 1 Samuel 7:1. It was the climax of a journey which had begun centuries ago at far off Sinai. Since 2 Samuel 6:14-15 and 1 Chronicles 15:28 also mention this event, it is likely that portions of this psalm have been borrowed from earlier compositions.

In verses 1 through 5, there is a unique glimpse of David's motive of bringing the Ark to Jerusalem. The focus was not political, not merely the *added touch* to Jerusalem, but rather a symbol of God, which was to make the people more conscious of their heritage and to follow the God of David at all costs. The emphasis of this prayer is on his attention to find a suitable place for the Ark. As the pilgrims approach the Temple, they seek entrance to the city, which belongs to God, based on God's promises to David rather than on their own goodness.

The second portion of the psalm is much more festive and includes promises made to God as well as God's promise to keep the family of David upon the throne forever. The beauty and warmth of these promises come from the love of the people and require a loving answer to reach fulfillment. Sometimes, humans tend respond in a cynical and trite manner, treating God's choice of Israel as His child as something they can exploit. The later usage of the Temple as a place of commercialism will give an example of this exploitation. This very incorrect attitude and its corresponding responses are seen in Matthew 21:12 among other places.

Note: The words "Arise, O Lord" were used each time the Ark left the Temple.

PSALM 133

¹A Song of degrees of David. Behold,
how good and how pleasant [it is] for brethren
to dwell together in unity!
²[It is] like the precious ointment upon the head,
that ran down upon the beard, [even] Aaron's
beard: that went down to the skirts of his garments;
³As the dew of Hermon, [and as the dew] that
descended upon the mountains of Zion: for there
the LORD commanded the blessing,
[even] life for evermore.

PSALM 133
Title: Twentieth Psalm of Instruction
Author: a Psalm of David
Superscription: a Song of Degrees
Theme: Unity of the Saints

This psalm, with all its colorful language, has been credited to David. History indicates that this psalm was written when all the tribes gathered to crown David, their king. Other possibilities drawn from history include the time after the influx of the refugees from the Northern Tribes during the Assyrian invasions, or a post-exilic gathering of Israel as told in the Book of Nehemiah. What specific moment it represents, there is no way of knowing.

What is known, however, is that *brotherhood*, in God's sight, would include everyone. Everyone includes the debtors, the slaves, the offensive and the oppressive. Until a man had chosen to deny Jehovah as his God, he was welcome in the *Kingdom brotherhood*. No amount of exaggeration is needed to portray the benefits to the unity of the people. They will be blessed as individuals and as a whole. God's blessings are for the many, not for the few. Blessings are freely given and meant to be shared, bringing all of God's people into the arms of fellowship.

The second half of verse 3, with its strong accent on God's love, gives a final glimpse into the psalm. In short, true unity, like all good gifts is from above, bestowed rather than contrived, a blessing rather than an achievement.

PSALM 134

¹A Song of degrees. Behold, bless ye the LORD,
all [ye] servants of the LORD,
which by night stand in the house of the LORD.
²Lift up your hands [in] the sanctuary,
and bless the LORD.
³The LORD that made heaven and earth,
bless thee out of Zion.

PSALM 134
Title: Sixteenth Psalm of Praise
Author: anonymous
Superscription: a Psalm of Degrees
Theme: Praising the Lord in the Night

Psalm 134 is a great conclusion for the songs used by the pilgrims. The nature of the psalm corresponds to the benediction at the end of each book at the Psalter. The position of this song in the collection suggests that it was sung at the close of evening worship. The Feast of Tabernacles is the most likely occasion. The songs of Ascents, alternately named the Song of Degrees, began in Meschech and Kedar in Psalm 120, where the people were living among strangers and it ends beautifully on the note of serving God day and night within His Temple.

The psalm begins with a call to "behold, bless ye the Lord, all ye servants." The voice comes from the High Priest, the Levitical Choir or perhaps even the pilgrims who have gathered. The last option makes greater sense and gives a reason for this psalm to be included in the collection. The Temple minstrels lift up their hands in an attitude of prayer and blessing the Lord. As verse 2 of this psalm and 1 Timothy 2:8 show, uplifted hands are an integral part of both Jewish and Christian worship.

The people know that God is creator and now His blessings will show forth from His holy city. The traveling songs directed toward the wonderment and blessings of God end the psalm.

PSALM 135

¹Praise ye the LORD. Praise ye the name of the LORD; praise [him], O ye servants of the LORD.
²Ye that stand in the house of the LORD, in the courts of the house of our God,
³Praise the LORD; for the LORD [is] good: sing praises unto his name; for [it is] pleasant.
⁴For the LORD hath chosen Jacob unto himself, [and] Israel for his peculiar treasure.
⁵For I know that the LORD [is] great, and [that] our Lord [is] above all gods.
⁶Whatsoever the LORD pleased, [that] did he in heaven, and in earth, in the seas, and all deep places.
⁷He causeth the vapors to ascend from the ends of the earth; he maketh lightnings for the rain; he bringeth the wind out of his treasuries.
⁸Who smote the firstborn of Egypt, both of man and beast.

⁹[Who] sent tokens and wonders into
the midst of thee, O Egypt, upon Pharaoh,
and upon all his servants.
¹⁰Who smote great nations, and slew mighty kings;
¹¹Sihon king of the Amorites, and Og king of Bashan,
and all the kingdoms of Canaan:
¹²And he gave their land [for] an heritage,
an heritage unto Israel.
¹³Thy name, O LORD, [endureth] for ever;
[and] thy memorial, O LORD,
throughout all generations.
¹⁴For the LORD will judge his people, and he will
repent himself concerning his servants.
¹⁵The idols of the heathen [are] silver and gold,
the work of men's hands.
¹⁶They have mouths, but they speak not;
eyes have they, but they see not;
¹⁷They have ears, but they hear not;
neither is there [any] breath in their mouths.
¹⁸They that make them are like unto them:
[so is] everyone that trusteth in them.
¹⁹Bless the LORD, O house of Israel:
bless the LORD, O house of Aaron:
²⁰Bless the LORD, O house of Levi:
ye that fear the LORD, bless the LORD.
²¹Blessed be the LORD out of Zion,
which dwelleth at Jerusalem. Praise ye the LORD.

PSALM 135
Title: Seventeenth Psalm of Praise
Author: anonymous
Date: Post Exilic
Superscription: none
Theme: Praise God for Creation and Loving-kindness

Almost every verse in the Book of Psalms is either an echo or direct quotation from another part of Scripture. This psalm is no different as verses 15-21 were first seen in Psalm 115 and other portions form a collage of quotations from the Old Testament. This psalm was specifically for Temple worship and included solo singers, the Levitical Choir and interaction with the people.

In verses 1 through 4 the call of "Praise ye the Lord" brings the people to worship the Lord's goodness and His choice of Israel as His own. The first *reason* for praise is that the Lord's name is good, that He is good, and further, that His name and the act of worship are delightful to both God and the worshiper. The love of God for His people is a reason to sing, especially in light of the majesty of His personal character.

Yahweh here is a powerful reference to Israel's covenant God as compared to the *gods* of the heathen. He is described as the God of nature (5-7) doing whatsoever he pleases in heaven and earth. He is the God of history (8-14), leading His chosen people out of Egypt and through the conquest of Canaan. Jeremiah 10:13 also gives a clear picture of God's workings in nature. They are more than mere quotations; they are truths by which to live. By avoiding reference to the physical world it becomes obvious that God's miracles are not confined by time, space or situation. Although these are important, God's miracles should not be relegated to such dimensions, as He is everywhere at all times. For Him, time and circumstance are of no importance.

"Bless the Lord" is the same call to praise found in Psalms 115 and 118. This psalm draws attention to the fact that grateful remembrance of God's mercy is important. God has begun a good work; it only makes sense that He will complete it.

Many Christian creeds have a similar pattern, progressing from the creation, to the acts of redemption and then forward to the prospect of the second coming of Christ. Here, the call to honor God is at the center of a man's being, shown through his trust, gratitude and praise. There can be no comparison of man's blessing God in praise to the blessings He bestows upon mankind. Matthew 21:16 offers the reminder that one should not be too proud in offering himself to God, for out of the mouth of babes comes perfected praise.

Note: "to repent himself" as used in verse 14 does not mean that God needs to repent. It indicates that God will defend His people against evildoers, oppressors and those who are Israel's enemies.

PSALM 136

¹O give thanks unto the LORD; for [he is] good:
for his mercy [endureth] for ever.
²O give thanks unto the God of gods:
for his mercy [endureth] for ever.
³O give thanks to the Lord of Lords:
for his mercy [endureth] for ever.
⁴To him who alone doeth great wonders:
for his mercy [endureth] for ever.
⁵To him that by wisdom made the heavens:
for his mercy [endureth] for ever.
⁶To him that stretched out the earth above the
waters: for his mercy [endureth] for ever.
⁷To him that made great lights:
for his mercy [endureth] for ever:
⁸The sun to rule by day:
for his mercy [endureth] for ever:
⁹The moon and stars to rule by night:
for his mercy [endureth] for ever.
¹⁰To him that smote Egypt in their firstborn:
for his mercy [endureth] for ever:
¹¹And brought out Israel from among them:
for his mercy [endureth] for ever:
¹²With a strong hand, and with a stretched out arm:
for his mercy [endureth] for ever.
¹³To him which divided the Red sea into parts:
for his mercy [endureth] for ever:
¹⁴And made Israel to pass through the midst of it: for
his mercy [endureth] for ever:

¹⁵But overthrew Pharaoh and his host in the Red sea:
for his mercy [endureth] for ever.
¹⁶To him which led his people through the wilderness: for his mercy [endureth] for ever.
¹⁷To him which smote great kings:
for his mercy [endureth] for ever:
¹⁸And slew famous kings:
for his mercy [endureth] for ever:
¹⁹Sihon king of the Amorites:
for his mercy [endureth] for ever:
²⁰And Og the King of Bashan:
for his mercy [endureth] for ever:
²¹And gave their land for an heritage:
for his mercy [endureth] for ever:
²²[Even] an heritage unto Israel his servant:
for his mercy [endureth] for ever.
²³Who remembered us in our low estate:
for his mercy [endureth] for ever:
²⁴And hath redeemed us from our enemies:
for his mercy [endureth] for ever.
²⁵Who giveth food to all flesh:
for his mercy [endureth] for ever.
²⁶O give thanks unto the God of heaven:
for his mercy [endureth] for ever.

PSALM 136
Title: Eighteenth Psalm of Praise
Author: anonymous
Superscription: none
Theme: God's Enduring Mercy

This psalm of thanksgiving is likely an extension of Psalm 135. Both have God's interaction with Israel as a focal point and both speak of God's mighty works of creation. "His mercy endureth forever" occurs in every verse. This psalm could have the Levite leader reading the recital and the choir or worshipers responding with the refrain. The psalm is much easier to read without the refrain, suggesting that the refrain was not always a part of this psalm. Yet the refrain gives it a distinctive character and an important place in Jewish worship. This was designated as a *Hallel* song and was used at Passover as well as a song of general worship at the Temple. More on this can be seen in 2 Chronicles 7:3 and Ezra 3:11.

Historical in nature, this psalm tells the story of Israel and God's actions on their behalf. The creation of the earth also holds a primary place within these verses. "Oh give thanks unto the Lord" is the invitation to join in thanking God for His goodness and His Mercy. It calls for a graceful and thoughtful worship, telling what the believer should know through God's glorious deeds and how nature testifies to His never-ending devotion.

Verses 4-9 bring together the two thoughts regarding creation. In the Book of Genesis, the day by day creation is focused upon. The second half of the creation story is that of God's love, wisdom and understanding which He used in putting the world together. Here in the Psalter, it serves as an invitation to Christians not to quibble over cosmological theory, but to take joy in His environment. To God, this earth is not simply a created mechanism, but a product of a devout and steadfast love.

Each event from Egypt to Canaan, witnesses the way God has manifested His loving kindness within Israel's history. It courses through time, stopping here and there to comment on a specific situation. The heart and soul of this psalm is not overshadowed by historical facts however, and the worshiper's love and praise for the mercy of God runs throughout the psalm. The Christian community has its history in the cross and the resurrection; the sayings of Jesus and the words of the Apostles. The heritage of Israel is also the heritage of the Christian, binding Jesus to the Father and the Father to His people and creation. It illuminates man's redemption and the parallel pilgrimage that leads to baptism as in 1 Corinthians 10:1-4.

God's steadfast love endures forever. The final refrain shows the relevance of every act of God to every singer of this psalm. The closing verse takes up the same style as verses 1-3, bringing the psalm full circle and back to thanksgiving.

PSALM 137

¹By the rivers of Babylon, there we sat down, yea,
we wept, when we remembered Zion.
²We hanged our harps upon the willows
in the midst thereof.
³For there they that carried us away captive required
of us a song; and they that wasted us
[required of us] mirth, [saying],
Sing us [one] of the songs of Zion.
⁴How long shall we sing the
LORD's song in a strange land?
⁵If I forget thee, O Jerusalem,
let my right hand forget [her cunning].
⁶If I do not remember thee,
let my tongue cleave to the roof of my mouth;
if I prefer not Jerusalem above my chief joy.
⁷Remember, O LORD, the children of Edom in the
day of Jerusalem; who said, Raze [it],
raze [it, even] to the foundation thereof.
⁸O daughter of Babylon,
who art to be destroyed; happy [shall he be],
that rewardeth thee as thou hast served us.
⁹Happy [shall he be], that taketh and dasheth thy
little ones against the stones.

PSALM 137
Title: Fifth Prayer/Testimony Psalm
Author: anonymous
Date: Post-exilic
Superscription: none
Theme: Trouble in a Foreign Land

The title of this psalm gives no indication as to its connection to the Babylonian exile, but the relation of this outcry to other parts of the Old Testament and the teaching of the New Testament is relatively obvious. While it is not certain where the psalmist was when he wrote this song, he appears to have been one of the exiles who returned to Jerusalem approximately 538 BC. As a previous captive, he relives the bitter cruelty of those who held him prisoner. His voice comes in sobs as he remembers, "by the Rivers of Babylon, we wept." When asked to sing for the amusement of their captors, they struggled, knowing that the songs of Israel were for worship and praise, not for entertainment. During the length of captivity in Babylon, the harps and lyres hung on the tree branches and very few songs were composed.

Verse 4 asks, "How shall we sing the Lord's song. . .?" for to do so would be a direct desecration of all things holy (Ezekiel 25:122). This may have been the prelude to a defeatist answer, repealing forever the hope of Israel, slowly allowing her to fade into the Babylonian landscape. However, this psalmist instead springs to life with an intense, burning loyalty to Israel. This outburst raises his love for Jerusalem and his hatred for his captors. Aside from the Babylonians, the psalmist also faces his anger toward Edom, a nation that gloated over the falling of the temple as seen in Ezekiel 35:15; 36:5.

The slaughter suggested in verse 9 was of the type used primarily in the sacking of foreign kingdoms, (Isaiah 13:6; Nahum 3:2-3). This is not the Israelite playing a judge, but reveals only vaguely what Babylon has done to this nation. This appears to be confirmed in verse 8 as it focuses on the appeal for retribution.

There is a very angry answer to the question, "What did perpetrators of such acts deserve?" Presumably, after imposing such suffering, no punishment would be too excessive for the Babylonians. Sadly, most responses come in white-hot anger, while God suggests a calmer response. A man should rethink an event back to its essence, as God did with the cries of Job and Jeremiah. He should study the impact of his choices and be willing to accept them. Following God's will and trusting in Him for retribution directs a man to the proper response after such cruelty. Therefore, this psalm goes beyond either ignoring or playing down the anguish inflicted upon Israel, giving it full voice to express anger, sorrow, frustration and bitterness. Although there is no formal ending, it appears that the psalmist has made his decision and relies on God to help him lay enmity and bitterness to rest.

Notes on Psalms 138-150

This collection of eight Davidic psalms ends the primary portion of the Psalter. While there are many psalms that seem to exceed David's lifetime, they clearly stand in the tradition and style of David, the reputed *Father of the Psalms*. This final Davidic collection contains the Psalter's two most magnificent expositions on the greatness and the goodness of God. The focus on God's relationship with an individual is found in Psalm 139, while Psalm 145 shows God's relation to all of creation.

Psalms 146-150 are *Hallelujah Songs* not meant to be separate from the Psalter, but added at its end to create a final burst of praise that will please God.

PSALM 138

¹[A Psalm] of David. I will praise the with my whole heart: before the gods will I sing praise unto thee.
²I will worship toward thy holy temple, and praise thy name for lovingkindness and for thy truth: for thou hast magnified thy words above all thy name.
³In the day when I cried thou answeredst me, [and] strengthenedst me [with] strength in my soul.
⁴All the kings of the earth shall praise thee, O LORD, when they hear the words of thy mouth.
⁵Yea, they shall sing in the ways of the LORD: for great [is] the glory of the LORD.
⁶Though the LORD [be] high, yet hath he respect unto the lowly: but the proud he knoweth afar off.

> ⁷Though I walk in the midst of trouble,
> thou wilt revive me: thou shalt stretch forth thine
> hand against the wrath of mine enemies,
> and thy right hand shall save me.
> ⁸The LORD will perfect [that which] concerneth me:
> thy mercy, O LORD, [endureth] for ever: forsake not
> the works of thine own hands.

PSALM 138
Title: Tenth Praise/Prayer Psalm
Author: a Psalm of David
Superscription: none
Theme: The Lord's Goodness

Once again, God has shown His faithful love. He is great and mighty, yet He cares for seemingly insignificant men and women. The psalm begins as a hymn of thanksgiving, but later turns into a song of trust. In some respects, this psalm is like Psalm 18, although far less intense. It also shares one third of the words used in Psalm 145. Many of the ideas and phrases of this psalm are reminiscent of other sections of Scripture, primarily from Isaiah 40-66. Several manuscripts of the Septuagint connect the psalm with the time of Haggai and Zechariah.

The psalmist has experienced a recent answer to his prayers, for which now he gives his thanks. For whatever reason, the psalmist has decided that he should sing publically and he does so, giving thanks for his deliverance before the congregation. This is very similar to Psalm 40:10. There is a wonderful mixture of humility and boldness found here. David is bold enough to come before God's throne, yet as he comes, he is bowing in humility. Once again, there is a reminder that God's glory is revealed in His responses to the lowly.

David had once felt rejected and under the pressure of other *gods* (1 Samuel 26:19) and like today's Christians, he felt the force of other ideologies, demonic powers or idols of foreign cultures. David did not give into the *gods* that surrounded him, but stood steadfast, holding on to God and His promises. He expresses his deep confidence that God will fulfill His promise and complete the deliverance of Israel. Although an individual speaks the whole Psalm in a very personal manner, he is giving thanks for Israel as well.

Note: For all of its beauty, the Scripture does not encourage making an idol of the Word of God. Instead, man is reminded of Paul, boasting always in the Lord and even in his own infirmities. By using the Bible as a guide, man can see that it is not always the situation that needs changing-often the man involved in the situation that needs to change.

PSALM 139

¹To the chief Musician, A Psalm of David. O LORD, thou hast searched me, and known [me].
²Thou knowest my downsitting and mine uprising, thou understandeth my thought afar off.

³Thou compassest my past and my lying down, and art acquainted [with] all my ways.
⁴For [there is] not a word in my tongue, [but], lo, O LORD, thou knowest it all together.
⁵Thou hast beset me behind and before, and laid thine hand upon me.
⁶[Such] knowledge [is] too wonderful for me; it is high, I cannot [attain] unto it.
⁷Whither shall I go from thy spirit? or whither shall I flee from thy presence?
⁸If I ascend up into heaven, thou [art] there: if I make my bed in hell, behold, thou [art there].
⁹[If] I take the wings of the morning, [and] dwell in the uttermost parts of the sea;
¹⁰Even there shall thy hand lead me, and thy right hand shall hold me.
¹¹If I say, Surely the darkness shall cover me; even the night shall be light about me.
¹²Yet, the darkness hideth not from thee; but the night shineth as the day: the darkness and the light [are] both alike [to thee].
¹³For thou hast possessed my reins: thou hast covered me in my mother's womb.
¹⁴I will praise thee; for I am fearfully [and] wonderfully made: marvelous [are] thy works; and [that] my soul knowest right well.
¹⁵My substance was not hid from thee, when I was made in secret, [and] curiously wrought in the lowest parts of the earth.
¹⁶Thine eyes did see my substance, yet being unperfect; and in thy book all [my members] were written,

[which] in continuance were fashioned,
when [as yet there was] none of them.
¹⁷How precious also are thy thoughts unto me,
O God! how great is the sum of them!
¹⁸[If] I should count them, they are more in number
than the sand: when I awake, I am still with thee.
¹⁹Surely thou wilt slay the wicked, O God: depart
from me therefore, ye bloody men.
²⁰For they speak against thee wickedly,
[and] thine enemies take [thy name] in vain.
²¹Do not I hate them, O LORD, that hate thee? and
am I not grieved at with those
that rise up against thee?
²²I hate them with perfect hatred:
I count them mine enemies.
²³Search me, O God, and know my heart:
try me, and know my thoughts:
²⁴And see if [there be any] wicked way in me,
and lead me in the way everlasting.

PSALM 139
Title: Eighth Psalm of God
Author: a Psalm of David
Superscription: to the chief Musician
Theme: God's Complete Knowledge of Man

Nowhere outside of Job does one find such a profound awareness of how awesome it is to ask God to examine every thought, word and deed, with no thought of hiding or fighting. From the standpoint of Old Testament theology, this is the climax of the thoughts in the Psalter regarding God's personal relationship to the individual. The psalmist does not engage in useless ideologies, but simply describes his humble walk with God and shares what he has learned about God. He calls for God to examine his heart and to see his history. Like Job, he firmly claims his loyalty is to the Lord.

"Oh Lord, thou hast search me, and known me." The psalmist is completely aware that God knows every motive behind every action, yet he also knows his own inability to have a full comprehension of God. In four stanzas of six verses each, the psalmist displays the attributes of God: omniscience (1-6) omnipresence (7-12) and omnipotence (13-18). God's love is personal and active; discerning man; (3) knowing his mind and as in Amos 4:13, always surrounding and protecting His people.

"Whither shall I go from thy spirit?" Using rhetorical questions, the psalmist clearly shows that there is no place in heaven or earth that God cannot reach. Verse 10 shows gratefulness that God's long arm is moved by love. The psalmist recognizes the wonder of his own creation and of how God always knew everything that was happening.

In verse 16 the Hebrew words mean that *the days of my life were mapped out in advance.* Verse 14 in Hebrew reads, *"I give praise to thee, for I am awesomely and wonderfully made."*

All of life is in the hand of God. There is an unbelievable amount of detail in the human body, all of it coming from the mind of God. Such divine knowledge is not only wonderful (6), but carries its own proof of the ultimate commitment: God will not leave the work of His hands to chance. The words "I am still with thee" in verse 18 shows that there is no limit to what God can do on behalf of man.

David's final statements regarding the evil men in the world become gentle as he realizes that wicked and evil thoughts may be lurking in his own heart as well. David's resolve to honor God always was not necessarily easy, since immoral men can become convenient allies and the scoffers can be daunting opponents. Aware of his own weaknesses, he begins to *search* himself. Self-judgment, he determines, is better than vengeance (Romans 2:1-16).

PSALM 140

¹To the chief Musician, A Psalm of David.
Deliver me, O LORD, from the evil man:
preserve me from the violent man;
²Which imagine mischiefs in [their] heart; continually are they gathered together [for] war.
³They have sharpened their tongues like a serpent;
adders' poison [is] under their lips.
⁴Keep me, O LORD, from the hands of the wicked;
preserve me from the violent man; who have
purposed to overthrow my goings.
⁵The proud have hid a snare for me, and cords;
they have spread a net by the wayside;
they have set gins for me.

⁶I said unto the LORD, Thou [art] my God: hear the
voice of my supplications, O LORD.
⁷Oh GOD the Lord, the strength of my salvation,
thou hast covered my head in the day of battle.
⁸Grant not, O LORD, the desires of the wicked:
further not his wicked device;
[lest] they exalt themselves.
⁹[As for] the head of those that compass me about,
let the mischief of their own lips cover them.
¹⁰Let burning coals fall upon them:
let them be cast into the fire; into deep pits,
that they rise not up again.
¹¹Let not an evil speaker be established in the earth:
evil shall hunt the violent man to overthrow [him].
¹²I know that the LORD will maintain the cause of
the afflicted, [and] the right of the poor.
¹³Surely the righteous shall give thanks unto thy
name: the upright shall dwell in thy presence.

PSALM 140
Title: Eleventh Prayer for Judgment
Author: a Psalm of David
Superscription: to the chief Musician
Theme: Deliverance from Wicked Men

David has constantly had a myriad of enemies surrounding him. Some wanted his throne, some his power, authority and some even wanted his life. What his enemies could not have foreseen, however, is that every time they drove him back, they drove him back to God. This psalm is linked with 141-143 and shows the strife in Israel. No opposing group or nation is identified, but the problems appear to come from within Israel. The plots of war are similar to those in James 4:1-3 and arising from greedy and wicked men in the nation. David's prayer makes several physical references to the heart, head, tongue, lips, hands, feet and tears and teeth, showing that men have many parts and tendency to use them all in one way or another.

David's plea is for God's help; he prayed, "Deliver me, preserve me, keep me, grant not the desires of the wicked." David makes no excuses for the wicked man, as they have chosen the alternate way instead of God's way. It is easy to see that the actions of the wicked have changed very little through the generations. Paul, in 2 Corinthians mentioned the pattern of hurting and slandering when he states, "He has delivered us from so deadly a peril and He will deliver us again."

The word for *"cause"* in verse 12 is a legal term, reinforced by *justice* in the second line. The duties of a national King are constant and the use here serves as a reminder that God, as the Great King, will keep watch over all things. God is the King to the king; His voice is the only one that needs to be heard. It is His administration and He will govern with supreme wisdom and justice.

At psalm's end, the psalmist is completely positive. His heart is free to find its true home and his last words match the climax to which the whole of the Scripture moves: we shall serve Him and we shall see His face (Revelation 22:3-4).

Note: The New Testament treats the Psalter as a major witness to human depravity (Romans 3:10-18), because it exposes His enemies spreading evil like a poison, which can be hidden and used in any situation as is seen in Psalm 69:4. Paul, who was also a target, uses this verse to show that Jews as well as Gentiles are guilty of sin and need a Savior (Romans 3:8-13).

PSALM 141

¹A Psalm of David. LORD, I cry unto thee:
make haste unto me; give ear unto my voice,
when I cry unto thee.
²Let my prayer be set forth before thee [as] incense;
[and] the lifting up of my hands [as]
the evening sacrifice.
³Set a watch, O LORD, before my mouth;
keep the door of my lips.
⁴Incline not my heart to [any] evil thing,
to practice wicked works with the man that work
iniquity: and let me not eat of their dainties.
⁵Let the righteous smite me; [it shall be] a kindness:
and let him reprove me; [it shall be] an excellent oil,
[which] shall not break my head: for yet my prayer
also [shall be] in their calamities.
⁶When their judges are overthrown in stony places,
they shall hear my words; for they are sweet.
⁷Our bones are scattered at the grave's mouth,
as when one cutteth and cleaveth
[wood] upon the earth.

⁸But mine eyes [are] unto thee, O GOD, the Lord: in
thee is my trust; leave not my soul destitute.
⁹Keep me from the snares [which] they have laid for
me, and the gins of the workers of iniquity.
¹⁰Let the wicked fall into their own nets,
whilst I withal escape.

PSALM 141
Title: Fourth Prayer Psalm
Author: a Psalm of David
Superscription: none
Theme: Protection from Evil Behaviors

Psalm 141 is an evening prayer, which matches the morning prayer referred to in Psalm 5:3 and was prompted, like its companion, by the example of daily sacrifices (Exodus 29:38). This is a continuation of David's plea for protection. He is slandered, the victim of falsehoods spread by his enemies in Israel. The tone set here is different from most laments in that he is not at war with physical enemies; it is much more of a spiritual war. He seeks out God's assistance to overcome the temptations that sin has put before him. He prays that even if surrounded by the evil actions of others, he will not allow them to become a part of his own behavior.

The opening verse shows how much concern he places on his piety. The rest of the psalm expands on this feeling of self-doubt. The Hebrew words used to describe this battle do not lend themselves to translation, but the purpose of the psalm still rings clear. This is David's prayer against insincerity and compromise. It is a plea for his very survival in the midst of his never-ending attacks by others. Similar to the previous psalm, the prayer uses many of the same references to the body: hands, mouth, lips, heart, head, bones and eyes.

Verses 7 through 10 describe David's plight and not that of his enemy. "Set a watch, O Lord, before my mouth," is his request to have the ability to double check what comes out of his mouth, knowing that the tongue is the most powerful weapon. Cursing and blessing must not come from the same mouth. He desires a pure heart, freedom from wickedness and an ability to refuse the wonderful tidbits offered by those who are impure in both action and desire. The prayer expands, going past speech to the mind, which guides his behavior. "Incline not my heart to evil" is the Old Testament equivalent to the New Testament petition "Lead us not into temptation" in Lord's Prayer.

He is fearful that he is becoming the same as those evil ones of which he speaks. He begins to worry that he will somehow assume their manner. It is not his desire to become cynical and skeptical, scheming and plotting like the wicked men of which he speaks. Unfortunately, those very attributes may become his, as mortals tend to turn into the type of people that surround them.

David determines to stand resolutely in his understanding of self-discipline and devotion. He continues to follow the way of God as in Revelation 5:8, with its golden bowls full of incense, (the prayers of the saints) and Hebrews 13:15, with its verbal sacrifice of praise. He will rely on good judgment to overtake his opponents and prays they will give heed to his words. He is looking ahead to a time when such a stand will prove that God will make no deals with evil.

PSALM 142

¹Maschil of David; A Prayer when he was in the cave.
I cried unto the LORD with my voice; with my voice
unto the Lord did I make my supplication.
²I poured out my complaint before him;
I showed before him my trouble.
³When my spirit was overwhelmed within me, then
thou knewest my path. In the way, wherein I walked
have they privily laid a snare for me.
⁴I looked on [my] right hand, and beheld,
but [there was] no man that would know me:
refuge failed me; no man cared for my soul.
⁵I cried unto thee, O LORD: I said, Thou [art] my
refuge [and] my portion in the land of the living.
⁶Attend unto my cry; for I am brought very low:
deliver me from my persecutors;
for they are stronger than I.
⁷Bring my soul out of prison, that I may praise thy
name: the righteous shall compass me about;
for thou shalt deal bountifully with me.

PSALM 142
Title: Sixth Prayer/Testimony Psalm
Author: a Psalm of David
Date: While David was Hiding from Saul
Superscription: to the Chief Musician *Maschil*

Alone and in trouble, this prayer comes from the early part of David's life, while he was hiding in the cave from Saul as seen in 1 Samuel 22:1 and 24:3. As David faces intense persecution, he voices his appeal, makes his complaints, states his petition and closes with a note of confidence in the Lord. When forsaken by all others, the Lord will remain as a safe and faithful refuge. David refers to prison in a figurative sense to define circumstances that close in on him, thus paralleling the next phrase "shall surround". Along with Psalm 57, this hymn gives an idea of David's ever-changing emotions during this period in his life. Psalm 57 is bold and animated, while this psalm shows the strain of being hated and hunted.

The verbs used in verses 1-5 should be replaced with the present tense, as the psalmist is not remembering, but rather *living* this event. His great need is emphasized by the vigorous terms he uses while crying aloud in the cave. Like Bartemus in the Gospels, he refuses to lapse into silence. Refusing to *talk* to God only leads to despair. *Supplication* is an appeal to someone's kindness while *complaint* refers to troubling thoughts. Beyond both of these, however, is the word "Thou"-for the truth of the matter is that regardless of any situation, all can say, "Thou knowest my way!"

Verse 4 reveals the friendless state of David; no one wants to be near him, or so he feels. Mercifully, however, he is aware that God does know and care about him. God appears to emphasize His love for David by sending David's brothers and his father's household to join him in his cave and then, by degrees, a company formed a that would become the nucleus of his kingdom (1 Samuel 22:1-2).

Verse 6 brings a second affirmation of faith later paralleled in Matthew 26:38 as Jesus speaks, "My soul is very sorrowful, even unto death." This is a useful reminder that the psalms, like all parts of scripture are for the instruction of the people. However, in this instance, David dares to visualize the day when he is no longer hunted, but adored and possibly even crowned as King. Or, perhaps he merely looks forward to bringing his offering to the Temple when he has at last become a free man.

PSALM 143

¹A Psalm of David. Hear my prayer, O LORD, give ear to my supplications: in thy faithfulness answer me, [and] in thy righteousness.
²And enter not into judgment with thy servant: for in thy sight shall no man living be justified.
³For the enemy hath persecuted my soul; he hath smitten my life down to the ground;

he hath made me to dwell in darkness,
as those that have been long dead.
⁴Therefore is my spirit overwhelmed within me;
my heart within me is desolate.
⁵I remember the days of old; I meditate on all thy
works; I muse on the work of thy hands.
⁶I stretch forth my hands unto thee:
my soul [thirsteth] after thee, as a thirsty land.
⁷Hear me speedily, O LORD: my spirit faileth:
hide not thy face from me,
lest I be like unto them that go down into the pit.
⁸Cause me to hear thy lovingkindness in the
morning; for in thee do I trust: cause me to know
the way wherein I should walk;
for I lift up my soul unto thee.
⁹Deliver me, O LORD, from mine enemies:
I flee unto thee to hide me.
¹⁰Teach me to do thy will; for thou [art] my God: thy
spirit [is] good; lead me into the land of uprightness.
¹¹Quicken me, O LORD, for thy name's sake: for thy
righteousness' sake bring my soul out of trouble.
¹²And of thy mercy cut off mine enemies, and
destroy all them that afflict my soul:
for I [am] thy servant.

PSALM 143
Title: Twentieth Prayer of Distress
Author: a Psalm of David
Date: When Absalom pursued David
Superscription: none
Theme: Appeal for Guidance

This urgent cry comes from David as he hides from Absalom and his army as told in 2 Samuel 17. In this prayer for God's help, David has truly reached the end of the line; he has no more reserve and no more resources. In his desperate situation, only one refuge remains and that is God Himself, (5-12). He comes to God as a repentant sinner-not one who is free of guilt, but still one who is in desperate need. He casts himself on the mercy of God. Remembering God's mighty works in the past has given him encouragement to make this appeal.

David prays for guidance three times in verses 8-10. Each of these three prayers has a slightly different meaning if read carefully. "The way I should go" gives an indication that he is looking at his own destiny in the world. "Teach me to do thy will" sets his priorities and makes the commandments of God far more important than self-fulfillment. The words "lead me" show the humility of one who know that he not only needs to be told, but also needs to be guided in doing right things. The apostle Paul in Romans 8:14 and Galatians 5:18 teaches that man is to look to God's spirit for this leading, to seek an inward work of inclining the will and focusing the mind. The plea for a *level path* implies a smooth course where no one is liable to trip, stumble or lose their way.

With his life in the balance, David appeals to God for a firm commitment to save him. This is the fourth of his appeals. David looks to God's deliverance based on His Name. God is committed to His servant, as surely as His servant is committed to Him. If God cared nothing for His name, His righteousness and steadfast love, for the cause of right or for His covenant, there would be no reason to believe in His goodness. Most importantly, David reaches out towards God as his Father, loving Him for who He is, not simply to do what David has asked. Personal devotion to God made David a great king. The greatness of his story flows through the Book of Psalms.

Note: The paradox of a righteous judge who nevertheless justifies the wicked (an act which Proverbs 17:15 calls an abomination to the Lord) would not be resolved until Jesus settled it on the cross at Calvary. Every phrase is laden with stress and no sufferer need feel unique in what he experiences. These needs are very similar to those describing the emotions of man in Matthew 26:37 and Hebrews 4:15. They are a reminder that no person will ever be alone or less than fully understood.

PSALM 144

¹[A Psalm] of David. Blessed [be] the LORD my strength, which teacheth my hands to war, [and] my fingers to fight:
²My goodness, and my fortress; my high tower, and my deliverer; my shield, and [he] in whom I trust; who subdueth my people under me.
³LORD, what [is] man, that thou take us knowledge of him! [or] the son of man, that thou makest account of him!
⁴Man is like to vanity: his days [are] as a shadow that passeth away.
⁵Bow thy heavens, O LORD, and come down: touch the mountains, and they shall smoke.
⁶Cast forth lightning, and scatter them: shoot out the thine arrows, and destroy them.
⁷Send thine hand from above; rid me, and deliver me out of great waters, from the hand of strange children;
⁸Whose mouth speaketh vanity, and their right hand [is] a right hand of falsehood.
⁹I will sing a new song unto thee, O God: upon a psaltery [and] an instrument of ten strings will I sing praises unto thee.
¹⁰[It is he] that giveth salvation unto kings: who delivereth David his servant from the hurtful sword.
¹¹Rid me, and deliver me from the hand of strange children, whose mouth speaketh vanity, and their right hand [is] a right hand of falsehood:

¹²That our sons [may be] as plants grown up in their youth; [that] our daughters [may be] as corner stones, polished [after] the similitude of a palace:
¹³[That] our garners [may be] full, affording all manner of store: [that] our sheep may bring forth thousands and ten thousands in our streets:
¹⁴[That] our oxen [may be] strong to labor; [that there be] no breaking in, nor going out; that [there be] no complaining in our streets.
¹⁵Happy [is that] people, that is in such a case: [yea], happy [is that] people, who is God [is] the LORD.

PSALM 144
Title: Eleventh Prayer/Praise Psalm
Author: a Psalm of David
Superscription: none
Theme: a Song to the Lord

This psalm begins with the energy of a warrior, worthy of David himself at the height of battle. The first seven verses include lines from Psalm 18. There have been questions as to the unity of the verses that complete this psalm. Verses 12 to 15 are from a previously unknown psalm and were placed here as the psalms were compiled. In fact, the entire psalm is a compilation. Occasionally other parts of the Psalter are seen here, which have caused many to believe that Psalm 144 is part of a compilation of psalms created solely for David's descendants. It is impossible to determine whether these psalms are post Davidic or if David has drawn freely on his previous writings.

Regardless, it is David's life, faith and poetry that ensure the timelessness and beauty of the psalms.

The often quoted lines of verse 3, "What is man that Thou takest knowledge of him or the son of man that thou makest account of him!" shows David's amazement that so great a God would bother about him or his problems. Man's time here is so swift and passes like a breath, yet Almighty God has chosen him to be worthy of His time and efforts.

While Psalm 18 looked back upon the things that God had done for the Israelites in the past, this psalm looks eagerly toward the future. The *right hand* mentioned in verses 8 and 11 are symbolic. The right hand was commonly raised in worship, when making an oath or simply shaking hands to complete a transaction or agreement. The Song of Moses, Deuteronomy 32:40, show Moses raising his hand in promise to God. The sons are seen as sturdy, well-established trees and the daughters the very picture of statuesque elegance and strength. This shows, that as with the Book of Psalms, t there has been nothing slipshod in their "upbringing".

At psalm's end, the people look toward the wealth and resources of the kingdom-both of which are gifts of God and are not to be something assumed, but instead, as a gift from a loving Father and the cause of great rejoicing. Having begun with human, nonmaterial values in the soundness of the family (12), the prayer ends at the source of the harmony it has envisioned. The final thanksgiving is reserved for God from a people grateful for their treasures. This, as a later man of God would declare in Habakkuk 3:17-19, the love of God will outweigh the loss of everything else.

Psalms 145 through 150, intended for public worship, sing the praises of God. Jews use them today in daily prayer. Psalms 146 through 150 each begin and end with *"Hallelujah—O, praise the Lord".*

PSALM 145

[1] David's [Psalm] of praise. I will extol thee, my God, O King; and I will bless thy name for ever and ever.
[2] Every day will I bless thee;
and I will praise thy name for ever and ever.
[3] Great [is] the LORD, and greatly to be praised;
and his greatness [is] unsearchable.
[4] One generation shall praise thy works to another, and shall declare thy mighty acts.
[5] I will speak of the glorious honor of thy majesty, and of thy wondrous works.
[6] And [men] shall speak of the might of thy terrible acts: and I will declare thy greatness.
[7] They shall abundantly utter the memory of thy great goodness, and shall sing of thy righteousness.
[8] The LORD [is] gracious, and full of compassion; slow to anger, and of great mercy.
[9] The LORD [is] good to all:
and his tender mercies [are] over all his works.
[10] All thy works shall praise thee, O LORD;
and thy saints shall bless thee.
[11] They shall speak of the glory of thy kingdom, and talk of thy power;

¹²To make known to the sons of men his mighty acts, and the glorious majesty of his kingdom.
¹³Thy kingdom [is] an everlasting kingdom, and thy dominion [endureth] throughout all generations.
¹⁴The LORD upholdeth all that fall, and raiseth up all [those that be] bowed down.
¹⁵The eyes of all wait upon thee; and thou givest them their meat in due season.
¹⁶Thou openeth thine hand, and satisfiest the desire of every living thing.
¹⁷The LORD [is] righteous in all his ways, and holy in all his works.
¹⁸The LORD [is] nigh unto all them that call upon him, to all that call upon him in truth.
¹⁹He will fulfill the desire of them that fear him: he will also hear their cry, and will save them.
²⁰The LORD preserveth all that love him: but all the wicked he will destroy.
²¹My mouth shall speak the praise of the LORD: and let all flesh bless his holy name for ever and ever.

PSALM 145
Title: Nineteenth Psalm of Praise
Author: a Psalm of David
Superscription: none
Theme: God's Love

This is the last psalm attributed to David and the final acrostic psalm as well. One letter of the Hebrew alphabet (*nun*) is lacking from the standard Hebrew text, but most ancient translations allow a text from

Qumran, which as translated at the end of verse 13 means "the Lord is faithful". The focal point is clearly expressing adoration for God's love and majesty. The psalm uses a collection of verbs here, including: praise, extol, declare, speak, say or meditate. In addition to its verbs, this psalm carries various descriptions of God such as rock, fortress, deliverer, great, terrible, righteous, holy and compassionate among others.

David's personal experiences have enlarged his understanding and his relationship to God. He is keenly aware of God's greatness and His care of the world. He has learned and has taught to others that God is not a God of time, but His love and goodness extend to all people throughout eternity.

Verses 10 through 13 repeat several phrases found in verses 4-7, but with a slightly different tone. While verses 4-7 show the mighty acts and character of God, 10-13 focus specifically on God's *Kingdom*. The importance of the Kingdom of God is shown by its usage four times in three verses. This highlights the theme of God's rule over the world, rather than the glory of redemption. In the Book of Daniel 4:3, Nebuchadnezzar speaks these words and stresses that the emphasis of the redemption God offers is just as much a cause for joy as is the compassion which David ascribes to God in verses 8 and 9. The reappearance of verse 13 in the book of Daniel 4:3 on the lips of Nebuchadnezzar confirms this as much a cause for joy as is the compassion proclaimed in verses 8 and 9.

The phrase "upholdeth all that fall" shows God's ability and willingness to help not only those who are stumbling, but to reach down and uplift those who have already fallen, either in body or spirit. He has the power to revive a man's lost hope or physical infirmities, regardless of how *deep* the malady has become. The term "nigh unto all" is not an indication that God is standing within earshot in an earthly sense, but includes the nearness of one's closest of friends.

Verse 20 is the only verse of this psalm that makes any mention of the evilness of men. Sadly, wickedness is a large part of the world; this could hardly be a psalm of David without a mention of the wicked ones. The righteous judgments of God are absent from this psalm.

David's contribution to the Psalter ends on a note of praise. His experiences and his words have been his own, but his thoughts are as wide as humanity and as unfading as eternity.

PSALM 146

¹Praise ye the LORD, Praise the LORD, O my soul.
²While I live will I praise the LORD: I will sing praises unto my God while I have any being.
³Put not your trust in princes, [nor] in the son of man, in whom [there is] no help.
⁴His breath goeth forth, he returneth to his earth; in that very day his thoughts perish.
⁵Happy [is he] that [hath] the God of Jacob, for his help, whose hope [is] in the LORD his God:
⁶Which made heaven, and earth, the sea, and all that therein [is]: which keepeth truth for ever.

⁷Which executeth judgment for the oppressed:
which giveth food to the hungry.
The LORD looseth the prisoners.
⁸The LORD openeth [the eyes of] the blind:
the LORD raiseth them that are bowed down:
the LORD loveth the righteous:
⁹The LORD preserveth the strangers; he relieveth the
fatherless and widows: but the way of
the wicked he turneth upside down.
¹⁰The LORD shall reign for ever, [even] thy God,
O Zion, unto all generations. Praise ye the LORD.

PSALM 146
Title: Twentieth Psalm of Praise
Author: anonymous
Superscription: none
Theme: Happy are the Lord's People

"While I live I will praise the LORD; I will sing praises unto my God while I have any being," This, the second verse of psalm 146 sets the tone for this short collection. These five psalms served as a small hymnal of songs used in the synagogue in daily worship. Like most of the psalms in this final book, Psalm 146 exhibits a reflection of Israel's past and is post-exilic in structure and language. In many ways, these psalms are a miniature of the history of Israel.

Based on experience, the psalmist begs others not to depend on the favors of the noble or rich surrounding them. As in Proverbs 19:6, he knows that no good or lasting help can come from trusting in man. Princes last for only a short time and soon either they or their kingdom is no more. The focus is to be on God, the hope and help of His people, utterly dependable, caring for all their needs. Man is far too fallible to be trusted, all too often lacking in desire or willpower. God reigns over all and forever!

The contrast in this psalm is the often seen *clash* between eternal justice and those who live in folly and put their trust in wealthy or immoral rulers. The kingship of the Lord in verses 5-10 shows just how foolish it would be to place one's trust in someone merely because they are influential. Too frequently, a visual backing may seem more solid and practical than the word of an *invisible* God. Isaiah 32:5 is a reminder that things are not always as they seem.

What is as it seems is the love of God. Those who choose to walk with and hope in the Lord are truly the recipients of His blessings. This hope based upon God's creation of the universe shows His loving care of man and His everlasting righteousness.

The final beatitude in the Psalter is in verse 5. This beatitude is for the man who understands what it means to be in personal covenant with God. "*Jacob*" is used here to represent the people on earth who rely totally on God. God takes them to Himself and transforms them into special recipients of His love. He protects guides and cares for His chosen ones in His own special way. The New Testament Apostle Paul, at his trial said, "All deserted me, but the Lord stood by me" (2 Timothy 4:16-17).

Note: The opening call "praise the Lord" is a summons to the world. The personal and lifelong praise of the individual now opens out into the praise of Zion, to all the people of God and to all of eternity. Whether or not the psalmist included himself in this timeline does not matter, for it was his destiny. God is not the God of the dead, but of the living.

PSALM 147

¹Praise ye the LORD: for [it is] good to sing praises
unto our God; for [it is] pleasant;
[and] praise is comely.
²The LORD doth build up Jerusalem:
he gathereth together the outcasts of Israel.
³He healeth the broken in heart,
and bindeth up their wounds.
⁴He telleth the number of the stars;
he calleth them all by [their] names.
⁵Great [is] our Lord, and of great power:
his understanding [is] infinite.
⁶The LORD, lifteth up the meek:
he casteth the wicked down to the ground.
⁷Sing unto the LORD with thanksgiving;
sing praise upon the harp unto our God:
⁸Who covereth the heaven with clouds,
who prepareth rain for the earth,
who maketh grass to grow upon the mountains.
⁹He giveth to the beast his food,
[and] to the young ravens which cry.

¹⁰He delighteth not in the strength of the horse: he taketh not pleasure in the legs of a man.
¹¹The LORD taketh pleasure in them that fear him, in those that hope in his mercy.
¹²Praise the LORD, O Jerusalem; praise thy God, O Zion.
¹³For he hath strengthened the bars of thy gates; he hath blessed thy children within thee.
¹⁴He maketh peace [in] thy borders, [and] filleth thee with the finest of the wheat.
¹⁵ He sendeth forth his commandment [upon] earth: his word runneth very swiftly.
¹⁶He giveth snow like wool: he scattereth the hoarfrost like ashes.
¹⁷He casteth forth his ice like morsels: who can stand before his cold?
¹⁸He sendeth out his word, and melteth them: he causeth his wind to blow, [and] the waters flow.
¹⁹He showeth his word unto Jacob, his statutes and his judgments unto Israel.
²⁰He hath not dealt so with any nation: and [as for his] judgments, they have not known them. Praise ye the LORD.

PSALM 147
Title: Twenty-first Psalm of Praise
Author: anonymous
Date: Rebuilding the Walls of Jerusalem
Superscription: none
Theme: Praise God for Salvation

This psalm gives praise to God, the Creator and Lord over all, for His special mercies to Israel. The Septuagint splits this psalm into two parts, verses 1-11 and verses 12-20. The reason for this division in the Greek translation is unknown. This is a *pure* psalm of praise, as it bears no hint of complaint, evil doers or petition for deliverance. Outlined here is God's power and understanding from beginning to end, along with His incomparable ability to provide for and eternally sustain the people of Israel. Common in Israel's worship, this psalm extols the many virtues of God while praising His glorious works among men.

The praise comes from the nation-the nation whose God commands the universe (4), the seasons (8), the nations (14) and all of nature (16-18) with a power that leaves no doubt that He is well above all that mankind could imagine. Yet His heart goes out to each man who is in despair or unhappy, as seen in verses 2 and 3. He is greatly delighted by man's respect and praise. His words provide a guide to life in verse 19. Verses 1-6 speak of His love of Israel. "The Lord doth build up Jerusalem" refers to the restoration of the Temple following the exile.

The promises of Isaiah 40:1, made to a wandering and weary people, are cause for celebration as they are fulfilled in the Jerusalem and in the lives of its people. Definite clarity of His magnificent power is in verse 4, where it is said that He has not only created the stars, but He knows their number and calls each by their name. The meaning here is that although God is greater than any imagination could comprehend, He also gives His attention to the tiniest parts of His creations.

The final verses of this psalm center on the Word of God giving its greatest function as the creation and communication between man and the universe. God's effortless control in terms that recalled Job 37:1-13 are in verses 15-18 and form a reminder that God is focused and diverse. Verses 19 and 20 are the crux of the psalm. While prayer and supplication are a means of reaching out to God as a way of getting things done, statutes and ordinances or even appeals can be uncertain tools. By speaking to man rather than programming man, God shows His desire for a relationship, not simply a set of behaviors. He desires relationship, not robotics.

The closing in verse 20 appears somewhat over confident, but is in reality an exclamation of wonder. If pride were to creep into Israel's praise, the very name of Jacob would bring a sobering reality. If Jacob had not aligned himself with the Lord, the future that was promised in Isaiah 49:6, to be a light unto the world, would have lapsed into everlasting darkness.

PSALM 148

¹Praise ye the LORD. Praise ye the LORD
from the heavens: praise him in the heights.
²Praise ye him, all his angels:
praise ye him, all his hosts.
³Praise ye him, sun and moon: praise him,
all ye stars of light.
⁴Praise him, ye heavens of heavens,
and ye waters that [be] above the heavens.
⁵Let them praise the name of the LORD:
for he commanded, and they were created.
⁶He hath also stablished them for ever and ever:
he hath made a decree which shall not pass.
⁷Praise the LORD from the earth,
ye dragons, and all deeps:
⁸Fire, and hail; snow, and vapors;
stormy wind fulfilling his word:
⁹Mountains, and all hills;
fruitful trees, and all cedars:
¹⁰Beasts, and all cattle;
creeping things, and flying fowl:
¹¹Kings of the earth, and all people;
princes, and all judges of the earth:
¹²Both young men, and maidens;
old men, and children:
¹³Let them praise the name of the LORD:
for his name alone is excellent;
his glory [is] above the earth and heaven.

¹⁴He also exalteth the horn of his people, the praise of all his saints; [even] of the children of Israel, a people near unto him. Praise ye the LORD.

PSALM 148
Title: Twenty-second Psalm of Praise
Author: anonymous
Superscription: none
Theme: All Creation to Praise God

This psalm is divided into two sections with a small two-verse *intermission* in the center. The first four verses are a call directed to the heavens to give praise to the Lord as the creator and keeper of all things. Verses 5-6 show some of the reasons that God is deserving of praise. He is the commander and creator of all things, and it is by His word and decree that they shall stand forever. Verses 7 through 12 command praise from all created things upon the earth and the accompanying reasons to glorify Him appear in the final two verses. All of creation is to give praise to the Lord, for His name is excellent, His glory reaches beyond the heavens and He exalts the horn of His chosen people, Israel.

Not only in Old Testament times, but in the Christian era as well, men have been tempted to worship angels (Colossians 2:18) who are not equal to God. Angels are fellow workers as servants of God as seen in Revelation 22:8-9. To worship and glorify the stars (or any of God's creations) as if they control destiny is also a folly. Two movements of this psalm show that stars, like man, were created with a single word. Part one of this psalm incites praise from all of creation that is above the earth, while part two demands praise from all that is within the earth. Clearly, his only potential joy will come from the bonding of man with the heavens and both in adoration of the One who has created them.

Instruction is found in the comparison of verses 13-14 and 4-6. The celestial bodies are called upon to give praise to God simply because of their existence at the hand of God. Yet in verse 13, man's praise must be made consciously, as it is to humankind that God has revealed Himself. Simply stated, God's glory in the world is the natural law, while to humankind, His glory and redemptive love deserve praise. He brings His children closer to Himself, as seen in Revelation 21:3: "He will dwell with them, and they shall be His people."

Note: The "exalting of the horn" of a man or nation may be translated as growth and prosperity given by God.

PSALM 149

¹Praise ye the LORD. Sing unto the LORD a new song, [and] his praise in the congregation of saints.
²Let Israel rejoice in him that made him: let the children of Zion be joyful in their King.
³Let them praise his name in the dance: let them sing praises unto him with the timbrel and harp.

⁴For the LORD taketh pleasure in his people: he will beautify the meek with salvation.
⁵Let the saints be joyful in glory:
let them sing aloud upon their beds.
⁶[Let] the high [praises] of God [be] in their mouth, and a two-edged sword in their hand;
⁷To execute vengeance upon the heathen, [and] punishments upon the people;
⁸To bind their kings with chains, and their nobles with fetters of iron;
⁹To execute upon them the judgment written: this honor have all his saints. Praise ye the LORD.

PSALM 149
Title: Twenty-third Psalm of Praise
Author: anonymous
Superscriptions: none
Theme: Praise for God's Righteousness

In its final verses, Psalm 148 called mankind to give God praise and worship; here, the focus is entirely upon Israel. The psalm appears in two segments: verses 1-4 deal with praise and verses 5-9 are centered upon judgment. By linking these two trains of thought together, it is seen that there is boundless power in worship and praise. The most powerful weapons in man's arsenal is praise, as it encourages God to deal with both the physical and spiritual needs of man. The enemies mentioned here are also found in Ephesians 6:12 of the New Testament.

Israel's has a unique honor among the nations. She was granted salvation (in fact and promise) and until the coming of Christ, God gave Israel the blessing of the Sinai Covenant. Having these blessings, she was armed to call upon God and use His power to go before them in battle. Under this arrangement, Israel served as the earthly contingent of the armies of the King of heaven.

"Sing unto the Lord a new song" shows the congregation gathering in the Temple, working together to create a new song to celebrate yet another victory of Israel's army. Verse 3, with its mention of dancing, brings with it the intensity of spirit with which they rejoice. Any victory indicates God's favor upon them and the vision of Israel's strongest warriors singing out in praise with the two-edged sword in their hands is symbolic of the victory that has been achieved in the name of God. Comparable in the New Testament is Ephesians 6:17 and Hebrews 4:12, which instructs Christians to wield the sword of the spirit, which is the Word of God.

Verses 6 through 9 are referencing a *holy war,* of which there are many. However, using the battle with the Canaanites as an example, the song is of the retribution with which God overtakes His enemies. As a nation, Israel was told to go and occupy the Promised Land. With God before them, they were successful. The earthly end to God's promise to them will be fulfilled when He comes with His heavenly army in the final judgment (2 Thessalonians 1:7, Revelation 19:11). The evil enemies of the church are not flesh and blood, but wickedness disguised as righteousness. In any battle, the two-edged sword of God must be used, for the weapons of evil are not of this world.

Just as in ancient Israel, the Christian's two-edged sword (6) is the Word of God, created to destroy pride and arrogance that tries to set itself up against God. In truth divined by the sword will take every thought and idea and bring it under the scrutiny of God. In 2 Corinthians 10:5; Hebrews 4:12 this is further referenced. The apocalypse, with its other-worldly imagery of the final judgment, carries the description of the final victory and the need for one last *new song*. The church, with its roots firmly planted in Israel, has conquered by the blood of Jesus and by their own testimony: for they loved not their lives, even unto death. The unholy as well as the righteous will face a final judgment, whose outcome is *written by the cross.* He has appointed glory for all His faithful ones at a higher level than was clearly visible in the Old Testament, yet voices itself loudly from the books of the New Testament.

PSALM 150

¹Praise ye the LORD. Praise God in his sanctuary: praise him in the firmament of his power.
²Praise him for his mighty acts: praise him according to his excellent greatness.
³Praise him with the sound of the trumpet: praise him with the psaltery and harp.

⁴Praise him with the timbrel and dance: praise him with stringed instruments and organs.
⁵Praise him upon the loud cymbals: praise him upon the high sounding cymbals.
⁶Let everything that hath breath praise the LORD. Praise ye the LORD.

PSALM 150
Title: Twenty-fourth Psalm of Praise
Author: anonymous
Superscription: none
Theme: Praise ye the Lord

Every instrument in the orchestra, everything with life and breath in the whole of creation joins in a mighty, crashing symphony of praise to God. As the final psalm and the doxology to the Psalter, this final hymn measures up to its position of honor. Here is a true *snapshot* of praise. Here lie instructions or reasons of where, why and how to worship the Almighty. In addition, there is a listing (not all-inclusive) which describes the instruments used to make praise and worship lively and diverse.

Where to worship God is simple-everywhere. The where of praise is the call to God's worshipers on earth to join together at His chosen place. Included in the call to praise is the reminder that He may be praised from anywhere in the created universe. Verse 2 is the reason for worship. Although specifics can be added by the worshiper, the basis of worship is always God's magnificent character and the things He has done for man, a result of His unfathomable greatness. Give remembrance to past actions of deliverance and salvation. His mighty deeds refer primarily to His saving acts (Psalms 20:6), remember also the personal strength he has placed within man.

The *how* of giving praise to God has one all-inclusive answer: praise with all that is within the soul, the spirit and the mind. Mentioned in the psalm is the trumpet blast, as was done in Leviticus 25:9 to announce the Year of Jubilee. Victories are celebrated with the timbrel and dancing; by simple music making and the use of the pipe and the flute (Genesis 4:21, Job 21:12). Every kind of instrument, voice and melody is to join in the praise of God. Praise and worship must include prayer, music, praise, honor and humility. God as creator must be acknowledged and as nothing can be hidden from Him, motives for prayer must be pure.

Even when one feels less than inclined to praise Him, the instruction is clear: everything with God's gift of life should praise Him. Praise not by memorization as do the Pharisees, not out of requirement like the priests and the Levites and not merely adding a voice to the congregation. From all that is within, all creatures of time and space that have breath are to be included in His choir forevermore.

Note: The use of the word "evermore" means literally "to the end of days" as is seen in Psalm 23. Both in Psalm 23 and in this final psalm the end of the length of days is left undefined. Until the coming of the New Testament men could not know of eternal life in heaven and that as God Himself is eternal, so it is with the length of days (Revelation 21:1-2)

NOTES ON BOOK FIVE
Major Themes

- God is consistent and unchanging
- God's word is infallible
- Wisdom is to be prized
- God's attributes reflect His Law
- Prayer speaks directly to God
- Remembrance of God's deeds is important
- Rely on God in every circumstance
- Do not trust in men or money
- Declare God's goodness openly
- Welcome the Holy Spirit

CONCLUSION

The Book of Psalms now comes to a close. The ending brings a quiet pause, perhaps a sign that there should be more to read and yet, all has been said. It has ended after its exposé on the life, struggles and joys of the people of Israel. The term "Israelites" includes thousands of people, yet through the verses one hears the tale of individual lives, revealing their hearts and hardships as they journeyed in the desert of their own faith.

There is virtually no circumstance of life that has not had its "say" in the Book of Psalms. Loneliness, praise, fear, joy, failure and frustration have each had their voice within these pages. Fortunately for mankind, each has been handed down with not only the situation, but with the solution as well. Adultery, murder and disobedience are shown along with God's corresponding condemnation and while the sin is forgiven, the consequences are clearly seen. Singing, dancing, love and obedience have brought forth visions of God's great joy and delight over His people.

David, Moses and Solomon, along with the Sons of Korah and the Sons of Asaph, have put into words the very essence of life itself. There are no saints to be found here, only sinners relying on God. Nowhere will there be found any who are worthy of God's great love and kindness. Within this book there lies only life—life on a daily basis with its joy, anger, hope and suffering. It is today's world in yesterday's setting.

The truth that rings through all 150 books, however, is this: God loves His people. God's people will continually fail and disappoint Him in spite of their best efforts. There will always be forgiveness because God loves His people.

Thus, as the last page is turned and the music of the last song is fading, the Book of Psalms comes to an end, leaving the reader to ponder the wisdom within.

RESOURCES

Dake, Finis Jennings. <u>Dake's Annotated Reference Bible.</u> United States: np, 1963

Halley, Henry H. <u>Halley's Bible Handbook.</u> Grand Rapids, MI: Zondervan Publishing House, 1995.

Hayford, Jack., ed. <u>Spirit Filled Life Bible (NKJ).</u> United States: Thomas Nelson Publishers, 1991

Howard, David Jr. <u>Fascinating Bible Facts</u>. Lincolnwood, IL: Publications International, LTD, 1997

Kidner, Rev. Derek. <u>An Introduction and Commentary of the Psalms vol 1 and 2.</u> Tyndale Old Testament Commentaries. D.J. Wiseman, ed. Downer's Grove, Illinois: Inter-Varsity Press, 1973.

Lockyer, Dr. Herbert. <u>All the Doctrines of the Bible.</u> Grand Rapids, MI: Zondervan Publishing House, 1964.

<u>NIV Study Bible.</u> Grand Rapids, MI: Zondervan Publishing, 2002.

Pfeiffper, C., and Harrison, E., ed. The Wycliffe Bible Commentary. Chicago, IL: Moody Press, Paperback Edition 1983

Vine, W.E., Unger, M.E. and White, William Jr. Vine's Complete Expository Dictionary. Nashville, TN: Thomas Nelson, Inc., 1996.

Whiston, William. Trans, The Works of Josephus. Peabody, MA: Hendrickson Publishers, Inc., 1987.

Wilkinson, Bruce., and Boa, Kenneth. Walk Thru the Bible Volume I. Nashville, TN: Thomas Nelson Publishers, 1983.

CPSIA information can be obtained at www.ICGtesting.com
Printed in the USA
BVOW02s1813081113

335822BV00005B/8/P